Everybody's Grandpa

Everybody's Grandpa

FIFTY YEARS BEHIND THE MIKE

by Louis M. "Grandpa" Jones

with Charles K. Wolfe

KNOXVILLE : THE UNIVERSITY OF TENNESSEE PRESS

Library of Congress Cataloging in Publication Data

Jones, Grandpa, 1913-
  Everybody's grandpa.

  Discography: p.
  Bibliography: p.
  Includes index.
  1. Jones, Grandpa, 1913-. 2. Country musicians—
United States—Biography. I. Wolfe, Charles K. II. Title.
ML420.J757A3   1984   784.5′2′00924 [B]   84-7225
ISBN 0-87049-439-2 (alk. paper)

Frontispiece: *Photograph courtesy of Grandpa Jones.*

Contents

Illustrations

Acknowledgments

Many people helped us in putting this book together, but some are due special recognition for their invaluable information and advice. Musicians who shared time and memories with us include the late Merle Travis, the late Kirk McGee, Bradley Kincaid, Joe Troyan, and Bill Grammer. A special help throughout the project, and a constant source of encouragement, was Ramona Jones. Norm Cohen, Ivan Tribe, Bill Malone, Neil Rosenberg, Bill Harrison, and Carl Fleischhauer offered suggestions and insights into the development of the book. Carol Orr, Director of UT Press, and Michael Lofaro, of the Press Board, were strongly supportive from the start, and Katherine Holloway did her usual fine editorial work on an unorthodox manuscript. For transcribing tapes, typing the manuscript through various stages, and helping with the index, honors must go to Susan Gay and Betty Nokes. Overseeing and co-ordinating the indexing was Mary Dean Wolfe, assisted by Stacey and Cindy Wolfe. A special list of scholars and historians who assisted in the preparation of the discography appears on page 236. Some of the writing and research was made possible through grants from the Faculty Research Committee at Middle Tennessee State University.

With only a couple of exceptions, the illustrations in the book come from Grandpa Jones' own collection of photographs accumulated over the years. When possible, we have tried to ascertain the name of the original photographer and to give proper credit; in many cases, though, it was impossible to determine the photographer of a particular photo, and in these cases we offer an apology for uncredited work.

June 6, 1984   GJ & CKW

Collaborator's Note

Many so-called "collaborations" between author and famous personality are little more than ghost-written accounts by the author based on interviews and research. It is a pleasure to report that my work with Grandpa was a collaboration in the true sense of the word. When Grandpa first discussed with me the idea of doing a book, he had already written about 75 typed pages himself, and had been gathering materials and notebooks from friends and relatives. Throughout the development of the manuscript, Grandpa continued to write some sections himself, send them to me, and respond to my editing or annotating. Similarly, in sections that I wrote based on extensive taped interviews with Grandpa, I tried to preserve as much as possible the oral flavor of Grandpa's speech, and then I submitted written copy for him to edit and annotate. (I early on learned to respect Grandpa's sense of detail and proofreading ability.) Grandpa also sent me a large number of "self-interview" tapes made at various locations while he was on the road; in these he responded at length to questions I had sent him, and dictated entire sections about subjects he considered important.

Grandpa's career is well documented, probably better than that of any other country music entertainer of his generation. He has always had a keen sense of history and is a knowledgeable student of folk songs and song histories. His files have preserved datebooks, diaries, old scripts, contracts, scrapbooks, and cartons of memorabilia, and this trove accounts for the many exact dates and details in the book. In cases where my own research into old songs and early music caused me to want to amplify or annotate some of Grandpa's remarks, I chose not to utilize explanatory footnotes, but to discuss the problem with Grandpa and with him develop a way to integrate my concerns into the narrative proper. Nonetheless, there are some names and personalities which play an important role in this story that the average reader—or the average non–country music fan—may not recognize. For these I have provided thumbnail biographical sketches briefly explaining their background.

By leaving the narrative proper unencumbered with notes and digressions, I hope I have preserved some sense of Grandpa's considerable skill as a raconteur, as well as the wit and warm personality that have won him friends from Maine to California.

Charles Wolfe

Everybody's Grandpa

One.

I came out of the bedroom and stood in front of the mirror and looked at myself. Whoever I looked like, it sure wasn't Grandpa Jones. I had my regular glasses on instead of my little spectacles. The suspenders, the old high-top boots, the little hat were all missing. In their place was this dark blue tuxedo, this frilled shirt, this big bow tie—what we used to call a monkey suit back in the old days. I had rented the outfit several days before from Bittner's, the big tuxedo rental place at the Rivergate Plaza in Goodlettsville, just down the road a few miles. Now here I was, standing all alone in our study, waiting on the rest of the family to get ready. I could hear my wife Ramona and daughter Alisa talking, and I hoped my son Mark was back in his room getting into his suit.

I sat down and glanced at the evening paper. The headlines read "CMA Awards Show Set for Tonight." Everybody in Nashville knew that those initials meant "Country Music Association," and that the annual awards show was country music's version of the Academy Awards, the Emmys, and the Pulitzer Prizes all rolled into one. Tonight's was the twelfth annual show, and it would be on television coast to coast over CBS. In the Nashville *Banner,* the columnist Red O'Donnel ran through the nominees and made a few predictions. A big category was Song of the Year, and the list included "Don't It Make My Brown Eyes Blue" (introduced that year by Loretta Lynn's kid sister, Crystal Gayle), "Heaven's Just a Sin Away" (an old-time country song done by a new father-daughter team called the Kendalls), "Mamas, Don't Let Your Babies Grow Up to Be Cowboys" (by Waylon and Willie), and "Take This Job and Shove It" (a hit by Johnny Paycheck).

A little further down in the story I came across my name. "A highlight of the 90-minute special, hosted for the second consecutive season by Johnny Cash, will be the induction of a new member into the Country Music Hall of Fame. The nominees are Cash, Vernon Dalhart, Grandpa Jones, Hank Snow, and the Sons of the Pioneers. (Cash is a good bet)."

Looking over the list, I saw several good bets. I had never known Vernon Dalhart, but I had heard his famous records of "The Prisoner's Song" and "The Wreck of the Old 97," and I had listened to his songs on an old Victrola when I was a boy; one of his hits, "Billy Richardson's Last Ride," I still used myself and had just recorded. I had heard the smooth harmonies of the Sons of the Pioneers since the 1930s, too, and back in my early days in West Virginia I even had a group that used those three-part harmonies and did a lot of western songs. Both Hank and Johnny I had known for years on the Opry; Hank and I shared a love for the old Jimmie Rodgers, and I recalled that right after Hank's hit of "Golden Rocket" came out in 1950, my recording boss, Syd Nathan, asked me to do a version of it. It's funny how many ties and connections you build over so many years in the music business.

It was getting on near six o'clock, and still no one had come out. I reached for my wallet and quietly unfolded the sheet of paper. I had started getting nervous about my nomination a week before, and decided it would be a good idea to have some sort of a little speech ready just in case. Without telling anybody, I had written out a few lines, studied them, polished them, changed words here and there, and gotten them just right. I hated to hear people ramble around and make a mess of a response on national television. I looked over the speech, and closed my eyes. I ran over it again, making sure I had it memorized and just right. It seemed to say what I wanted to say, to thank the people I wanted to thank, to say what I felt about country music and what it had given me over the last 50 years. I should know it by now—I had read it to myself every day during the past week—but just to be on the safe side, I folded the paper and slipped it into the inside pocket of my suit.

Ramona and Alisa came into the room, ready to go. They both looked fine; Alisa, our youngest, was still in high school, but she had her mother's good looks and was already making a name for herself playing the hammered dulcimer and singing. Pretty soon Mark appeared, dressed in a suit and looking uncomfortable; he was our middle child, and was getting good on a claw-hammer banjo and the bass. Someone asked me if I was nervous. "Like a cat at a dog show," I muttered. We all loaded into our Lincoln, and drove out the gates from our ranch house and along the little gravel road that led to the highway.

We got to the I-65 intersection and turned south toward Nashville. I-65 comes from Louisville into Nashville and goes straight on down to Birming-ham, and a lot of the musicians use it to get to work, since many of them live up in the hills north of Nashville, around Hendersonville and Goodlettsville and Gallatin. When we first moved up there, the towns were small and there was a lot of good fishing and hunting. Now Nashville has grown out so much that there are giant shopping centers and apartment developments in a steady stream all along the highway. We stopped at Hendersonville and met Eloise, our older daughter, with her husband Larry Hawkins. Eloise sings, too, and runs our music publishing and booking company. She and Larry followed us on down in their car. By six-thirty we were down to Briley Parkway, and we turned there and headed across the Cumberland River to the new Opryland complex near Gallatin. Pretty soon we could see the high wings of the Opry House over on our right, and I tried to imagine what it would be like inside. I had often been there as a performer, but being in the audience was a new experience for me. Four thousand seats in the auditorium, every one of them sold out weeks and months before. Everybody in black tie or formal clothes. I didn't mind telling anyone that I would rather have played ten personal appearances than go through that night. It made me even edgier when we drove through the big gate behind the Opry House, where the performers park, and were met by a young man who took our car and parked it. They'd not done that before, either.

When we got to our seats, I relaxed a little bit, but when the curtain

Bud Wendell (right), president of WSM, *and Hal Durham, general manager of the Opry, helped me celebrate my 1978 induction into Country Music Hall of Fame.*

went up, the big cameras turned on, and the show got started, I began to get nervous again. I barely remember Crystal Gayle and Don Williams getting Vocalist of the Year awards, and I didn't even pay too much attention when Dolly Parton's dress split down the middle and she had to borrow a mink stole from Kenny Rogers's wife, Marianne Gordon. The closer to the end it got, the jumpier I was. Ramona whispered that my hands were as cold as ice. I told her I knew that.

I tried to think of something to take my mind off it, but all I could think of was how nervous I was getting. After 50 years behind the mike, doing shows almost every workday, why was I acting so unprofessional? I remembered the only other time in my career when I had been this nervous. That was at another big show, a long time ago in Akron, Ohio. March of 1929. Wendell Hall, the Red-Headed Music Maker, the man who had a hit with "It Ain't Gonna Rain No More," had come to town. It was advertised around that he would hold a week-long amateur show, and that at the end of the week the winner would get $50—in ten-dollar gold pieces. I had just moved up to the big city of Akron from Henderson, Kentucky, and I had been impressing the girls by singing and playing the guitar. I was impressing my Aunt Polly, too. She saw the ad and told me if I didn't go and try out, she would drag me down there. She meant it.

I hadn't played much in public before. At the high school assemblies in Akron, nobody sang the kind of music I was singing; the boy who was considered the good singer was studying opera. I didn't think there was much sense in going down to Wendell Hall's show with my cheap guitar. But I finally got up enough courage—a combination of fear of Aunt Polly and brashness on my part. It turned out that about 450 contestants signed up for the contest, and some were to be weeded out each night. The winners for the night were chosen by audience applause. I stood off stage waiting for my turn to come, and my nerves got worse and worse. Finally I was the next in line. I looked down to tune my guitar one more time and shook my head at what I saw. I had chewed the end of the guitar while waiting, and I didn't even realize it; now it looked like some cat had sharpened his claws on it. And it was a good $12 guitar that my sister Louise had bought me. But it was too late to do anything. They were calling my name, and I took my chewed-up guitar

Charles Wolfe explains to me about putting a book together. Photo by Carl Fleischhauer.

and walked out on stage and did my two songs. They were both imitations of Jimmie Rodgers, who was the biggest singer in the nation then: "My Dear Old Sunny South by the Sea" and "Going Back to Texas." My secret weapon was my yodel, and I had practiced it night and day.

I made the finals, and Friday night I had to go through all of it again. Again the waiting, again the nervousness, again wondering if I had my guitar in proper tune, again wondering what the audience—and Mr. Hall—would think. I don't even remember what I did or how it sounded, but as soon as I'd sung the songs, I took off and went home. I didn't find out until the next day that I had won first prize and that Mr. Hall had been unable to find me that night to give me the prize money. He awarded it to me the next day, and talked to me about being nervous: "A lot of nights I have to go out there and do ten minutes on my own before the show starts, and I hardly ever know what I'm going to do," he said. I stared at him in wonder. It was bad enough to go out with guitar in hand and song rehearsed, but to go out with no plans at all was just crazy. Was that what being a professional meant? Later that day Mr. Hall had all the winners on his radio show, and when I got behind the mike I wasn't nearly as nervous. And I took my chewed-up guitar and those gold pieces and traded them in on a better guitar. . .

Ramona was nudging me, and I came out of my daydream and looked up at the stage of this huge Opry House in 1978. This place might have intimidated even Mr. Hall. The cameras were swinging back, and the show was just getting ready to start up again after a commercial. They were introducing Glen Campbell to do the honors for the Hall of Fame award. Several other nominees were sitting near us, right up toward the front, and they looked as shaky as I felt. Glen talked for a few minutes, and then I heard him mention "little spectacles and leather boots." I almost fell out of my seat, because I knew no one wore anything like that but me. When he finally called my name out, I jumped up and kissed Ramona and got up the steps to the stage, managing not to miss one, or stumble. I stood there looking at Glen and staring into the bright lights and wondering what I would say when the applause died down. Finally I caught my breath and began. "I certainly didn't expect this," I said, and took off, improvising some speech that I had never thought of before and don't remember today. I didn't even have time to read the plaque they unveiled. Before I knew it, the show was over, and everybody was congratulating me and taking pictures.

One of the first people I ran into backstage was Minnie Pearl, who had gotten a plaque like mine a few years earlier. She took me by the arm and looked at my plaque and giggled. "Oh, yours is just great," she said. Glen was standing next to me when a reporter asked him about me. "He has this one thing young performers look for all through their careers. He has an honest heart." Someone asked me how I felt. "I think the honor comes with my Social Security," I joked. In about three weeks, I would turn 65, and I had just finished filling out my Social Security papers. There were more pictures and more interviews, and a lot of nice things were said about me, and we stayed at the Opry House talking and visiting until nearly midnight. I was tired, but it was a good tired; the evening had made me glad that I had been in this business of picking and singing for 50 years, and I remember thinking that if I had the chance, I'd do it all over again. At least I told several reporters that.

We drove back up the interstate and pulled into our driveway about twelve-thirty. It was a warm night, and I was glad to get out of my tuxedo and frilled shirt. As I took it off, a piece of paper fluttered to the floor. I picked it up, puzzled. It was my speech. I had totally forgotten about it. All the careful polishing and practicing had gone for nothing. I thought about reading over it to see what I had left out but decided not to. I had said just what I thought and felt that night, and that was better than any speech. I tossed my paper in the wastebasket and went into the kitchen for a drink of cool well water. So now I was in the Hall of Fame. It was select company. Did this mean I was a certified country music legend? I didn't feel like one, but I had spent a lot of time entertaining people over the years, and in a lot of places, from dusty old country schoolhouses in West Virginia to muddy foxholes in Korea. I know a lot of stories, some good, some not so good. And I had known a lot of good musicians whose names are all but unknown to the people who had been congratulating me tonight at the Opry House. I had seen some good times and some bad times—times when I'd had hit records and couldn't fill all the show dates I had requests for, and other times when I didn't have enough to buy wheel-tax stickers for my car and had to sneak out of town before daylight to go on tour. There were no great scandals in my life—no drugs, no drinking problem, no tragic accidents or messy divorces or scrapes with the law. Still, it was a rich, full, and complicated story, and maybe somebody would be interested if I told it. I was 65, the age most people retire; I had just been given the highest honor my profession could award. Maybe it was time to take stock, to look back and try to sort out some of the history. Maybe it was time to write a book.

Two.

SWEET DREAMS OF KENTUCKY

About the first thing that I can remember is tobacco. My father, David C. Jones, grew tobacco until he got too old to follow a walking plow, and I still saw him do that while he was in his seventies. But raising ten children wasn't an easy task, even though all we bought at the grocery was sugar, coffee, flour, and coal oil. There were eight boys and two girls. By age, they ran like this; Wilmer, Homer, Letcher, Velma, Aubrey, Gordon, Louise, Spurgeon, Eugene, and me. I was the last one. There never was a time when all 12 members of my family were together. My brother Letcher left home when I was seven months old. He came back to see us when I was 24. I had to be introduced to him.

But even though some of the older boys were gone from home by the time I got old enough to remember things, I *do* remember my brother Wilmer bringing home some mementos of World War I. He was in the National Guard (brother Letcher did his time in Hawaii, where he trained troops for overseas duty). I remember a hat like the Boy Scouts wear, and a pair of wraparound leggings that started at the shoetops and ended just below the knee, where they tied with a string that was attached to them. Wilmer brought home an old Kreg-Jorenson rifle, too, a 30/40-caliber. I wish I had it now; it is still a good deer rifle. Once the boys were cleaning the rifle before the open fireplace, and somehow it went off; the bullet went through the door of the closet where Mom kept her canned fruit and broke 13 quarts of good blackberries. Mom ran them out of the house—gun and all.

I can remember my grandmother and grandfather well, although my grandmother died not long after I turned five years old. Back then a lot of old folks had hardening of the arteries, and their minds didn't work well; my grandmother was one of them. I remember one night when she was spending some time with us, we were all sitting around the wood fireplace, and my grandma walked over to the window. She said to my brother Spurgeon, "Come here, Spurgeon, the moon's on fire." Spurgeon didn't pay much attention at first, but finally went over to make her happy. "The Higgins barn is burning up!" he shouted. We all rushed to the window to see, and Grandma said, "Well, I didn't tell all of you to come."

My grandpa was a carpenter and when my grandma died, he made her a casket and lined it with silk.

Grandpa was an ardent fisherman. When the time came when he thought the fish would bite, he would lay down his tools and go, no matter how much of a hurry somebody else was in to get a house built. These were my mother's family. They were great "put it off till tomorrow" folks. My mother told me her grandfather was also a carpenter, and that they had lived at Niagara, Kentucky (where I was born), in an old log house. The front room had a window facing west. They decided to build another room on the west side for a kitchen. They finally got the room built, but something came up before they cut the window into a door. They kept putting it off, and the women who cooked the food had to straddle those logs to bring it into the room where they ate. They did this so long that my mother said the logs were worn slick from being climbed over. There were only two logs to be cut into to make the door, but they never did find time.

Niagara is located in Henderson County, about eight miles north of Sebree, Kentucky. The land around Niagara is very fine farming land. During the time we lived there, it was tobacco and corn that was raised. Now soybeans are a little ahead of tobacco, I think. My great-grandpa Dorris had a farm there, and during the oil boom around Niagara a few years ago, there were 11 big wells pumping on that farm. I'm sorry to say it was owned by others, then and now.

When I was five years old, we were living at the Gooch place in Smith Mills, Kentucky. Eugene and I were the youngest, and we rolled hoops for miles around that place. The hoops came from the hub of a farm wagon, about the size of a pie pan, and we would make T-shaped sticks to push them with. We got a lot of exercise, got out of a lot of work, and stubbed a lot of toes on roots that were sticking out of the ground around big trees. A Dr. Gooch owned the place, and we rented it from him. He had a Dodge roadster and drove it about 10 to 15 miles an hour. All the kids would grab hold of the bumper of his Dodge when he cam by and run along behind him. The Methodist church was across the road, and a four-acre lawn in front of the Gooch place was full of beautiful maple and sweet gum trees. When any of the churches would have a pie supper or barbecue, it was on our lawn. Homer, my next to oldest brother, had three girls—Eleanor, Frances, and Venata. We played together every day. They lived right close to us. The day after one of the pie suppers or barbecues, we would be down there early, looking for change people had lost the night before. Sometimes we would find nickels and dimes, occasionally even quarters.

My dad had 23 stands of bees at one time. He also butchered beef and sold it, along with produce from the garden, to folks in Henderson. He would drive along the street and ring a little bell, and people would come out and buy whatever he had. He said he always sold beef to the folks that owned the Chinese laundry. He said they would always buy the neck, but not before one of them went around to all the others with the meat and they all agreed.

One day I heard my parents talking about a sale. I didn't know what they meant, but I was soon to find out. They were planning on selling everything but the household goods and moving to Evansville, Indiana. It was nine miles farther than Henderson, and I think I had been to Henderson only three times by the time I was six years old. Anyway, they had heard about a lot of work over there in the ironworks, and money was short at the Gooch place, so the decision was made. Velma, my older sister, was already in Evansville, working in a ten-cent store.

We moved in August of 1920, after having a big sale at the Gooch place.

We wound up living in Evansville 13 months, and I guess it was the most unhappy part of my childhood. Coming right out of the country and never having lived in the city, I was scared to death at the thought of going to school with strange children and having strange teachers.

Well, they started me out to school by having my brother Aubrey take me on his bicycle. I hated going, and I screamed and fought every day until it got to be a show for the neighbors; when school time came, women would sit at the windows all down the street to watch. One day Aubrey took me into the room—I wouldn't go in unless he took me—and the teacher, Miss Thimble, told him he could go, that I'd be okay. I had a different idea. I was screaming, "I want to go back to Kentucky." The other kids must have thought I was crazy. After my brother had gone, Miss Thimble grabbed me and set me down hard in the seat. I grabbed her leg and pinched it as hard as I could. She jumped back, and I didn't quite make out what she said. I found out later that Aubrey came back home and told my mother he was going to take me back to Kentucky as soon as he could. Maybe that was the turning point. I managed to go for a while without incident, even though I did not learn a thing. Sometimes when the teacher would ask a question, I'd know the answer but wouldn't talk because the other students laughed every time I said a word. I really sounded backwoods. And we were so poor that I thought everyone was better than I was. It was much later that Bradley Kincaid, with whom I worked for years, finally helped get me out of that kind of thinking. He said to me one day, "Grandpa, you are just as good as anyone else—you're no better, but you are just as good." I think that did me a lot of good.

I finally got acquainted with some neighbors up and down the street and found they were fine folks, just like in Kentucky. One family named Lindensmitt lived right across the street. One of the boys was about my age, and we became great friends. But one day when he and I were playing in the gutter after a rain, a car hit him and knocked his head against the curb and killed him. It was a shock to everyone, especially me.

After 13 months, you can imagine my joy the day I heard them talking of going back to Kentucky. (Work had gotten so slack in Evansville that Pop, Eugene, and Spurgeon were going around mowing grass with a push lawnmower that they carried in a little two-wheeled cart aong with the other tools

Kids in a tobacco field back home: I'm in front (left) with my niece Eleanor; behind us are my sisters Louise and Velma, and their friend Bessie.

That's me on the pony, with a neighbor girl in Evansville, Indiana.

they used. Pop made the cart.) Aubrey got hold of an old truck somewhere, everything was loaded on it, and we set out for Kentucky. With bad roads, bad tires, and a bad engine, we arrived at the old Baldorff place about five miles out of Weaverton, near Henderson. The place belonged to Uncle Willie Todd. He was no kin to us, but Pop's folks had raised him, so we all called him Uncle Willie and his wife Aunt Nan. Uncle Willie had grown up and done well, and by now he owned quite a few houses around Henderson. The old Baldorff place, where we would stay in 1921 and 1922, was destined to be my favorite place of the many we lived on.

We arrived at about eleven-thirty at night. Ice was half an inch thick on the trees, and they were cracking and popping like a new oak wagon. The old house had stood empty for a long time, and it was dreary. We got a fire started in the old fireplace, and Mom made some coffee on the hot coals and whipped up some sandwiches from somewhere—boy, were they good. We all finally got bedded down anywhere we could, and when I got up the next morning and saw all those beautiful fields and woods, it made me soon forget that night before. It was sure a better sight than those asphalt streets. And to this day I have never wanted to live in town again.

The next morning Pop started the almost impossible task of trying to mend the old farm tools that were left there by the last family that went broke on the place. He had to make ready for tilling the crops of tobacco and corn that he was to raise in the coming year. We were to farm on the halves: we got half of the crop, and Uncle Willie got half. That year was the leanest I can remember. We had an old cow giving milk, and we had some corn in the crib. Things got so bad that Mom got some of the corn and shelled it and parched it in the oven, then ground it up in the coffee mill and poured milk over it, and for three weeks we ate that and nothing else. Gordon, one of my brothers, ran a three - horse plow on that food for two weeks. I didn't think anything about it, though; I thought everyone was as poor as we were. I was too busy making roads under the tobacco plants and running make-believe cars on them when I was supposed to be worming and suckering tobacco.

Henry and Lawrence Lindensmitt, our friends from Evansville, had a friend named Cyril Brock. They also had a mandolin and fiddle. They soon learned where we lived in Kentucky and would come out nearly every

Sunday. Mom would cook them a big dinner every time, as she thought she must do that for the "city folks" that came to visit us. We always had a big garden and put up a lot of canned vegetables, but she had to cook a chicken or some kind of meat with it. So her frying chickens were going fast.

Uncle Willie liked to make money, so one day he sent a sawmill crew in, and they cut nearly all the trees in the big 20 acre lawn in front of the Baldorff house. I got acquainted with the folks that ran the sawmill, especially with Si Mitchell, the cook, and I'd eat a lot of meals with them in the tent where they ate. When the sawmill shut down for the day, Si Mitchell would be at his little woodstove in the tent, cooking supper. Many evenings I was there, watching him stir up the biscuits and make the coffee. With the wood burning, the coffee boiling, and the biscuits baking, I thought it was the best smell I ever smelled. Even better, though, was that two of the crew, Wilbert and Joe Lee Howard, had a guitar. And that was how I came to love that instrument. (A lot of people think I've only played the banjo, but the guitar was my first love and my only instrument for many years.)

The Howard boys would leave their guitar at our house, because they thought the damp tent was bad for it, and I'd slip in there and play on it. I thought it was the finest-sounding thing I ever listened to. Wilbert Howard played the guitar tuned down to Spanish style, I call it, and chorded it with a bottle neck on his little finger. He would wrap a twine string around the neck of a bottle, soak the string with turpentine, and set it afire. When the turpentine burned out, he would tap the neck gently and it would break off where he wanted it to. It was from Wilbert that I first learned the tune "Sweet Dreams of Kentucky," which I recorded some 50 years later.

The Lindensmitt boys often brought their fiddle and mandolin along, and we would all gather on the front porch after supper. The Howard boys would come up. Joe Lee played a little steel guitar (a dobro, as they call it now), using his pocketknife for a steel, and Wilbert seconded on his guitar. We played almost every night if it was warm enough, and I became fascinated with the old tunes they played.

The sawmill was there about two or three months. One of the workers was a crippled fellow who was mighty good at the end of a crosscut saw; they called him Toddle Edwards. When he walked, he would throw his leg out and

This is Mom, cleaning a duck on the old Shepherd place in Kentucky.

My childhood pal Randall Sellers (left) and I were trying to look serious—maybe wishing we could drive that old Ford.

around. Later that year our old cow stepped on one of the little chickens and mashed his leg. I felt sorry for him, so I took him to the house and took care of him until he could walk. But he threw his leg out, and my sister Louise said he walked just like Toddle Edwards. So the name stuck, and my chicken was called Toddle Edwards from then on. As I told before, Mom's frying chickens were getting scarce. One Sunday the boys were over from Evansville, and we sat down to dinner. When they passed the chicken to Aubrey, he took a leg, looked at it, and said, "Aw, aw, Toddle's dead!" Well, I jumped up and ran out of the house. I was really hurt.

There was one tree—a beautiful maple, out in the field north of the house—that had a lot of big limbs close to the ground. We used to climb up there, and we could actually walk around because the limbs were so big. We called it the "House Tree." I've spent many happy hours in that tree. I wrote a poem about it and the old place.

The Old House Tree

The highway runs across the yard,
The two big pines are gone,
But things are almost bound to change
As old Time marches on.

There still stand some old locust trees
And a knotty pine around,
Close to the place on top of the hill
Where the old frame house burned down.

The weeds have taken the old front lawn
Where the beautiful maples grew,
But they went like the ash and the white oak
To the sawmiller and his crew.

It makes me sad when I stop and look
From the new highway they made
Through the lawn where the beautiful trees once stood,
And the coolness of their shade

Would beat any air-conditioning
Ever invented by man,

Just sitting on the grassy bank
Where the little spring branch ran.

Why, I remember one old tree
That was so big around
And the limbs spread out—great big limbs—
Just a little ways off the ground.

Us kids would walk around up there.
It was a sight to see,
Just like a room of branches—
We named it "The Old House Tree."

But the old House Tree, it too is gone,
And a fine home stands on the spot.
Some folks say it's a beautiful place,
But to me it's just a blot.

For I saw that place when the House Tree stood
High on that beautiful hill,
And a building won't take the place of a tree,
I don't think it ever will.

But as I said one time before,
Old time marches on,
And many things of our childhood days
Are already past and gone.

But who can say, maybe these same things
Might appear again somewhere,
And a House Tree may be growing
When we all arrive up there.

We had some goats there on the place, and one day Pop butchered one.
We didn't like the meat at all. I guess we didn't fix it right. When we milked
nanny goats, all we could use was two fingers and thumb; but the milk tasted
richer than cow milk. And the nanny goats didn't kick like a cow: they would
just stamp their feet. In Evansville we had a friend named Joe, who could
have won any eating contest that ever was. He got hungry between bites. At
the farm we had a black dog that was the same way, so we named him Joe, too.

When Pop butchered the goat, he took the head way over in the field and threw it away. That night Joe, the dog, was sitting on the front porch. All at once he stuck his nose in the air and took off. We watched, and he went as straight to that goat head, straight as a martin to his gourd.

Pop had some funny sayings. One day he came out of the kitchen with the sheep shears and started for the barn. I asked him what he was going to do. He said, "By gad [that was his byword], I'm going to shear the old mule. She looks like a she-buzzard up a crab apple tree."

There was a lone apple tree on the very top of the hill behind the house, old and all twisted by the wind. I found a lot of arrowheads up there. And a little farther back was an old barn built of logs that had fallen partway down. In the end of one of the logs was a large bumblebees' nest. With nothing else to do, we kids decided to run them out. We started throwing clods of dirt at the hole. Finally, I guess they got tired of it, and here they came. Hundreds of them. Everyone scattered, and I took off toward the pond, which was about 150 yards away. About the time I got there, the bumble did too. He nailed me on the back of the neck. We let them alone after that. I guess they were there when we moved away.

My brother Aubrey, in his younger days, helped operate a still down in Hollow Stump, Kentucky. All of us kids thought moonshine was something, so we begged him into making some to show us how he did it. Soon he had some mash working—the first step in making moonshine. He never did finish it, though, as he would have had to construct a still to cook it off, and he was afraid someone would catch him. We were out in the country but not really far back in the hills. So we got the bright idea of feeding that fermented mash to the hogs, and they loved it. Just in a few minutes we had a whole lot full of drunk hogs. They would try to walk, and then sit down and squeal.

Another trick we did to the hogs was to shock them. There was always a Model T coil and a Hot Shot battery around. Hooked up the right way, those made the best shocking machine that ever was. We would put soaked corn in the trough and wet the ground around it and hook the wires up and call the hogs. When they got a mouthfull, it gave them a jolt, and they would squeal and run. We had one old sow that was what you would call a glutton. She ate everything she could find. We shocked her four or five times, but she kept coming back. She got so she would start running toward the trough and squealing, knowing she was going to get shocked but unable to resist another bite.

Those unfortunate hogs also had a large bumblebees' nest in a stump near them in the barn lot. We would shell corn all around that stump, and then call the hogs. They would start rooting around that stump, and the bees would start doing their work and get all over the poor hogs. Like me, some would head toward the pond, sliding on their hind ends, and never stop until they were under water.

Even the chickens didn't escape our tricks. Aubrey was always fooling with electricity. He would wet the ground around the chicken pan and hook wires to it, and when a hen would peck into the pan, she would yell and fly ten feet high and come down running and cackling. Mom got mad at Aubrey; she said it would make the hens quit laying. He even hooked up the iron gate, and when someone would come and take hold of the gate, Aubrey would let him have it, and whoever it was would jump back and look at his hands and maybe try again. Aubrey got a lot of laughs that way, but somehow no one ever got mad.

I was 12 years old when we moved away from the old Baldorff place. It hadn't been very good to us financially, so I guess Pop did the right thing. It seems we moved an average of once every couple of years back then. I don't see how I ever got through high school. My grades were pretty poor. Anyway, we moved next over to the Shepherd place, owned by Mr. Jim Shepherd. It was a large log house covered with weather-boarding. It had four 20-by-20-foot rooms with a hall in the middle. Long ago it was probably an open dogtrot. That was a cold house; I remember sitting in front of the fireplace, looking through a crack between the chimney and the logs and watching the chickens walk around. I don't really remember getting there, I just started living there.

I know I started to a new school called Posey Chapel. It was a two - room school, one on top of the other. The first, second, third, and fourth grades were downstairs, and the fifth, sixth, seventh, and eight grades were on the top floor. It was four miles up what used to be US 41, except then it was a gravel road. It didn't take long for us to get acquainted with the Sellers family:

Randall, Jane, Dorothy, and Randall, Jr. Junior was to become one of my best friends, and we ran all over that part of the country. The Sellerses had about 150 acres of the finest land around Henderson. Junior and Dorothy used to come over and ask if I wanted to ride to school each morning with them in their pony buggy. The school had a shed and manger, so the kids that drove horses could bring hay and feed the horses at noon. One bunch of kids drove a farm wagon and two fine mules. They brought a gallon of buttermilk every day, and four of them drank it with their meals. Our meals those days usually consisted of some bacon or jowl between a biscuit and some blackberry jam between a biscuit. Maybe two of each. The biscuits with the jam would always be blue by the time the bell rang for lunch (or dinner, we called it). Sometimes we would spread our lunch: everyone put his food out on the grass, and everybody shared. One boy by the name of Robert Poff always had a nice lunch, some things that a lot of us hadn't eaten before—even stalks of celery. So we would try to get him to trade with us, but he soon got on to that. Trading good peanut butter or tuna fish sandwiches for an old cold biscuit with jowl wasn't too good, he thought. And he could run faster than any of us.

One day just before Christmas, the teacher told William Ward, Junior Sellers, and me to go cut a Christmas tree for the school so the girls could decorate it. William Ward came with his dad's farm wagon and two horses, and we started out. I can't remember where we went, but it was far enough so that we didn't get back till almost time to go home. William had his pockets full of parched corn, and we ate it all day. We got the tree and brought it back and decorated it the next day. There was practially no studying until after New Year's Day. They were hard times, but they were good times, growing up in that little corner of northwest Kentucky in the 1920s. They were golden years.

In 1976 I finally got a chance to record the song I learned from the Howard boys on that big old front porch of the Baldorff place so many years before, "Sweet Dreams of Kentucky." I wrote a couple of verses to it that sums up a lot of the way I feel:

> Sweet, sweet dreams of Kentucky,
> I hear you calling for me,

Sweet, sweet dreams of Kentucky,
That's where I'm longing to be.

I know there's a gal that's a-waiting,
By the red rose that grows by the door,
Dear old Kentucky, I know I am lucky,
To be returning once more. *

Three.

THE YOUNG SINGER OF OLD SONGS

I've been Grandpa for so long that it's hard to believe I started out billing myself as the "Young Singer of Old Songs," but I did. I was a young skinny boy with curly hair and a work shirt and suspenders, and I was using my middle name, calling myself Marshall Jones. Let me try to tell you how it all came about.

By the time I graduated from the eighth grade, I still had not been able to get a guitar, but I had never stopped wishing for one. In addition to listening to music by our neighbors, I heard music from my pop and even from my mom. Pop was an old-time fiddler, and I remember him playing old tunes like "Bonaparte's Retreat." But he played it a lot different from the way people play it now, more like a schottische. My mother was the daughter of another old-time fiddler, and she sang old songs and played the concertina. In fact, several of the songs I later recorded I learned from my mother. She used to sing the old ballad "Daisy Dean" and said it was supposed to be based on a true event. And she used to sing, "Don't Make Me Go to Bed and I'll Be Good." And later on, when she heard me do my version of it on records, she criticized the tune I used; she said, "Where'd you get that tune?"

The years 1927 and 1928 were in the heyday of Jimmie Rodgers, the Blue

Yodeler, and all of us loved his records—along with millions of other Americans. My brother Gordon bought every Jimmie Rodgers record that came out back then, and we played them on an old Graphaphone that my oldest sister Velma had gotten from Larken and Company years before. Gordon watched for new Jimmie Rodgers records like a hawk, and when he got one, for the first few days he wouldn't let us play it because he was afraid we would get our hands on the grooves and make them greasy. We had records by other artists, too, some country and some not. Mom liked old-time singers like Henry Burr and opera singers like Alma Gluck, and my sisters liked recordings by bands and orchestras. But Gordon and I were really stuck on Jimmie Rodgers. I used to listen for hours to how Jimmie did his yodels, and before long I'd learned the words to a lot of his songs.

Then, finally, my brother Aubrey came across. He was working at the Myer Brothers garage in Henderson, and one evening he came in and said, "Son [he always called me son], go out there and look in the cab of the truck." I expected to find a sack of candy, but you can imagine my joy when I looked in and there on the seat of the truck lay an old guitar. It was warped a little, but it looked like gold to me. I don't think it even had a brand name on it; Aubrey had bought it at a secondhand place called Cheap John's for 75 cents.

That night I didn't eat any of my supper, even though Mom had a lot of good things on the table—including a plate of her beautiful biscuits. I began practicing and kept it up in the weeks to come, picking up what little I could from watching anybody that played a guitar—even the blind street singers that sang on the corners in Henderson.

The people built what they called a community building right by the side of the old Posey Chapel school that I have been talking about, the one I finished the eighth grade in, and they'd have dances there. I'd go and watch the players pick. I remember one night three black men were playing for the dance; it was really cold that night, and the building was large with only a potbellied stove in the middle for heat. The boys would play square dance music, and between numbers they would strike matches and hold their fingers over the flame to try to get them warmed up enough for the next dance.

I kept going and watching the different bands, and finally one night one of the groups asked me to sit in with them. I nearly fainted, but I got up there with my 75-cent guitar and played. I really thought I had it made. I'd watch the other guitar player and make the chords he made. That's the way I eventually learned to chord the guitar. And then when I could get away somewhere so no one could hear, I'd try to sing the Jimmie Rodgers songs. Finally I got up my confidence and came out in the open with it, and got to where I didn't mind if people heard me.

Meantime, I had started to Barrett Manual Training High School in Henderson. I went in style. A friend of the family who had stayed with us a long time didn't have any money when he left, so he said he would leave his old Model T Ford coupe with us, and if he didn't come back after it for so many months, it was ours. The family gave it to me to drive to high school. Since the Sellerses had let me ride to school in their pony buggy, I told Dorothy that she could ride with me to high school in the Ford coupe.

Then one day when I came home and started to pick up my guitar, I sensed an uneasiness in the family. It was hard to put your finger on it, but it was there. And I knew what it meant. It was time for another move. But where to this time? I soon found out that it wouldn't be in Henderson County, where I grew up—in fact, not even in the state of Kentucky. We were going this time to Akron, Ohio. The reason for this was that my oldest brother, Wilmer, worked with the telephone company there, and he thought he could get jobs for all of us boys, and our sisters too. (And, in fact, he managed to do just that later on.) Louise, Eugene, and Spurgeon had already gone up there to work, and Pop had no one left but me to help him make a crop. The move made sense to him.

But school would be starting there before the family was ready to go, so I went up early to live with my sister Louise in her apartment. Aubrey drove me up in his old Model T, which was a little the worse for wear. It had been hit in the front and the radiator mashed in. After we crossed over into Ohio, we stopped at a little station for gas. The attendant took a look at the front and said, "Does your radiator leak?" Aubrey said, "Not a drop." The attendant replied, "It looks like it wouldn't hold shock fodder." We laughed, but I began to wonder if we would have the same trouble adjusting that we had had when we moved into town before. Would they think we were hillbillies up here, too?

It wasn't all that bad, though. I ran into Rex Stephens, a boy from Henderson, and we began to run around together. After a while, the folks drove up in a car called a Baby Overland, pulling a big trailer filled with furniture. I met them with some bad news: when I enrolled in West High School in Akron, I found they wouldn't give me credit for the year of high school I had taken in Henderson. I had to start out as a freshman again. But I stuck it out.

Things were better at home, and best of all, we were getting to hear more music. My brother Wilmer had studied radio from the time the first ones came out, and he knew quite a bit about how to build them. Once in 1923, when we were living at Grandpa Wise's old place, Wilmer brought his family to visit us and brought along enough parts to build a radio. No one in Smith Mills had one at the time, so when he got it built and the word got around that it was working, there wasn't a night went by that the house wasn't full of people waiting to hear the radio. But that first little crystal set he built was not very powerful, and besides, you had to use earphones to hear it. So many people got to coming and wanting to listen that we had to figure out some way to let more than one at a time listen. Finally, he got the idea of laying the headphones in a washtub to amplify the sound. It wasn't exactly stereo, but it sounded great to us then. At least we could all listen.

The first station we caught clearly was WOS in Jefferson City, Missouri. (In those days, all the stations had call letters that stood for something. WOS, they said, stood for "Watch Our State"; WLS in Chicago stood for "World's Largest Store" because it was then owned by Sears, Roebuck; WSM in Nashville was owned by the National Life and Accident Insurance Company, and it stood for "We Shield Millions.") The first barn dance music I remember hearing on the air came out of WOS in Jefferson City. There was some fiddling and banjo picking, and there was one man they used to let out of prison each day so he could be on the show. He was serving time in the state prison there, but he was a great old-time piano player. His name was Harry Snodgrass, and later on, after he got paroled, he played a lot of personal appearances around the country.

Aubrey soon learned how to make these radio sets himself, so when Wilmer went to Akron, Aubrey would get him to send him back the parts,

"The Young Singer of Old Songs" at the tender age of 23.

and he would build radios. He got to where he was selling them regularly to the farmers around where we lived. One time he built a neutrodyne receiver (which was a considerable improvement over the crystal sets but was eventually superseded by superheterodyne receivers); it had three dials on it, and you had to tune each one to a certain place to get it right. When Aubrey got it going, some fellow around there gave him $250 and a good Jersey milk cow for it. And at that time $250 was a lot of money.

By the late 1920s we had started listening pretty much to WLS in Chicago—we could get it better than a lot of the stations in Nashville or Atlanta. And WLS had good country music in those days, with the old *National Barn Dance* still going strong. We heard people like Bradley Kincaid, Chubby Parker, the Maple City Four, the Hoosier Hot Shots, Arkie the Arkansas Woodchopper, and many more. It was *the* country show then and a long time after that. (It continued to be very popular for years after I got into the business, but then somebody got the idea to put a pop orchestra in back of it, and it lasted about as long as a June frost.) As I watched my brothers build these funny-looking radio sets, and I hunkered down listening to the far-off sounds of fiddlers and singers I had never seen, I had no idea that I someday would make my living over this strange new gadget.

It took me only a few days to figure out that nobody in Akron was going to make fun of us for being "hillbillies." All of Summit County, where Akron was located, was full of people who had come up from Kentucky and West Virginia—because of the rubber factories. In fact, where we were, West Virginia was first in population, Kentucky I believe was second, and Summit County itself was third. A lot of the families that moved up there would have these get-togethers and pickings. These people didn't live in one particular place—they lived all over the area. In fact, we were poor as Job's turkey, but we lived out in the west end, which was not so much a ritzy neighborhood itself, but out a little farther was.

I played for a lot of square dances, but they were in dancehalls, you know. For instance, one of them was called the Whispering Pines, and there was the Land O Dance—two or three of them—but they all held square dances, with country music.

As I worked my way through high school (the only subject I really liked

One of our early radio bands up in Akron in 1931 included Davy West on the fiddle, Joe Troyan with the harmonica, George Coleman on banjo, a boy named Tuttle in the spats and light coat, and me with guitar and bow tie. I don't remember why we were so dressed up.

was woodworking), I kept singing and playing the guitar. Pretty soon I had managed to copy down by hand a lot of the old songs and some of the current hits. One day they asked me to sing in a high school assembly. I did a couple of old songs, and the opera student sang "Old Man River" and "Give a Man a Horse He Can Ride." Then a cute little girl I had been making eyes at did what she called a gypsy dance. The kids really liked it all, and after that all three of us performed quite a bit. I also entertained at a neighborhood boardinghouse where we used to live. I was overcoming my shyness about singing in public but still hadn't thought about doing anything else with my music.

That's when Wendell Hall came to town and held his talent contest, and that's when I won my first fame singing "Dear Old Sunny South by the Sea" and "Going Back to Texas." That was March 1929, and that was my first time on the radio—and I've been on the air off and on ever since. My prize money from that talent contest bought me my first good guitar, a brand-new little green Gibson, and I still have it today. I also got a chance to start playing on the radio there in Akron.

One afternoon WJW in Akron (it's in Cleveland now) sent me a card saying I was scheduled to do a radio show at 3:30 P.M. for 15 minutes. My announcer was Wayne Johnson, and he had to do the talking between numbers, as I was too scared to talk on the mike. Naturally, I did a lot of Jimmie Rodgers songs, as he was so popular then. I thought I had done well, but when I got home, Pop said, "Well, your program was all right if you hadn't done so much of that 'huy-huy'." Of course, he meant yodeling. My feathers fell when he said that.

In my first days on WJW I was nervous as a cat at a dog show before every broadcast. The announcers were not much interested in what I was doing—they would usually read the paper or something while I was singing. I would give them a list of my songs before I went on, and usually one would just say, "Now here's Marshall to sing 'Dear Old Southern Home,'" and as soon as I got done with that, he would say, "Now here's Marshall to sing 'The Roane County Prison Song.'" That would go on for 15 minutes, and when it was over, I'd be completely given out—I didn't have any time between songs, and some of them were pretty long. Finally, after I had been on the air for about a year, I got a "commercial"—that's what we used to call a radio show with a real sponsor. My first sponsor was Dr. Pennington, who billed himself as "Akron's leading dentist," and would pull your tooth for 50 cents. He had long office hours—from 9:00 A.M. to 8:00 P.M. Monday through Saturday and even from 10:00 to 1:00 on Sundays. It's sort of unusual to hear a dentist sponsoring a show today, but not back in the late 1920s when radio was just getting started.

The commercials for Dr. Pennington made it a little easier on me—at least I had time to catch my breath between numbers—and I found I needed to get up more songs, since I was on every day. I got a WLS song book and sang most of the songs in that, and then a lot of Jimmie Rodgers tunes and anything else I heard that I liked. I began collecting songs at that time, and writing them down in a big notebook. After a while I had a sheet printed up with the words to eight songs on it, along with my picture and an ad for the dentist. I wrote under my photo: "I'll sing one of these songs in each of my radio programs and I'd like to have you sing right along with me. You can't beat these old-time songs—nothing fancy about them, but they make mighty pleasant singing." The songs were "Eleven Cent Cotton and Forty Cent Meat," an old one about hard times; "Corrina, Corrina," and old blues number; "Twenty-One Years" and "Eleven More Months and Ten More Days," both old-time prison songs; "Silver-Haired Daddy of Mine," which was a big hit that year (1932) by Gene Autry; "Old Pals Are the Best," a sentimental tune with a Jimmie Rodgers yodel; "Blue Ridge Mountain Blues"; and "The Bum Song," written by the old hobo singer Mac McClintock. In a sense, you could say this was my first song book, but it wasn't any more than a sheet of paper printed on both sides. Still, it was a start.

Dr. Pennington paid me all of $14 a week. The Depression was really on then, and I was giving Mom $11 of this for groceries and keeping $3.00 to go to school on. I somehow managed to keep up in high school while I was on the radio. Finally, I got a better commercial deal with a radio store as the sponsor; it was called Bator Radio, on Exchange Street, and Mr. Bator paid me $16 a week. But I still found I needed to get more work with my music, and this led to the only time in my life when I didn't play country music. For years all the popular dance orchestras had had a tenor banjo to keep rhythm with—a four-string banjo that was strummed for rhythm. All of a sudden in the early 1930s, the tenor banjo went out of favor, and all the orchestras were replacing them with guitars. So one of the local dance band leaders came to me and said, "I want you to play guitar in my orchestra." I said, "I can't play with you. I don't know the chords to all these modern songs." "Well," he said, "it will be right in front of you there on the bandstand." I did know some chords, so I went on and played—played about six months with trumpets and saxophones and everything. I got to where I could play in there pretty well.

I also started playing some local theaters with a girl's trio headed by a woman named Josephine Dye; I did a lot of the car driving to dates around the area. Our booker was a man of about 70 who had been an important showman in his time, and he tried to be master of ceremonies for us, but did a poor job. He was crippled up and walked with a cane, and what resulted wasn't much of a show.

Before long, though, I found a regular partner. His name was Joe Troyan, though thousands of country music fans remember him as Bashful Harmonica Joe. In early 1931, Rudy Vallee, the famous singer and bandleader who is known for "The Whiffenpoof Song," held a show and an amateur contest in Cleveland. Since Akron was only about 35 miles from Cleveland, I went up to audition for it. Rudy Vallee picked out the seven winners; he chose me and my yodeling as one, and Joe and his trick harmonica playing as another. And it was some bunch of tricks, too. He would flip the harmonica and keep it in his mouth; he would play it using a little glass tumbler like a mute; he would play what he called the world's smallest harmonica; he would play by blowing into a rubber tube and directing its open end into the harmonica. And he did all sorts of animal imitations.

Joe and I became fast friends. He was about the same age I was, and had been born in Pleasant City, Ohio, though he was then living in Cleveland. He was Slavic, and had four brothers and a sister. His mother was one of the best cooks I ever met. I never could talk to her directly, since she didn't speak English (Joe acted as an interpreter for me), but she cooked all kinds of dishes that seemed exotic to someone like me who had been raised on hog meat and potatoes, and she made some of the best pastries I have ever eaten. After Joe and I started playing dates together, I got to sample them often. In our act, I

The Pine Ridge String Band on the Lum and Abner show in 1933: standing (from left) are George Coleman, Joe Troyan, Davy West, Andy Patterson, Marshall Jones, Warren Caplinger; seated are Lum (left), the Josephine Dye trio, and Abner.

would sing, yodel, and play the guitar; Joe would play the harmonica and do all sorts of comic imitations. We worked wherever we could, for a time we played two different night clubs on the same Saturday night, and "bicycled" (drove back and forth). And we were on radio at WJW in Akron as well as WHK in Cleveland. Between all this, we got up a pretty good income, for a time when so many were out of work and 20 cents would buy a good meal. We had to practice a lot, though. Joe recently wrote about some of those days, and said, "Grandpa could practice eight hours a day, he had such a strong voice. And good pitch. One day we were riding along on a bus in Akron, and they had a little fan in the bus to keep us cool, and Grandpa leaned over next to the fan and cocked his ear, and told me, 'Joe, dad-burn, that fan's in the key of C.' "

We worked wherever we could. A famous country promoter named Larry Sunbrock came to Akron twice a year; he'd rent the armory and have it crammed full every time, doing nothing but country. He'd always bring Natchee the Indian, the most popular trick fiddler of that day, and hold a big fiddling contest. But Larry booked the local Akron talent, too. I worked for him some, and that's where I met Cowboy Copas. We were both 19, and he was playing an act with Natchee.

Putting it all together, Joe and I weren't doing too bad. When I graduated from high school in the spring of 1932, I was able to wear two-tone white and black shoes, white pants, and a dark coat. I thought I was something. Herbert Hoover was still president, about 12 million people were out of work, and the Army veterans were marching on Washington trying to get their bonus money.

While I was on the radio in Akron, I met another pair of musicians who had had a lot more experience at country music than I had: Warren Caplinger and Andy Patterson. Andy was from Petros, in the wild part of east Tennessee, and Warren—or "Cap," as they called him—had been born on the Kanawha River in West Virginia. Andy told me that he and Cap first got acquainted at Brushy Mountain Penitentiary while Andy was assistant warden there in the 1920s. (I always said there was a thin line between musicians, preachers, and criminals—they might go either way.) Andy was a big, jovial, red-haired boy, and soon he and Warren were playing at dances around the area. (One of the songs I learned from them was "Roane County Prison" or, as it's more commonly known, "The Hills of Roane County"; it's a famous Tennessee murder ballad, and some of the verses Cap and Andy used to sing mention "Big Brushy" as the prison where the killer is sent.) They made quite a few records in the next several years, with a band they called Caplinger and Patterson's Cumberland Mountain Entertainers. By the time I met them, they were pretty well known, and I was really happy when they asked me to join them in show dates, singing the third part of a trio.

Later they took on a boy named Flip Strickland; as Cap, Andy, and Flip, they got a really huge radio audience, though they are about forgotten today and seldom mentioned in country music history books. Flip sang tenor, Andy lead, and Cap the third part. They later moved down to West Virginia and worked in Wheeling, Charleston, Fairmont, and across the river in Ashland, Kentucky. While they were at Wheeling, they started doing gospel songs and got to where they specialized in them; they would perform at area churches and "all-day singings," and later on they played at what we used to call "hillbilly parks." But more about that later.

In Akron I was proud to be a part of Cap and Andy's act. They were singing a lot of gospel songs even then, and I had sung gospel songs in church as a boy. Now I was finding that people liked to hear them on the radio and at concerts, too. Then one day in the late fall of 1932, Cap came to us and said that the team of Lum and Abner needed a string band for the new radio show they were starting over WTAM in Cleveland.

This was real news. Lum and Abner's show had been started just the year before by a couple of young businessmen from Mena, Arkansas; they were Chester Lauck (Lum) and Norris Goff (Abner), and in the show these two played country types who spent most of their time at the Jot'em Down Store in an imaginary Arkansas town called Pine Ridge. The show had become a nationwide success, and on Thanksgiving night they were going to move to Cleveland (from Chicago, where they started) and begin a new season. Along with their regular show about the Jot'em Down Store, they were going to have a "Friday Night Social" program which would be broadcast from an imaginary country schoolhouse. They needed the old-time string band for this part of the show. The sponsor would be the Ford dealers around the country—someone said it was the first time Ford had gone in for radio advertising. And though the sponsors really aimed the show at residents of Ohio and Pennsylvania, it would be heard on some 44 different stations. That's why we were excited about the news. It would really be the big time.

We had already been playing in a little string band, so we just formed it up and went down to audition. It was a good band. Andy and a guy named Davy West played fiddle, Cap and I played guitars, Joe did the harmonica, a man named George Coleman played the banjo, and some older man whose name I don't recall played the bass fiddle with a bow. As I said, Cap and Andy were both good enough that they had made quite a few records, so we weren't exactly an amateur group. After the audition, Lum and Abner wanted to know how much we would charge. Cap told Lum he didn't know what to charge, so Lum said they could give us $10 a man and pay our expenses. Cap said later he nearly fell over; he had been set to ask for $25 for all six of us! We struck a bargain and went out of the studio to pile into Andy's Nash Twin Ignition Six; on the way home we were feeling pretty good. It looked like a good Christmas.

It was really fun working with Lum and Abner. Though they dressed up in mustache (Lum) and goatee (Abner), they were in real life nice-looking young men. We became the Pine Ridge String Band: I played guitar and sang solos; Joe, besides playing harmonica in the band, did all the imitations of farm animals needed for the radio show's sound effects. We did a lot of live theater dates with Lum and Abner as well. The first was in Warren, Ohio. We played in between their acts. They came out and did a sketch and then introduced our band; we did a little show, and then all the lights in the place would go off; Lum and Abner would go out in front and discuss why the lights went out—they'd argue about who ran out of coal oil and all such as that—and all the while they were changing into the most beautiful white suits that could be bought. When the lights came back on—all they had to do was flip the switch—there they were in the latest of clothes, in direct contrast to the old clothes they started the show with. They looked grand. (The band dressed in country clothes, but nice ones: I used to wear a white shirt with tie and suspenders.)

Because Lum and Abner were so popular on radio, we always drew good crowds in the theaters. About the only place I remember that we didn't have a good crowd was a little theater somewhere in Ohio; for some reason there were sparse pickings, and Lum and Abner decided to joke around. When they came out, Lum had on Abner's false goatee, and Abner had on Lum's mustache. I remember thinking that Abner looked like General Grant. And he may have felt like him that night. But most of the times we did good shows, and the people really liked them, and we were all sorry when Lum and Abner moved their show back to Chicago in 1934. Even today I still occasionally hear recordings of old Lum and Abner programs on some radio stations.

Four.

Harmonica Joe kept a diary of a lot of our early show business, and he says the date was February 24, 1935, when the next part of our careers started. After Lum and Abner went back to Chicago, and Andy and Cap lit out for West Virginia, Joe and I went back to playing the local clubs wherever we could find them, at $5.00 a night. On this night, though, we were part of a special show at the Akron Armory; it was called the Milk Fund Show, a charity affair to raise money to get kids milk. In 1935 times were still pretty lean around the country. Gene and Glenn, the famous duet singers from the old WLS days, came down from their new base at WTAM, Cleveland, and headlined the show, along with one of my idols from years past, Bradley Kincaid.

I had listened to Bradley over WLS on those little radio sets my brother Aubrey had built, and in 1935 he was about the most popular folk singer in the country. He had been born in the mountain country close to Lancaster, Kentucky; he told me that he started in the fourth grade when he was 19 and worked all the way up through Berea College while he was waiting tables at the Boone Tavern Hotel there in Berea. Later on, he attended a YMCA college in Chicago, and while there he was invited to sing with the college glee club over WLS radio. Someone told the program director that Bradley could sing mountain ballads and play the guitar, and he was invited to sing the following Saturday night on the *National Barn Dance.* One song he did was "Barbara Allen," and it drew so much mail that he had to sing it every Saturday night for the next two years. He started playing theaters and selling song books, and did very well. After WLS, he moved on to other large stations—KDKA Pittsburgh, WTIC Hartford, WLW Cincinnati—and began making records. He had several hit songs like "The Fatal Wedding," "Methodist Pie," "Liza up a 'Simmon Tree," and "Some Little Bug Is Goin' to Get You Some Day."

We watched Bradley play for the Milk Fund that night, and then Joe and I got up and did our act. We didn't know it at the time, but Bradley had stayed around to watch us. After the show he came up and introduced himself. He was a big, tall, handsome man with wavy black hair and an easy smile. "How would you boys like to join me in West Virginia" he asked, "and then go on up to New England and play on the East Coast for a while?" We didn't know what to say, we were so bumfuzzled. We managed to tell him we would go ask our folks, and Bradley said he would send us a wire where and when to meet him. Since we had never been away from home for any length of time, Joe went home to Cleveland, and I went home there in Akron, and that night we had long talks with our families. Finally, it was decided we could go. Bradley's wire told us to meet him at the Palace Theater in Huntington, West Virginia.

So, on March 6, 1935 (according to Joe's notebook), we played our last date in Ohio, Joe and I, at a place called the Zeppelin Inn at Peninsula, Ohio, from midnight until two o'clock in the morning. I had a 1932 Plymouth that was in pretty good shape, so Joe and I started for West Virginia right after the show. We set our speed at 45 miles per hour, a good clip for those days and those roads, and we drove all night. Bradley was coming in from New York and was to meet us at the theater for a matinee that afternoon. When we got to Pleasant City, Ohio, Joe's hometown, we stopped for breakfast and a good visit with his uncle. Then we pushed on toward the Ohio River through the Wayne National Forest and pulled into Huntington at ten-thirty in the morning, just a few hours before the matinee was to go on.

Even though we were bone tired, we started getting excited, but we couldn't find the theater at first; we drove all over downtown looking for it.

Finally, we turned a corner and there it was: a marquee for the RKO Palace. "Why, by doggies, Joe, lookie there," I said. "They've got our names in lights. Dad-burn. How do you like that?" We stopped at the theater and looked up. It said: "Bradley Kincaid, with Marshall Jones and Harmonica Joe, from the Lum and Abner Show." We got a big kick out of that—our names up in lights for the first time. But we didn't have long to savor it: Bradley drove up a few minutes later, and we were off to rehearse the first show.

That day we did one at 2:00 P.M. and the next one at 5:00 P.M. We hardly had time to catch our breath from that before we went over to the local radio station, WSAZ, for a 6:30 P.M. broadcast, then back to the theater for a show at 8:00 P.M. We staggered to our rooms at the Frederick Hotel at 11:00, about as ready for bed as we had ever been. We'd been going for over 24 hours straight, had driven over 200 miles, and had done five shows since we'd last slept. Who said show business was easy work?

The next day we repeated the same schedule of three live shows and a radio spot, and the day after that we did it all once again. Then on Sunday morning we drove up to Madison, Indiana, and did three shows that afternoon. I got to meet another star there; Gene Autry came over and visited Bradley between shows. They had been on WLS Chicago together, and now Gene was on WHAS in Louisville. "I'm not making enough money to feed my horse," Gene said, and asked Bradley what to do. We didn't hear the advice, but in a few months Gene got his call to go to Hollywood, where he became the country's most popular singing cowboy.

I was still pretty much a country boy. One morning we were all three having breakfast—bacon and eggs—and I was holding down a thick piece of bacon with my fingers and breaking it with a knife. Bradley said, "Marshall, you're supposed to use a knife and fork to eat the bacon, especially a fork." I looked up at him and said, "Well, dad-burn, Bradley, what in the world did people do before there were knives and forks?"

We kept up the touring, driving through Indiana and Kentucky where Bradley had lined up dates. We played several shows at Owensboro, where my brother Homer lived, and visited Henderson, my old home place. Homer put us up one night and saved us $1.00 on the hotel bill, even though eight of us

I had just gotten my mustache and started doing Grandpa bits when this publicity shot was made in Boston about 1936. Bashful Harmonica Joe is practicing a comedy bit on Bradley Kincaid, while I try to see what's going on.

*Here's an informal shot of
Bradley and the New Grandpa in
New England.*

had to sleep in one room. By April 2, 1935, we had moved on to Piqua, and then headed out for Parkersburg, West Virginia. Sleep caught up with us first, though, and we stopped for the night in Lancaster, Ohio. There was no one on duty at the hotel, though the doors were all open and the lights on. We waited around for a while, getting sleepier and sleepier, and finally we picked out our rooms and got the keys and went on to bed. When we got up the next morning, we sure found someone on duty, but I made a point of telling Joe, as we checked out, "You know, we could have walked away with that hotel." It's something you sure wouldn't see today—a self-service hotel.

We worked at Parkersburg and then drove on toward Elkins—through nothing but hills and hills and more hills. I remember saying to Bradley, "I wonder what they grow down here." Bradley said, "Just about the same things they grow in Ohio, Marshall." "Well," I said, "if I lived down here I'd plant hills. They always come up—and then disappear faster than a June frost." But the hills got to us a couple of nights later when we hit a bad late winter storm and could hardly drive. We were due in a little town called East Rainelle, West Virginia, for a midnight show, but we didn't get there until nearly two in the morning. Boy, we've blown this one, I thought. But we found the theater packed—packed with sleeping people, dozing in their seats and in the lobby, waiting for us. It was quite a night. We woke them up, and worked extra hard to give them a good show. Not only were we grateful to them for staying, but it was the last show in this area we were supposed to do with Bradley, and we wanted to go out big.

That night on the way to the hotel, Bradley and Joe and I discussed our future. Bradley had plans to start broadcasting over WBZ in Boston (on the NBC network) in two weeks; he wanted Joe and me to join him. Joe and I talked it over. The last six weeks had been hard work, but it had been fun, and we knew what a great trouper Bradley was; he was fair and honest, and drew the kind of crowds we could never hope to draw by ourselves. On that foggy night in the mountains of West Virginia, we decided that unless our parents objected, we would go with him.

We went home for a week's rest, then on April 17 left for Boston, where we met Bradley at the LaSalle hotel. Within a few hours the three of us had rented an apartment in the Roosevelt Apartments on Forsyth Street. We got settled in, and Bradley decided to teach us thrift. He brought in an empty cigar box, and said, "Each time we play a date, we each put one dollar into this box for the rent." That worked all right, but there were a few other things to get adjusted to. We shared the cooking duties, but Bradley soon took over making the coffee—he said we jerked the pot off too fast. There was only one bedroom, and I had a cot, which I didn't like too well; even on mornings after I got ten hours' sleep, I'd wake up tired. And to top it all off, we were homesick. "We must be five million miles from home," I'd tell Joe, and at times like those I'd think about going back, back to WJW radio in Akron, where I knew I always had a job waiting for me. But Joe and I stuck it out.

Country music had not really become very popular in New England yet, and Bradley sensed this. His plan was to go on the air and play a regular radio spot for a month before we started playing theaters; that way people would get to know us and show up at our concerts. As it turned out, we had been on only a couple of weeks when the mail started piling in, and we started getting requests to play show dates. Back in those days, a country singer made his real money from show dates, not from radio pay, so we decided to go on and start booking dates ahead of Bradley's schedule. We tried our first concert at Gardner, Massachusetts; we played three shows there and never did get all the people in who wanted to see it. We couldn't believe our luck—these New Englanders liking our type of music! But that first night was no fluke; in the next few weeks, turning away crowds became the rule more than the exception. We even played fashionable Newport and had a good crowd. And the people in New England were some of the nicest I ever played for. Every night somebody would say, "Now you just come home with us, and we'll fix you supper." And it would be fine. If we couldn't go home with them, they'd often put a pie or a cake in our car, and we'd find it when we got ready to leave. And these weren't people who had moved up from Kentucky or Tennessee; they were northerners who had lived there all their lives, just good old-timey people. In fact, I guess they're some of the oldest-timers in the United States.

We worked our stage shows down to a pretty tight routine. To start with, Joe did his bashful act, pulling Bradley's pant legs up and all such silliness, and then he would straighten up and play the harmonica really well. Then I would come out and sing a few songs. I still did a lot of the old Jimmie Rodgers tunes

Here I am with Harmonica Joe somewhere in New England. We took a lot of snapshots with our little Kodak in those days.

that my folks had sung, and some others that I learned from Bradley. Joe and I liked to do a yodel song that two boys from Switzerland had taught us; we called it "Tritzem Yodel." It was supposed to be in Swedish, but I doubt if it would have made a Swede very homesick. It went over well, though, and we used it on almost every show. After we had done our songs, Bradley would come out and do his solo numbers. (He also usually acted as emcee.) He wore a plaid shirt and high-top boots, just like the ones I still wear. In fact, that's where I got the idea of using them. A lot of times we would stage a little amateur contest before we did our show—something to get up a little local interest and stretch out the evening. This always worked well, except for one wild evening in Woonsocket, Rhode Island, when we had something like 27 amateur acts show up. Believe me, we were late getting off that night.

In fact, it was after one of these late nights that I got the name Grandpa—even though I was only 22 years old. We had begun booking out as far away as northern Maine, and had to drive back late at night and then go on the air early the next morning at WBZ. Bradley was the emcee and had to act like he wasn't at all sleepy, but we *were* sleepy, and it was hard to hide it. To make matters worse, I was still fighting that old cot in our room, and I was a little grumpy. Bradley said one morning, "Get up to the microphone. You're just like an old grandpa." And the way I talked, the same way I still do, made me sound older than I was, and pretty soon people were writing in and saying, "Just how old is that old fellow? He sounds about 80." So we decided to play this up. There was a famous old-time comedy team in Boston then, Bert Swor and Lou Lubin; they had been in vaudeville doing a blackface act for years and years and knew something about makeup. (Lou became the barber in the famous *Amos 'n' Andy* radio program later on.) They took me down to a store that had wigs and makeup of all kinds and bought me a false mustache and a pencil to draw lines in my face to make me look like an old man. Bradley gave me some leather boots that were all of 50 years old, and I started talking all the time on the radio in my whiny voice, and I've been Grandpa ever since. (I've worn those same boots every show I played since then; I have to resole them regularly, just wearing them from the dressing room to the stage and back.)

In spite of the homesickness, being in New England was exciting for two country boys. One day Joe and I walked down to the beach just to wash our

This is Bradley's famous LaSalle, with me looking like I owned it.

hands in the Atlantic Ocean; we thought it was unbelievable. And we visited dozens of historical sites and clicked hundreds of pictures with our little cameras. I was amazed to see all those places I had read about in history books—I had always like history in school—places like the Old North Church and Bunker Hill and Paul Revere's house. But we were still country boys. One night up in Bidderford, Maine, Joe and I checked into the hotel, put our pants on a chair, and crashed into bed. Bradley came in later and found us sound asleep—with our pants on the chair and the door wide open. He took our pants and left the door ajar, and waited for nature to take its course. The next morning when we woke up, we were dumfounded. We didn't know what to do; we couldn't even go out in the hall or up to Bradley's room, since we didn't have any pants. Worse yet, I'd had $7.50 in my pocket, and that was gone. We didn't even have a phone. So we waited, and talked, and hoped. Finally, Bradley appeared at the door. "How did you guys sleep?" he asked. We told him what had happened, and he listened with a straight face, really making us sweat it out before he smiled and confessed what he had done. But then came the sermon. "You're not at home now. You can't trust all people. You've got to hang your trousers in the closet and not only close your doors but *lock* them." Then he gave us back our pants, with the $7.50 intact. It was another lesson from Bradley.

In Akron, I had gotten acquainted with a family named Holder, from Tennessee. Mrs. Holder made the finest biscuits I've ever eaten, so I had dinner at their house quite a lot. The Holder kids all went to the First Baptist Church in Akron, and they got me to go to BYPU (Baptist Young People's Union) with them. When I went to Boston, I missed this. After a Saturday night concert, Joe would always ask people where the nearest Catholic church was, and I would always ask people where the nearest Baptist church was. But one day I decided to walk out and find one on my own; I walked to Roxbury, which wasn't very far from our apartment, and sure enough, found a Baptist church right away. I saw a bunch of young people milling around, so I asked one of them if they were having BYPU there, and he said they were getting ready for choir practice. I said we had just moved to town and I was hunting for a church to go to, and he told me to get a robe and come on in. "I don't even know the songs," I said. "Don't worry," he replied. "There will be a person on each side of you singing what you are supposed to sing." Well, while I was singing away up there, Joe and Bradley came looking for me. They had proceeded by checking through every Baptist church in the area. They looked up and down the aisles and all over the church, and were about ready to leave when Joe glanced up toward the choir loft and broke into a big grin. He nudged Bradley and pointed up my way, and they both smiled. They hadn't expected to find me there, choir robe and all.

Later on I got to know my friend in the choir pretty well. His name was McGlofflin, and his whole family were hymn singers. At his home, Mrs. McGofflin would play the pump organ while all the rest of us sat on the floor and bellowed out the old hymns. And Mr. McGofflin was not only a powerful singer—he was powerful, period. So were his sons, but he used to take them on one at a time in wrestling matches, and he usually won.

Hymns were popular on our radio show, too. Bradley would get a lot of letters asking him to do old hymns—people really liked his nice clear tenor voice. I remember one summer morning in New Hampshire in 1935, we all three gathered to read our fan mail before doing a show that afternoon at the theater. We took our time and opened more than 40 letters that had come to the station. Most were asking Bradley and me to sing hymns. That afternoon Bradley asked the manager of the theater if it was all right with him to sing hymns on stage during our show. "Hail, yes," he barked. "Sing 'em a hymn!"

Bashful Harmonica Joe took religion seriously—religion and baseball. (He had been a semiprofessional ballplayer, and a lot of afternoons he spent watching the Boston Red Sox.) Of course, he would never eat meat on Fridays. This was all right when we were playing up in Maine because you could get fresh lobsters for $1.25 a dinner then. One Friday at lunch Bradley asked Joe, "Why is it that you can't eat meat on Fridays?" "I really don't know," Joe replied. "We never did at home. We thought it was a sin. Maybe the good Lord *made* fish and lobster and other seafood to be eaten on Friday." Bradley thought about this for a while, and then said, "You know, maybe you're right. The change sounds good. I think Grandpa and I will stop eating meat on Fridays, too. It'll be good to lose some weight." I didn't mind this too much, as long as we were in Maine and getting fresh lobsters and clams every meal—I don't mean just on Fridays, either—but after a month of it, I said, "Joe, maybe we ought to get back to eating meat again some of these days."

On July 15, 1935, we left Boston driving in Bradley's big LaSalle on a two-week trip of show dates. We were booked to do 14 towns and 35 shows in all. We were to start out in Pascoag, Rhode Island; go on to Northampton and Amherst, Massachusetts; then to Rochester, New Hampshire; and on up to Maine, where we were to play Waterville, Portland, Bath, Rockland, Fort Fairfield, Houlton, Bangor, and some smaller places. They didn't allow Sunday shows in the state of Maine back then, and we got worried when we noticed that one of our bookings was on a Sunday afternoon. We pulled into the little town expecting the worst, but when we got to the theater, the manager met us smiling and ready to go. "Don't worry," he beamed. "I've already paid the fine in advance!" Sure enough, we had a full house, and everything went fine—for about 15 minutes. Then a huge storm hit and knocked out the lights all over town, including the theater. We didn't know what to do, but those Down Easters weren't about to give up after having come this far with our illegal show. About 25 of them lit out of the theater, and in a few minutes they had brought in their flashlights and even a couple of floodlights. They beamed them on stage, and we did two full shows in a nice, warm, soft light from a couple of dozen eager fans who were willing to wear out their batteries for a little country music. But that's the way we found the people up there, and it amuses me to hear people today talk about how New Englanders are only now beginning to hear some country music.

We were always looking for new comedy material for our act, but some of the best ideas never did get on the air or on stage. Jokes that could be used later, on a show like *Hee Haw* on national television, would never have been permitted back in 1935. I remember one time we had stopped for a red light in some small town. I looked over and saw a dog sitting on the curb. "Look at that dog, Bradley," I mused. "Why doesn't he cross? He's got the light with him." Bradley was sleepy and didn't say anything. Joe was half asleep in back. I went on. "Bradley, I kicked a dog once." This brought Bradley up. "What? Why, you ought to be ashamed of yourself, Grandpa." "Don't worry," I said, "I kicked him in self-defense. He had raised his leg to kick me first." When he had finished laughing and wiped his eyes, Bradley shook his head. "It's too bad we can't use that one on stage."

Joe and I were young, and we did a lot of courting up there. One of the girls I dated worked in one of the largest jewelry stores in Boston; her name was Ethel Jackson. Once I wrote a note to her and spelled her name "Ethyl." Boy, was she mad; she told me in no uncertain terms that she wasn't gasoline. Another night I went over to pick her up in my old Plymouth. I was being the gentleman, so I hopped out and walked around to the other side to open the door for her, and stepped where a dog had been. Well, when I got in the car it was plumb awful. And both of us were too bashful to say anything, so we spent the whole evening with that smell and never did mention it.

Bradley sometimes let us borrow his big LaSalle to take our girls out in. Driving that big car around, we really thought we were it. One day I drove the LaSalle down to WBZ to get our mail, and coming back, I ran through a stop sign I didn't see. There was a big Irish cop up on the stand at the corner, and he hollered at me to park at the curb. He took his time and let me sit there and stew, and then finally walked over to me. "Well," he said, "you thought you could sneak through that stop sign, didn't you? I know your type. You're probably out in your rich father's car. But your grandchildren will be sneaks just like you." I didn't say a word, since I didn't even have a driver's license yet. He raved for five minutes. I started to tell him that I was the Grandpa on Bradley's show at WBZ, but he was having such a time thinking I was some rich brat that I let him puff on. After he blew off enough steam, he let me go.

I was anything but a rich brat, though. I was comfortable, all right; after a year with Bradley I was making $50 a week, and for 1936 that was good. But the touring was hard on me, and there were times when I couldn't really see that I was getting any place. Several times I had decided to go back to Akron radio and work for $25 a week. Joe Troyan recently described one of those times when I really got fed up: "It was March 13, 1936. Bradley, Grandpa, and I left at 9:00 A.M. to play show dates in Vermont. We arrived in Rutland at 1:00 P.M. and did one matinee and two evening shows. The next day, after the matinee, Bradley suggested we go for a long walk. We did just that, walking down Main Street and window-shopping. In the show window of an auto dealership, we saw a beautiful canary yellow Packard with the top down.

Bradley looked and looked at the car, and Grandpa and I looked too, saying nothing. We finally left and walked another block, but Bradley said, 'Let's go back and take another look at that car.' We did, and he asked us how we liked it, and we both said it was fine, and pretty soon we were inside looking it over. The more we saw, the more we liked. Finally I said, 'Brad, I can ride in the rumble seat.' He replied, 'That does it. Grandpa, go up to the theater and get the LaSalle.' Grandpa got back, and in 20 minutes Brad had the new car out on the street. We rode to the theater in the new car, and after we got out Grandpa says to me, 'Joe, did you see what he just did? We can't do that with a new pair of shoes. They wouldn't give us anything on a trade-in! We'll have to drive that Plymouth of mine for 500,000 miles! Joe, before you and I can buy a new car, other people will be buying two of them, and when you and I can have two cars, other people will be buying aeroplanes or there won't be any gas left for us! Dad-burn the luck! I keep telling you we won't amount to a hill of beans!' "

But later on I learned otherwise, and that young man who was so impatient to get rich would later sing a different song.

BILL'S A MILLIONAIRE

I knew him when he was just a kid,
For I was little too.
We laughed and played and roamed the fields.
That's all we had to do.

Then we grew up and went to school,
And he learned mighty fast.
Now I was slow at figures,
But I got through at last.

By the time I had finished school
And a week or two gone by,
I saw him and the "dollar sign"
Was shining in his eye.

As weeks went by he had no time
To laugh and talk and dream,

His mind seemed always occupied
With some big money scheme.

Then one day he woke up to find
Himself a millionaire.
I thought—Now Old Bill is fixed for life,
He'll never know a care.

But it didn't turn out that way at all,
His worries had just begun.
His face took on a worried look
Like he'd turned his back on fun.

One day I met him on the street
In front of his own bank.
I said, "Come on Bill, let's you and I
Play a little prank.

Tomorrow let's just slip away
And fish like we used to do,
And run the fields round the old home place—
It'll be good for me and you."

His face lit up for a little while,
Then took on a look of woe.
"There's a meeting in Chicago
All next week and I must go.

Maybe some other time I can
I know 'twould do me good.
If I can ever get caught up I'll go,
And I really know I should."

Now that's been goin' on for years,
Since Bill was in his prime.
I ask him once or twice a month,
But he never has the time.

Lately I have noticed
Bill's color's very bad,

And I've heard he's seeing a doctor
For a hacking cough he's had.

Today I called—Why, haven't you heard
Bill passed away last night—
I knew the news was coming soon,
I knew he'd lose the fight.

Today I went a-walkin'
In the fields where Bill and I
As kids had spent so many hours
Just watching time go by.

As I sat beneath an old oak tree
I heard a robin call,
And I got to thinkin'—was old Bill
So wealthy after all?

Five.

HILLS OF WEST VIRGINIA

In 1937 I had my first real hit song. I was still playing the guitar then—in fact, I couldn't even play the banjo yet—and I was known mainly as a singer. I had a good yodeling voice and did well with novelty songs, but I didn't think I really had the perfect voice for the kind of slow ballads and love songs that Bradley did so well. But one of the big hit songs in 1935 was a record by a North Carolina band headed by J. E. Mainer, one called "Maple on the Hill." Though a lot of people didn't know it at the time, it was actually an old song from the 1880s that had been written by Gussie L. Davis, the first really successful black songwriter to work in what we now call Tin Pan Alley. It started off:

> Near a quiet country village stood a maple on the hill,
> There I sat with my Jannetta long ago.

It was popular on the radio then, and I got to doing it so much that I wrote an "answer song" for it.

Answer songs were popular back in the thirties; if anyone had a hit, then someone would write a follow-up to it, usually with the same melody and names but different lyrics. The lyrics would continue the story, and the song would be sort of a sequel to the original. Some songs went on for three or four sequels. Anyway, I decided to do a follow-up and wrote "Answer to Maple on the Hill." It started off:

> Since you left me, my Jannetta, all the world is sad and drear,
> And everything is desolate and still,
> The whippoorwill is singing oh so sad and plaintively,
> For he knows you've left the maple on the hill.

The song went on about how Jannetta had died, and about how her boyfriend wanted to be with her in heaven; it was really sad, but people back then liked them sad, and before long I had published it with one of the big national sheet music companies, M. M. Cole in Chicago. (I never got to record the song, but sheet music publication was about as good.) I hadn't been using the name "Grandpa" very long then, so the cover read "Words and Music by Marshall Jones" and had a picture of me with my plaid shirt, suspenders, hat, and false mustache. It wasn't that much of a song, but it was a boost to my ego when I really needed it.

I learned a lot from Bradley: simple things like how to travel, how to eat on the road, how to get on and off stage, how to dress, and much more. He had helped me realize that music, singing and entertaining folks, was an occupation very much worthwhile. I had always thought before my time with him that entertaining was somehow not real work, and that I should be training myself for some other "realer" occupation. But now I was learning that the entertainment business was one of the hardest jobs you could have, and that I never need fear that I hadn't put in an honest day's work for my $50 a week. In fact, by 1937 I was getting tired of the grind of the tours, and my stomach was giving me a little trouble. Besides, I was wanting to go it alone. Joe had gotten an offer to go work for a singer named Pie Plant Pete as a full partner, and so we decided to break up our three-man act.

I had been listening a lot to WWVA in Wheeling, West Virginia, and I liked the way its performers sounded on the air, as if they were having a lot of fun playing the kind of music I liked. And on Saturday night at the *Midnight Jamboree,* the audience seemed to be enjoying the show so much, and liking everything that was done, that I just wanted to be a part of it. When I broke the news to Bradley, he and his wife Erma both tried to discourage me. "You can't just walk up to a station out of the blue and get a job on it," Bradley said. But my mind was made up, and they couldn't change my plans.

When I arrived at WWVA, I was referred to the director of the *Midnight Jamboree,* Pat Patterson. I told him, "Mr. Patterson, I want to appear on the *Midnight Jamboree,* and I don't even care about the money; I just want to sing on it." (There were no unions down there at that time.) He sort of grinned, and said he would arrange an audition. He did, and after I had sung and told him I had been with Bradley Kincaid, he said I could do a spot on the coming Saturday night. Other acts on the show included Cowboy Loye, Doc Williams, the Leary family (who were Wilma Lee Cooper's family), Floyd Houser, the Hoosier Merry Makers, and a host of others.

Most of these had 15- or 30-minute shows of their own on WWVA every day. The station came on the air at six in the morning and ended about six in the evening each weekday. The acts would sing and pick, announce their dates, and if they had a commercial they would read it themselves. When I got my own show later, I did two long commercials for Hamlin's Wizard Oil. This was a well-known liniment of the day that was supposed to "relieve muscular aches and pains due to rheumatism, neuralgia, lumbago, and chest colds." It was also good for bruises, sunburns, frostbite, insect stings, athlete's foot, and burns—not to mention stiff neck and what they called "housewife's back," caused by lifting, scrubbing, and ironing. it was good for about anything as long as you didn't drink it. Its motto was "Rub it on, rub it in," and I delivered many a commerical for Wizard Oil.

WWVA was only 5,000 watts then, but it reached all over the U.S., every province in Canada, and even some foreign countries. I started by doing the *Jamboree* and some spots through the week, and I soon began "playing out" (doing personal appearances) with Floyd Houser and the Rhythm Rangers. We averaged about $5.00 each a night, and the *Jamboree*— well, the *Jamboree* divided half the take from its ticket sales among the performers; I've made as high as $69 on Saturday night and I've made as low as 69¢. But money was money in 1937, and I managed to save some. My folks were in Akron renting a house, so I bought two houses there, one in the back of the other; they moved into the front house while I rented out the back one.

At first in Wheeling I roomed with a tenor banjo player by the name of Walter James, who played with the Hoosier Merry Makers. He was a fine guy and an amateur photographer. We had an apartment you wouldn't believe. It was so dark that we named it "the Tomb." (He now has a studio in Helena, Montana). But I didn't spend a whole lot of time there. Pretty soon I was playing out every night with the Rhythm Rangers, and then doing a 30-minute show at six in the morning. In 30 minutes alone, you have to sing a lot of songs, even with two commercial spots. The engineer was the only other person there until six-thirty, so I had to sign the station on and do my program, and then the announcer took me off. It was hard to get up so early after playing and driving until one or two o'clock in the morning. I had an old alarm clock, and I'd set the alarm and then place it on the edge of the table so it would vibrate off and hit the floor, and that noise would wake me if the bell didn't. It finally broke the glass out, and then the legs broke off, then the bell came loose, but that clock never did stop running.

As I said, the broadcast day was filled with 15- and 30-minute shows, all live (except the Sons of the Pioneers, whose shows were on large transcriptions). As the morning acts that followed me got finished, many performers would go to the Wheeling Hotel or the Dinner Bell to eat breakfast. Most of the time I'd go along, and some days I'd eat breakfast four or five times. It's a wonder I wasn't fat as butter. But I ran it off on the hills, I guess.

Wheeling is the site of Fort Henry, where Betty Zane ran out during an Indian attack and brought back an apronfull of powder from the powderhouse just outside the fort. She was the heroine of Zane Grey's three books about Fort Henry. Colonel Zane commanded the fort, and his main scout was Louis Wetzel. Betty Zane is buried up in Ohio, and Louis Wetzel was buried on the banks of the Ohio River, though I'm told they have built a factory of some kind on the site. But I learned a lot of this sort of history while I was in Wheeling. I used to take long walks in the mountains around there after my six o'clock show (and breakfast); there isn't a mountain in the area that I haven't hiked on. One mountain had 11 springs. In fact, right in downtown Wheeling on 16th Avenue there was a large spring coming out of a hill. People used to line up for a block with jugs and buckets to get some of that water.

Just after I went out on my own, I had this picture made up as a postcard for fans in West Virginia; on the other side was the message, "How Many Biscuits Can You Eat This Morning?"

Life was never dull in Wheeling. One winter while I was playing with Floyd Houser, he bought a new 1937 Ford. The first snowy night when the roads were slick, he put a new set of chains on the car, but there were some clear places in the road; when the chains hit them, sparks would fly off. They lasted about three miles, but we made the date. Another time Floyd tied the bass fiddle, in its canvas cover, on the top of the car. Coming home, he rolled the car over. He wasn't hurt, but he sure turned a good bass into a sack of stovewood. Some of the boys who played with Doc Williams lived in an old hotel by the swinging bridge there in Wheeling, and one morning early there was a fire; his comedian, Rawhide, jumped out the window on the second floor onto the sidewalk, and it put him in the hospital for a long time. Nearly every act then had a comedian with baggy pants, suspenders, slouch hat, and no shoes. Doc Williams also had a girl vocalist, Sunflower, who was a fine singer and a pretty girl.

Others who were there included Hugh Cross and Shug Fisher, who had a fine group that was on for a cereal company called Georgie Porgie. Shug later went out west and showed up in a lot of cowboy pictures. Then there were the Arizona Ranch Girls, who did close harmony; they sang "Trouble in Mind" better than anyone I ever heard. They could almost sneeze in harmony.

And there was Jake Taylor with his band, the Rail Splitters; he did some fine shows and wrote some good songs. One, "There Ain't Nobody Gonna Miss Me When I'm Gone," was recorded by Cowboy Copas; then the tune was stolen, and new words were written to it. I wonder if Jake ever got anything out of it. Jake also had a comedian. He was billed as Quarantine, the Ugliest Man in Radio. One night after the show, someone gave the band a big chocolate cake. Coming home, Quarantine had the cake in his lap in the back seat. They had a wreck, and Quarantine ended up with his face down in the cake. They said it was the only time his face looked pretty.

One of the top groups on WWVA was Frankie More and the Log Cabin Boys. There was a girl working with them who went by the name of Cousin Emmy. She was especially popular with the kids and the old folks, because she played the old-time drop-thumb or frailing style of banjo. A lot of people think that there is only one type of banjo picking, the three-finger, Scruggs, or bluegrass style, in which the thumb, index, and middle fingers (and picks)

Here's the 1939 version of Grandpa (with the guitar) and the Grandsons (Pete Rentcheler, Lenny Aleshire and Biff Bledsoe), when I was working on station WMMN.

are used to get the sound. But before that was an older style of using the thumb and first finger to brush down across the strings. Cousin Emmy went at it with her entire forearm and picked down with that first finger. Her five-string picking fascinated me to the extent that I would follow her around the studio to watch and listen. I worried her so much that she finally said, "Okay, I'll show you how it's done." After a few lessons I managed to get me a five-string banjo out of a pawn shop up in Akron. (My parents were still living there and I made weekly trips home.) I brought the banjo back to Wheeling and got Cousin Emmy to play on it to see if it was all right. It was a Vega, and I think I paid about $10 for it. She approved, said it was a good banjo, and so I started practicing every day. Cousin Emmy really encouraged me from day to day, and this made me practice extra hard.

Still, it was a long time before I had nerve enough to play the banjo on stage. I felt safe with a guitar, but I didn't trust my banjo playing. Emmy taught me songs like "Cripple Creek," "Little Birdie," and "Ground Hog," and she tried to teach me "Johnny Booker," which was one she did a lot, but I couldn't get that one right for a long time. As I said, Cousin Emmy was very popular. She was at WHAS in Louisville for a long time, and she passed away in 1980 in a nursing home in California. But I'll never forget the style of banjo she taught me, and there'll never be another one like her. It's sad that such people are hardly ever mentioned in books on country music by these so-called experts.

Another character on the station back then was Silver Yodeling Bill Jones. He had a fine voice, and he really could yodel, but he did a deadpan act that was one of the funniest I have ever seen. One Saturday night on stage he was supposed to be wiring up the refrigerator and the radio. When he opened the refrigerator door, it started playing music; then he opened the back of the radio, and there sat two quarts of milk.

The *Midnight Jamboree* was always having some kind of slapstick routine that really tickled the audience. Sometimes people listening to the radio show would hear a full minute or two of nothing but laughing. But that was all right; the next week the people who had been listening would come down to the theater to see what all the laughing was about. The old Market Street Auditorium was full almost every Saturday night. I think radio and stage shows miss a lot nowadays by not having some of those old skits in place of "Now here's my latest hit. Now here's the flip side." They were a lot more entertaining. A lot of the real humor has gone out of country music in recent years.

On Saturdays, after the *Jamboree* at the auditorium, we all went back to the WWVA studios in the Stahlman Building and broadcast for another two hours. (One time during this late broadcast I got a long-distance phone call from by brother Spurgeon, who had been out of touch with family for over two years. He was up in Bangor, Maine, working for a power and light company, and was picking up our program all the way up there.) We would perform until two o'clock in the morning, and there was always something going on in the studio while you were singing at the mike. One particular night Jake Taylor was doing his song when the big double doors of the studio opened, and in came Hugh Cross and Shug Fisher and a half-dozen others with their shirts turned around backwards so they looked like doctors. They had an old marimba or xylophone on stage there, and they had Yodeling Bill Jones laid out on this so it looked like a hospital stretcher. They wheeled him up right in front of Jake, who kept bravely singing on, and proceeded to make like they were performing an operation on poor old Bill. They took out old shoes, bottles, cans, books, and everything you can imagine from under that sheet, all the time pretending that these were things they were removing from the patient. No one at home knew what all the ruckus in the studio was that night, or why Jake Taylor did such a punk job singing his sad song; maybe they thought he was getting carried away with emotion, but now the truth has been told.

Jack Suppler was an engineer at the station. His folks owned a big farm outside of Wheeling, and that was where the WWVA tower was located then. I remember one time I was on the air singing, and there was a storm going on. I was doing some old sad song like "Barbara Allen" when someone came in the studio and said that I was off the air, that the tower had fallen down. I never did know if it was my singing or the wind that did it. Anyway, we used to go out to Jack's farm and rabbit-hunt. His mother was a fine cook, and she never failed to have a good meal for us when we came in. The farm was located on one of the highest parts of the county.

Jack wasn't my only hunting partner. One of the real stars at the station, and someone that you never hear much about today or in history books, was Cowboy Loye, whose real name was Loye D. Pack. He was a coon hunter besides being a great on-the-air salesman and a good singer. He had lots of coonhounds, and some were good and some not so good; he would lose a dog nearly every time we went out hunting. But all he had to do was announce on his show next morning that he had lost one of his dogs. Most of the time it would be Old Nig. He'd say, "If anyone sees an old black hound that answers to the name of Nig, please call Cowboy Loye at WWVA." And he would always get Nig back; someone would always bring him in.

One night when Cowboy Loye and I went hunting, it was really cold, and there was a thin snow on the ground. After we got well into the woods, we stopped so the dogs could work out the section for coon tracks. Close by there was an old hollow snag about 15 feet high, with a hole in the bottom. We built a fire in the hole, and with the snag acting as a chimney, it was really roaring pretty soon. It melted a ring around that snag and we had a warm fire for about three hours. There was an old abandoned mine shaft going into the side of the mountain close by, and we wanted to see what was in there, so we walked in and found a lot of bats hanging from the roof. They were so cold that they couldn't move. We took one and put him close to the fire. Soon he got warm and was going to fight both of us; then all at once he flew away. Cowboy and I watched him fly out into the cold night, and we wondered if he ever found his way back to the protection of the shaft.

In 1938 Bradley Kincaid was in Hartford, Connecticut, and wanted me to come back up and do some more shows with him. He was at a big powerful station there, WTIC, and he was persuasive, so I spent a few more months in beautiful New England. That fall I decided to try my luck at Fairmont, West Virginia; I had come to like the radio work down there, and the people really responded well to the music. Besides, it was a beautiful country. On the way down to Fairmont, I stopped over in Charleston, West Virginia, to visit some old friends from Ohio—Andy Patterson and Warren Caplinger. They were known as Cap, Andy, and Flip now, and were specializing in gospel music on WCHS there. Andy said, "Why don't you try to get on at WCHS instead of going on to Fairmont?" Andy and his wife Lena had a niece staying with them then, a pretty girl named Eulalia Marie Losher, and we hit it off pretty well. In fact, that helped me make up my mind to stay.

I got a job at WCHS on a show called the *Old Farm Hour.* The master of ceremonies was Buddy Starcher; he had played on a lot of different stations, and I had known him before. He was one of the stars there in Charleston, and before long I was working with his group, doing a lot of shows and personals. About this time I put out my first real song book, a little book of some 16 pages that I had printed up myself. (In those days a lot of radio singers had their own song books printed up to sell by mail and at personal appearances for 10 or 25 cents; Bradley Kincaid put out a new one almost every year and sold them by the carload. In fact, I guess it was Bradley who first thought up the idea of a singer selling song books to fans.) I had begun to try to write my own original songs by then, and most of the ones in this book were originals—though when I look back on them today, some of them seem pretty sorry efforts. The book was called *Harmonies of the Hill Country,* and it had 15 songs and three poems. (I have always liked to write poems, and was writing them even back this early.) Most of the songs were gospel songs with titles like "On That Great Judgement Morning," "I Know My Lord is Coming," "Prepare to Meet Your Saviour," and "Send Me Your Address from Heaven."

A boy was writing a letter
To his girl in the valley below.
His letter said, "Darling, your last note
Came more than three weeks ago."
From this letter he received no answer,
So he went down to her house that day.
He found she'd been taken to Heaven,
Then an angel heard the boy say:

Send me your address from Heaven,
So I can write you up there.
Tell me that you still love me,
Tell me that you still care.
Mail it on a golden street corner
As you did on earth here below.

Send me your address from Heaven,
Of your home on that bright golden shore.

Well, sentimental songs were big then, and my book had a mother song, a prison song, a "black sheep come home" song, and a song about the mountains. I didn't keep too many of these early ones in my shows, but I was starting to come up with some that did stay around.

Meantime, I had been seeing more and more of Andy's pretty niece, Eulalia, and in the fall of 1938 I asked her to marry me. She said yes, and Andy and Lena stood up with us. A few months after that I decided to move on to Fairmont and work on station WMMN. We didn't have too much to live on at first; I scraped together enough cash to have some pictures of me printed up and offered them for sale on my show, and we managed with the help of that money until I got enough of a name to start playing out. On December 8, 1939, we had a baby girl, Marsha Marie Jones, and this made things even more complicated for someone still just starting out. But we thought the new baby was pretty swell.

On WMMN I was on a program called *Sage Brush Round-up* and had my own program sponsored by Cocoa Wheats. I put together my first band, a group called Grandpa Jones and his Grandsons. Two of the boys I had known from my Wheeling days. Pete Rentcheler, who played fiddle, was from Patricksburg, Indiana, and had come to Wheeling as part of the Rhythm Rangers. He was tall and thin, wore rimless glasses, had a weakness for pitching horseshoes, and planned to own a chain of dime stores some day. Loren (Biff) Bledsoe played banjo (I still didn't trust myself much on that instrument), and he was from Indiana, too; he and Pete had played a lot together before I met them. (Biff later changed his name to Dale Parker.) The fourth member of our band was one of the finest showmen I have ever known, Lenny Aleshire. He was the real veteran of our group. Lenny was from Missouri, and had lived with the Creek Indians when he was a teenager. Though he'd lost three fingers in a fight with a circular saw, he mastered almost every instrument there was, and then some. Ten years before we met him, he had joined the Weaver Brothers and Elviry, a well-known country vaudeville act, and had played in the big theaters from coast to coast. His hobby, believe it or not, was catching snakes.

Lennie could do a fast tap dance, and a square dance alone with imaginary partners. He played a weird set of homemade instruments: he had a dresser drawer strung up like a steel guitar, a push broom with one string on it that he played with a fiddle bow and noted with his old hat, halfful bottles that he would bang on, and a cowbell act where he tied cowbells to his hands and feet and rang out tunes on them. (I still do this on stage today, with Ramona's help.) Once Lennie made an instrument out of a square five-gallon oil can; he stuck a stick down in one corner of it and played it with a fiddle bow. We had Pete play his fiddle along with it, and then Biff joined in on clarinet for a weird three-part harmony. We had a contest where our listeners would try to guess what instruments we were using; if they were right, we sent them some Cocoa Wheats. We got guesses that ranged from a pipe organ to a harmonica.

One time we worked out a trick we called the cross-up: one of us noted the banjo and picked the guitar; a second noted the fiddle and picked the banjo; and the third noted the guitar and bowed the fiddle. We had been practicing it for a long time but didn't have it right yet, when one night, driving to a date, I told the band, "Let's try the cross-up." Everybody said no, but I begged them all the way there, and finally they consented. So on stage we gave it a big buildup and launched into it. Not only did we mess it up royally; we didn't even play the same tune we had been practicing the trick on! On the way home that night we began talking about how we messed up, and we all got to laughing so hard that we had to stop the car because we couldn't see for the tears in our eyes.

We did a lot of gospel songs at WMMN, so we got calls to sing in churches, usually on a 70/30 basis (we got the 70). Some of the little country churches around there didn't even have paint on them, but one minister told us that by having three concerts (they called them concerts) and had made enough money to paint the church inside and out. One night we played in some little church up in the hills, and since it was pretty cool outside they had built a roaring fire in the stove and really warmed up the place inside. About the time we started playing, I looked up and gasped; there were dozens of red wasps up on the ceiling. I've never seen so many red wasps in one place. As the evening went on, and things got warmer and warmer, the wasps started crawling down the walls. When one would get down far enough, one of the old mountain men would quietly reach up and, not missing a beat, pinch it with his fingers. Nobody got stung, but it was a little nerve-wracking.

People at Fairmont were just as full of jokes as the old gang at Wheeling. One day a bunch of the musicians were standing on the sidewalk outside the station getting some air when a fellow stumbled down the street toward them. He held a guitar in one hand—no case—and there was no doubt that he had been into the mountain dew. He said he wanted to get on the radio, and the boys were willing to oblige. One of them led him up to a parking meter and told him that it was an "outside microphone" for the station. So the old boy began to bellow out a song to the meter. Then someone else came up and twisted the meter handle and told him that he had to tone it down, that it was too loud. I never did find out if the old boy passed his audition.

I was also coming up with better songs and to do some that later became favorites. My 1940 song book, *Harmonies of the Hill Country Number 2*, had "Happy Little Home in Arkansas" (though I didn't know then how much it would come true), "You Done Me Mean and Dirty" (which I later recorded), and "Upon the Blue Ridge Mountain," a fine old outlaw ballad I learned from Lenny Aleshire, who called it "Been All Around This World." But the most popular song in that book was one I wrote called "The Tragic Romance." It starts out:

> Nestled in the heart of the Tennessee hills,
> Midst peaceful pines, midst the rocks and the rills,

and goes on to tell of a man who sees his girlfriend in the arms of another man and leaves town, never to return. One day years later he runs into her brother and finds out that the girl has pined away, and that the man in her arms was himself. The song later became quite a hit when Cowboy Copas recorded it and the Morris Brothers, an act from North Carolina, recorded it; I even sold quite a few copies of my own record of it, and it is still sung a lot today, especially by bluegrass bands.

It came about one evening when we were returning from a show date; I had been singing the old 1890s song "After the Ball," and I borrowed the story from that and the tune from the old folk song "Naomi Wise" and began to work it out. The four of us worked on it that night parked under a streetlight, and I started singing it soon after. I put it in my 1940 song book as the lead number, and through 1941 it was the most popular song that I performed. Both the Morris Brothers and I have copyrights on it; the Morris boys got their copy from some listener who had heard mine and mailed them the words. They thought it was an old folk song, so they adapted and arranged it, and filed a copyright. That's why the song is listed by different composers yet today.

Six.

THE GALLOPING GOOSE

September 1, 1939, was a Friday. I had just gotten off three days' vacation after playing for 14 straight nights at little towns in and around Fairmont. That night the Grandsons and I drove 60 miles to play a date at the high school in Sardis, Ohio. The talk all day was of the war in Europe; Germany had invaded Poland that morning, and the fighting was intense. Everyone was saying that the war we had all been expecting was finally here. At the time, I didn't know it might change my life. I was all of 25 years old; we were expecting a baby in a couple of months; and a lot of people were saying that the U.S. would never get in the war. That night in Sardis I was more worried about my share of the gate, which was $6.70.

The rest of that week we continued to play the little towns as President Roosevelt one day declared a "limited national emergency" and the next pledged U.S. neutrality. On September 2, we drove 50 miles to play at the Talbot Community Fair for a "house" of $30 and a personal share of $7.50; Sunday we played the Adolph, West Virginia, M.E. Church for a gate of $20.83; Monday, the Weston Fair Grounds for a big gate of $330; Tuesday, a church at Booth for $23.50; Wednesday, the Baptist church at Liverpool for $23.40; Thursday, St. Leo's church at Metz for $19.15; Friday, the Union

Hall at Valley Head for $37.48. Saturday we were back on the air at the *Sage Brush Round-up*. That's the way it was going, week in and week out. We were booked nearly every night, but most nights I netted less than $5.00 and averaged, with my *Sage Brush* pay, less than $30 a week.

I kept on playing over WMMN through 1940, appearing some with the Grandsons, and playing a lot of personals with Jake Taylor, and even a few with Cap, Andy, and Flip; Bill Cox; Salt and Peanuts; and others. If you wonder what one of the live shows back then was like, here's a lineup that I found in one of my old notebooks, dated August 29, 1940:

1. The Unclouded Day
2. At the End of the Lane
3. Banjo
4. Yodel—jokes
5. Farther Along
6. Fiddle tune—riddle joke
7. We Shall Rise
8. Rattler
9. Pete sings "Whispering Hope"
10. Turn Your Radio On

Looking over my old notebooks, I see that I was still singing more Jimmie Rodgers songs than any other kind—and this was seven years after he died. I also did a lot I had learned from Bradley Kincaid, a lot of Carter Family songs (they were popular then, broadcasting over border radio stations in Mexico), a lot learned from Scotty Wiseman (whom I had listened to for years over WLS), and a lot learned from another Chicago act, Karl and Harty. I also did gospel songs by Albert Brumley (who wrote "Turn Your Radio On" and "I'll Fly Away") and others published by the Stamps-Baxter song book company, which was then about the country's biggest gospel music publisher. I was also singing a song that was to become my biggest hit in later years, "Old Rattler." But more of that later.

In the spring of 1941, I went back to WWVA in Wheeling and took over a program that began at 6:25 A.M. every day. A lot of the people who had been on the station in 1937 were gone. Radio entertainers were always moving from one station to another in those days, sometimes staying only a few months or a year and then moving on. There was a good reason for that, though. Radio entertainers had to make their real income from doing personal appearances, since radio sponsors really paid very little; they would be allowed to announce their concert dates on their radio shows, and they could play out on nights they didn't broadcast and charge 25¢ or 50¢ a head at a schoolhouse or church or fair. Out of that income they had to pay gasoline and expenses (sometimes we had to drive 80 miles round trip to a show date), and it didn't take long to "play out" an area—to get to where the people were sort of tired of seeing your show and where they wouldn't turn out too well for personals. West Virginia had the very best country music audiences I have ever played for, but even at that we found we had to move around. So by mid-1941 I was playing the Wheeling area again with a band called the Grandchildren.

Meanwhile, the war kept getting closer and closer. Monday, December 8, 1941, was crisp and cold in Wheeling, and when I arrived to do my early morning program, the wire services were clattering with the news of Pearl Harbor. No one could doubt that we would be in war now. I started the show off that morning with a new song written by Ted Daffan and Jimmie Davis that reflected the way a lot of us felt: "Worried Mind." Then I did "Picture on the Wall," an old sentimental number; a Jimmie Rodgers tune called "Treasures Untold"; a Carter Family song, "I'm Thinking Tonight of My Blue Eyes"; a sort of honky-tonk song called "It Makes No Difference Now"; and another Jimmie Rodgers–Clayton McMichen favorite, "Peach Pickin' Time in Georgia." Even though I was singing the old songs that we had enjoyed for years, I couldn't help feeling that things were going to be changing a lot.

A few weeks after that, I ran into an old friend, Roy Starkey, and learned that he was working at WLW in Cincinnati. He was a singer and storyteller— he would sing a cowboy number and then tell the story of the song. He was talking up his new station and its new show called the *Boone County Jamboree.* It had started in 1939 when George Biggar and Bill McCluskey came over to Cincinnati from the WLS *National Barn Dance* and brought a lot of the big acts with them, like Lulu Belle and Scotty, and the Girls of the Golden West, WLW was heard all over, since it started out broadcasting at 500,000 watts, more power than any other radio station in the U.S. When Roy told me that I might get on WLW, it really tickled me, because I had never been on a 50,000-watt, much less a 500,000-watt station. I went up for an audition, and I guess I did okay, because they hired me. And there I was, alongside the biggest country names I had ever worked with since my days with Bradley: Merle Travis, the Delmore Brothers, Curly Fox and Texas Ruby, Lazy Jim Day, the Girls of the Golden West, and a lot more.

The next couple of years at WLW we had lots of fun; the station used an old bus we called the "Galloping Goose" to take us to personals. It was an old Studebaker truck chassis with a bus body on it, and was even equipped with a 110-volt generator run by a five-horse engine. We used to shave with an electric razor and laugh because we were using a five-horse engine to pull it. A lot of times we would get in as late as two in the morning, and have to do our first program at three-thirty, so there was really no sense in going home. We would just sleep in the lobby for an hour or two, do our early shows, and be finished with our day's work by six-thirty. It got to be such a routine that I wrote a little poem about it; later Merle had it hand-lettered and illustrated.

THE HILLBILLIE CYCLE
by Gran'pa Jones

At three o'clock 'most every morn
We rise up to dish out the good ol' corn.
Hillbillie alarm clocks everywhere
Disturb the peace and rend the air.
Landlords turn and toss in bed
And hate themselves for having said,
"This apartment is nice as can be
Only forty-five a month, heat and water free."
He remembered well on that sad day
The hillbillie handed him a check for pay.
A Crosley check of high esteem
For it was Wednesday . . . if you get what I mean.

We stumble around, and stump our toes,
Seeking the place we left our clothes
When we came home three hours before.
Are they on the dresser, or throwed on the floor?

We stumble and stalk, and cuss a bit
Trying to get the direction of it. . . .
The closet, I mean—oh, there's the door.
It's hit you in the head before.
You fumble and feel all around
To see what outfit can be found
To wear to Garfield's, and get a cup
Of "battery acid" to wake you up.

We flash our badge and ascend the stair
To grab a "box" and hit the air.
We sing and play and hope we're heard,
For we're earlier than the early bird.
But when it's over we steer our trails
To Dennison's place to tell tall tales,
Drinking coffee until we're full,
Cause you have to do something while shooting bull.
We wait around till ten or so—
For that's when the "Galloping Goose," you know,
Takes it's departure with us aboard
To entertain somewhere with "boxes" and "goards."
Once on the bus, the battle is on
To get the best seat before it is gone.
But the poker players don't worry us,
For they're away in the back of the bus.
You know they're there, you can hear so plain—
"Check . . . I'll call you . . . by God, deal again!"
We sleep, we sing, and play the guitar.
Some laugh, some gripe, some thoughts are afar
Over the ocean with loved ones true
And wonder if we'll ever get over too,
Cause McCluskey promised that we might go
And make the trip as an army show.

The bus bounces, swerves, clatters, and squeals
Till you swear it will never stay on its wheels.
We're nervous and jittery after the ride;
We have a little fit and jump out of our hide;

We gripe because it's such a ghastly experience
To ride in that bus to a personal appearance.
But we wouldn't miss it, you can bet your last dime.
We're always there and often on time
To ride away on the Galloping Goose
When we've eaten our breakfast, with "no juice . . . ?"

We arrive back in town on the Galloping Goose,
And it looks like the wrath of Jehova' broke loose.
We all look so terrible after the ride
That the guard don't even want to let us inside.
We try to get comfortable—no one looks neat;
Some run around in their rusty bare feet.
We're hardly awake till we're off the air
And so nervous we're tearing our hair.
When we get back home and ready for bed,
Then we're woke up, and always see red
If anyone says a word out of the way,
'Cause it's sure nerve wracking to get Crosley pay.
Now in that cycle, the Hillbillies run.
We don't make much money, but we have lots of fun.

Looking back over this epic after so many years, it dawns on me that there are a few things in there that might need some explaining. That "Crosley check of high esteem" referred to the Crosley Company that owned WLW, and Garfield's and Dennison's were cafes near the studios, where a lot of us hung out. Even back in 1940, WLW had a union for musicians that we all had to join. But there were separate unions for the hillbilly performers and the regular popular performers because a lot of the regular musicians' unions didn't want to accept country pickers and singers in those days; they felt that unless you could read music, you couldn't play. And it didn't take us long to figure out that the scale in the hillbilly union was a lot lower. (I didn't join the regular musicians' union until 1953 in Washington). The "McCluskey" in the poem was, of course, Bill McCluskey, who was the manager for the *Boone County Jamboree.*

Merle Travis and Alton Delmore became two of my best friends, and two of the most influential musicians I have ever met. Merle already had a reputation as one of the best guitar pickers in the business, even though he was barely into his twenties. Merle had learned his thumb-and-finger-style picking down in Muhlenberg County, Kentucky, where they take their guitar playing seriously, and had worked with Clayton McMichen and the Georgia Wildcats before coming to WLW with a popular band called the Drifting Pioneers. Merle was a rough-and-tumble boy in those days, and he and Red Phillips used to go out and get in fights just for the exercise of it. Sometimes they'd come in pretty banged up, but they would be able to do their show and pick as clean as ever. Merle could also write songs easier than anyone I've ever seen (he cooked up his famous "Smoke, Smoke, Smoke That Cigarette" one afternoon out in his garage as a favor to his pal Tex Williams, who was looking for a new song), and those of us who had the privilege of traveling with him got to hear the imitations and see dozens of the cartoons that he was also famous for. Merle and I got along fine and began singing together as early as 1943; he had a nickname for me that I can't print here, but he said it had to do with my ability to ride for hours without getting up and stretching or reaching for a cushion.

Alton and Rabon Delmore had been on the Grand Ole Opry back in 1933, and were known all over the country for their "Brown's Ferry Blues," "Gonna Lay Down My Old Guitar," "Southern Moon," "When It's Time for the Whippoorwills to Sing," and others. They had been through some hard times when they landed at WLW, but they were soon drawing in mail and making a lot of new friends. Rabon, the younger, had bad eyes and squinted a little; he played the little tenor guitar that made their breaks and turn-arounds sound so nice. Alton did most of the song-writing, but not all. One time I remarked to them, "Boys, you wrote a good song when you wrote that 'Blow Your Whistle, Freight Train.' I really like that." Rabe said, "I wrote that one, Grandpa." And Alton snapped, "You wrote the verses, and I wrote the choruses." And Rabe said, "All right—you're the Billy Hill of the outfit!"

Like a lot of brother acts, Alton and Rabon had their share of fights and at times would resort to punching each other. But a lot of their squabbles were more subtle—and funny to those of us who knew them. One day Alton had car trouble getting downtown to the studio; Rabon was already there, and it was getting near time for them to sing. So Rabe just picked out something he could sing by himself and started to go on. Alton, meanwhile, was racing up the street; he rushed into the lobby and didn't even wait for the elevator, but took out running up the stairs. The studio, now, was on the fifth floor, and Alton made it just a few seconds before air time, blowing and puffing, totally out of breath. As he told it, "I couldn't believe it. Rabe had 'Smoky Mountain Bill' up there on the stand, one of the hardest songs we sang. Nowhere in it to catch your breath. It looked just like a bear to me."

Alton had a strange, dry sense of humor, and Merle and I used to laugh for hours on end at things he said. Even years later, when Merle and I got some time together, we always shared a few Alton stories. I was destined to record a lot with the Delmores after the war, but when I left Cincinnati, I didn't see as much of them as I did of Merle. He and I kept in touch, worked together, hunted together, and remained good friends. I saw the Delmores have their big postwar hits like "Blues Stay Away from Me" and "Hillbilly Boogie," and I knew that Rabon's death in the early 1950s hurt Alton a lot. But Alton kept on writing good songs; the last time I saw him, he had come down to Nashville with some to sell. That afternoon in front of the old Sam Davis Hotel in downtown Nashville I bought a song called "Tuesday Morning" from him for $25. I never recorded the song for some reason, but it's a good one, and some day I want to preserve it for him. Alton's son, Lionel, inherited a lot of the Delmore talent, and as I am writing this (1983), Lionel's song "Swingin' " is number one in the country, on both country and pop charts. Alton would have been proud.

During the early 1940s gospel music was getting popular on WLW, and Merle had gotten to singing with a quartet that included Buddy Ross, as well as Bill and Walt Brown from the Drifting Pioneers. They had to sing really early in the morning, and they found themselves reading hymns that they didn't know too well out of old books. Early one particular morning, Bill had a tenor solo with the words "way down in my soul." He got a little mixed up and started to say "heart" instead of "soul," then realized his mistake and tried to catch himself. But what came out in his nice tenor voice was "way down in my *hole.*" There was no tape at that time; it was all live, and out it went over the air. Everybody in the studio broke up, including the quartet, who got to laughing so bad they had to stop singing. The announcer, between gasps for breath himself, finally got a record on the turntable to take up the dead air. Later on, Merle and I would be getting involved in gospel music at WLW with slightly better results.

I had so much leisure time that I went out and got me a job at a loading dock; it was wartime for real now, and we were loading milling machines. They were really heavy, and we had to roll them into the trucks on wooden rollers. The first two weeks it nearly killed me, but I got used to it, and after a while I could keep up with the rest of the workmen. I tried to learn to chew tobacco like them, too, but I never could get the hang of it; I had spent too many hours working over tobacco to really enjoy chewing it.

Meanwhile, big changes were happening in my life. In 1944, I lost my father; he was 86 when he died and had been living in the house I had bought for my folks in Akron while I was working in Wheeling. I had a big song book in 1941 and another in 1942, put out by M. M. Cole Company in Chicago; they listed my name as "Grandpa Jones, The Kentuck' Yodeler," and they had a lot of good songs, but few of them were ones I really sang very often. Some of them I hardly even knew; they were chosen by the publishers from older songs that they owned. I had made my first records—more about that later—but they weren't doing much, and to top it off, things weren't going well at home with Eulalia and me. And I figured that even though I was 31 and a father, the war folks probably needed me. So I enlisted and went off to see what the fighting was all about.

Seven.

THE MUNICH MOUNTAINEERS

I went to Camp Swift in Austin, Texas, for my basic training. That was a lonesome place. From there I went to Fort Sam Houston in San Antonio to train for Military Police. That was what I was all the time I was in the Army. I wrote home pretty often at first, and then the letters got fewer and the answers got fewer.

At Fort Sam we had good barracks; they were World War I leftovers, but they were comfortable. Then we got orders to move the entire company to Camp Livingston in Louisiana. So all the packing had to be done and all the vehicles made ready, and when we finally got there, the weather was so sultry that I broke out in prickly heat. That was the first time I'd ever had it, and it scared me; I didn't know what was the matter. One day the officer that I drove for—I had a jeep assigned to me and drove this lieutenant around—said he and I were going out in the boondocks and look for a place to do some night work with the troops. He told me confidentially to buy some tackle so we could fish a little. About the time we were all set, the captain came up and said he was going with us. We figured that would sure mess up our plans, so we just told him what we had in mind. He said, "Fine, I'll fish with you." We not only caught a few fish but killed one of the largest cottonmouth moccasins I ever saw.

Finally, one day in late 1944 we got overseas orders. I think some of the officers were a little more scared than we were. We packed and went to New York to board the *Queen Mary,* which had been converted to haul troops. I had brought along my guitar, and we did some singing on the way. The ship had to zigzag all the way across so she'd be more difficult for submarines to hit. In six days we landed in Greenock, Scotland. We unloaded and had a meal of some kind of sausage, hard rolls, and tea. From there we went to Chippenham, England, in a train that had been strafed by a German plane. We knew then that we were pretty close to the fighting. It was muddy and foggy most of the time in Chippenham, but they had the best fish and chips I have ever eaten. I ate a lot of them, and maybe that was what gave me appendicitis; after a group of us went to Swindon, England, for special duty, I had to be operated on. The young doctor gave me a spinal injection on the wrong side, and when the incision was made, it was like being in a knife fight. (I played the same hospital later when I went over to entertain the troups in 1955.) I left the hospital two weeks early, as my company was going into Germany, and I wanted to go with them; the doctor gave me a note saying that I was not to lift anything. So I had it pretty easy going over, but when I got into Germany, the jeep shook me up quite a bit. The roads had been all torn up by bombs.

We were sent first to Aachen. This town had been flattened by bombs—we couldn't even find a house with enough rooms intact to live in—and a lot of boys, including me, saw our first dead German soldiers. They hadn't picked them up yet. We didn't stay in Aachen long before we were ordered to Cologne to guard the Rhine river bridge. One fellow was put on the bridge with an M-1 30/06 rifle, and he had to shoot at everything that came floating down the river for fear it might be a floating bomb designed to blow up the bridge. Other boys had to stand at the bridge and delouse German citizens as they came across; there was very little pure water available, and they couldn't keep clean. This really bothered them, because there have never been any cleaner people than the German people, and they were doing the best they could.

When we got to Cologne, we were hunting a place to stay, as we were going to be there for a while. North of Cologne, in the little town of Merheim, there was a restaurant and hotel all in one building. It was owned by a Mr. and Mrs. Hause, who wanted us MPs to billet there because they said if the infantry got in, they would tear the place up. So some of us moved in—all that could get in—and the rest stayed in houses up and down the street. The restaurant was called the Golden Pflug (Golden Plow), and the hotel had pink bathrooms and running hot water. It was really good to be in a nice place. I got a letter not long ago from Bill Birdsall, one of our group, and he said that he had been to Europe and had gone to the Golden Pflug, and the Hauses' daughter Lorie (now Lorie Roberts) still operates the place.

After we got settled, we used the restaurant for a messhall. Mr. and Mrs. Hause did the KP, and we gave them the same food we ate. They were happy with that arrangement. Once I saw some strawberries in the back yard, and I told Mrs. Hause that I really liked strawberries. So when they got ripe, here she came with a big bowlful for me, even as scarce as food was for them.

When we first got there, Edgar Lacy and I walked around to look at some of the damage that had been done to Cologne and found a little puppy that had somehow escaped the bombing. We took him back to the barracks with us and fed him, and he grew up to be a nice dog. Of course, we named him Adolf, and we took him with us everywhere. At times we would be in a crowd, maybe 400 troops standing around, and Adolf would go through the crowd until he found me or Lacy. He didn't have much to do with the other men. I still enjoyed hiking; Lacy and Adolph and I walked a lot on Sundays, and it is a wonder we didn't get blown up by land mines or leftover explosives. (I remember once we came upon an ammunition dump. There were lots of 8-mm shells and "potato mashers" [German hand grenades] in the dump, and I know there were land mines around it, but we somehow missed them.) There were little porcupines in Germany—a lot smaller than ours—and Adolf would tree them under old lumber piles. When we helped him get them out, they would ball up, and Adolf would get mad because he couldn't get to them. Later, we took Adolf on to Munich with us, and he always rode in the jeep with Lacy or me. We hated to leave him when we came home, but they wouldn't let us bring him back to the U.S.

In Cologne we were in charge of eight DPs (displaced persons), all Russians, and they gave us trouble even though they were supposed to be our allies. After the war ended, they went around killing Germans for no reason at all. We tried to stop them, but we couldn't find them; by the time we found out that they had killed someone, they'd be gone. One day we heard that they were in a small patch of woods, so we machine-gunned it, but they weren't there. A few days later I was walking down the *Autobahn* (a road like our freeways) and came upon a man from our outfit, a big Indian named Haurey, whom we called Chief. He was standing with one foot on a dead German. At first I thought he had shot the man, but he said the DPs did it, and he was guarding the body until the ambulance came. The German was an old man who had been fighting at the front; since the war had ended by then, he was walking home, and these eight DPs killed him for no reason; he didn't even have a weapon.

Not long after that I was walking back to camp and came to one of the bridge overpasses that the Germans had blown down onto the *Autobahn* so that our artillery could not go either way, and I had to walk up to the road that had crossed the Autobahn and then down again. When I started up the path (made by other people doing the same thing), I saw blood trickling down the path. I went on up a little farther, and there lay a German woman about 40 years old who had been shot in the back of the neck five times. I didn't want to leave her there, so I waited a little while, and a German man came along on a bicycle. I asked him if he was Russian. He quickly informed me that he was German and produced a bunch of papers to prove it. He told me that the eight DPs (the ones we were looking for) had shot her and run off with her wrist watch. I told him to go and get the German ambulance, and I'd guard the woman. It was getting dark, and it was pretty spooky until the ambulance got there. We never did track down those DPs, as far as I know. But they were a bloody bunch, and in ordinary times their deeds would have made front-page news.

Chief Haurey was quite a character. He would go on a little bender and disappear for a few days, and no one would know where he was. Once when he had been gone for three or four days, he came in with an old German pulling him in a little wagon behind a bicycle. The cyclist was almost

Going on guard duty at Camp Livingston, Louisiana.

By the time I got to Munich in 1945, I had grown a real mustache; MPs have to look serious, after all.

exhausted, but Chief had his rifle on the man, making him pull; when he got there, he gave the German a cigarette and told him to go. The GIs would have fun anywhere they were. One day in Cologne, with the Germans right across the Rhine, along came a tank retriever, which was a big machine-like a caterpillar tractor. It was pulling an old horse-drawn hearse with the top torn off, and sitting on a beautiful couch in it were four soldiers with high silk hats and umbrellas. It was a funny sight. I guess if the Germans had telescopes and saw that, they were laughing, too.

After the German surrender, we were sent to Munich—or München, as the Germans spell it—and moved into a building that had been occupied by a Panzer unit. We met a lot of nice German people, and by that time I could talk a little German, and they could talk a little English. Dachau, which had been one of the worst concentration camps, was just 12 miles away, and we would go out there and get some German prisoners to do our KP, dishwashing and cleaning up.

I was appointed assistant cook, and a fellow by the name of Goosby was the head cook. I helped him as best I could; one day I made about 500 biscuits for the outfit. (It gave me the experience I would need for one of my record hits, "How Many Biscuits Can You Eat This Morning?") The men really went for them. Behind our headquarters some German had planted a garden before he was interrupted by the Americans, and I went out there and gathered a lot of greens to cook, too. One was called kohlrabi; at the time I didn't know what it was, but it looked good, so we had some. It was fine.

The good part about being assistant cook was that I worked three days and got off two. Those two days were spent hunting, if the season was right. The boys knew I liked guns, so almost every day I'd find a different one on my bed when I came in. As a result I had any kind of gun that I wanted to hunt with, and there was some beautiful workmanship in a lot of those guns. I'd hunt pheasants and bring them back to camp and cook them on the stove we had in the room. As assistant cook, I could get whatever else we needed out of the kitchen; many times Cox and Beaty (my roommates) and I wouldn't even have to go to the messhall. The fields there around Munich were long and narrow, separated by a row of trees. I had a jeep assigned to me, so I'd put it in the lowest gear and start it down the field and walk in front of it to the other end, then ride back and try another field. I killed a lot of pheasants. Once I got a big snowshoe rabbit, and coming home I met a German woman with a little girl. I offered her the rabbit, as I knew food was short for civilians. She was afraid to accept it until I made her understand I was Military Police; then she took it and kept bowing to me till she was out of sight.

In our room in Munich, we always had a crowd of boys because I had carried a guitar with me, and we sang a lot. When we got tired and wanted the others out so we could go to bed, one of us would get a 30/06 rifle cartridge, back up to the stove, ease the door open, drop the cartridge in, close the door, and come back and sit down. In about ten seconds the cartridge would explode and blow both doors of the stove open, and we three would have the room to ourselves.

There were several boys who played country music. Mike Rocus played the fiddle, and there was a bass player from Pennsylvania. Alex Campbell played guitar; he told me that when he got home he and his sister, Ola Belle Reed, were going to start a band. Now they have a very popular band around Oxford, Pennsylvania; it's the staff band of Sunset Park there.

Anyway, Mike Rocus and I and three other boys sort of drifted together, and before long we had formed a little string band. I did most of the singing, but Mike, playing fiddle, was really more the leader. The boys in our outfit got to where they liked our music pretty well. One day a fellow who had dropped by to listen to us introduced himself as a representative of the AFN—the Armed Forces Network that covered all of Europe—and he wanted us to come and play on a regular program. We checked with our superiors, and they agreed to free us up for an hour each morning to try it out.

I don't remember whose idea it was, but we decided to call ourselves the Munich Mountaineers, and for five months we had a regular program over AFN from eight to nine in the morning. Pretty soon we started getting stacks of fan mail from lonely GIs who hadn't been able to hear any real country music since they got overseas; most of the military music was brass bands, and the touring show troupes consisted of pop singers like Al Jolson. Our shows got more and more popular, and before long we were doing remote live broadcasts from Munich beer gardens and the Red Cross Hall—always drawing wall-to-wall crowds. And we started getting requests for personal appearances at night; guys from other outfits wanted us to come and play for their affairs near Munich. Once we played for a rodeo: some boys who had done rodeo work borrowed a few steers and horses, and put on a show for a crowd of happy GIs and very puzzled and confused Germans. We usually played within a 75-mile radius of Munich, and we would ask that the hosts pick us up and deliver us. They were always glad to, and before long I was doing about the same sort of thing I had done in West Virginia—piling into a vehicle and driving to personals, getting back in time for an early morning radio show. The difference was that now I was in uniform; the vehicles were big Army trucks; and the next morning after the broadcast I had to go back to being another MP and do a full day's work.

Of course, we got hold of some people who hadn't heard much country music. Some liked it, and some didn't. I got myself in trouble one day with a black American officer because I had used the word "darky" in some old-time song, maybe "Darling Nellie Gray." I tried to explain that words like that were a part of the old songs, but he was still offended, and I guess I can see why. Another soldier wasn't so easily pacified. He wrote me a long angry letter in which he said: "I wish, when you get your release from the Army, and get halfway across the Atlantic on the way back, that you would dump all of your music and your banjo in the ocean." Well, I was feeling ornery, so I just took his letter into the station and read it on the air. Talk about a response! When I got completely out of the Army months later, I was still getting letters cussing that man out. And I had reminded him, when I read his letter, that there was a little knob there on his radio, and that people who had enough sense to know what it was for could turn the sound on and off at will.

A lot of the German residents seemed to like our music, but few of them ever wrote us letters, so we didn't know exactly what they thought of it. There was one time when I did, though. After the war ended, we had a number of German friends who would invite us home for supper. There was this one big good-natured fellow who must have weighed 250 pounds and could drink a gallon of beer at a time; he was an old guy but a lot of fun. I had never learned to speak German well, but for him I managed to figure out a way to sing "Mountain Dew" in German. It wasn't great German, but this old man knew no English, and it was enough that he could get the drift of the song. When he got the picture of what the song was about, he just blew up laughing. The longer I sang, the louder he laughed. I guess they must have made a little homebrew in the Black Forest back in the old days, just like they did in the mountains over here.

Of course, all this time I continued to try to write songs, and I came up with 15 or 20 that were decent enough to keep. I found that the most popular songs I wrote were about current events; the one I got the most mail for was one I did about the ETO (European Theater of Operations) called "It's Rough in the ETO." I don't suppose I did that song one time after the war, but I sure did it a lot when I was in Germany. Another one, which I wrote as more and more of the boys finished their stints and started for the States, was called "Get Things Ready For Me, Ma, I'm Coming Home," and it was one of the first songs I recorded when I got back. It also was a song for its time, but even today both of these songs tell something about the way things were back then.

It's Rough in the ETO

When I first received my greetings
From dear old Uncle Sam,
I didn't give much though to
A far and distant land,
But now that we are over
I find it to be so
That no matter where we travel
It's rough in the ETO.

It's rough in the ETO.
It's rough in the ETO.
When I used to hollow, "P–O–E," *
All the boys made fun of me,
But now we're on the deep blue sea
It's rough in the ETO.

All day long we're watching
The planes up overhead.
Keeping all our eyes peeled

So we won't stop no lead.
If we get too much closer
To that front line, I know
My knees will be a-knocking.
Oh, it's rough in the ETO.

It's rough in the ETO.
It's rough in the ETO.
Back in the days of Old Ft. Sam,
The boys didn't much give a damn,
But now it's C or K or Spam.
It's rough in the ETO.

It's rough in the ETO.
It's rough in the ETO.
The boys all say you got to be tough
It don't take long to get enough,
Like the talking dog said "Rough, rough, rough."
It's rough in the ETO.

*Grandpa says every serviceman will know that POE stands for "port of entry."

Get Things Ready for Me, Ma

Once Uncle Sam said, Get your hat
And come along with me,
We got a little job to do, far across the sea.
And now that I have done two years . . . the hardest ever known,
Get things ready for me, Ma, for I'm a-comin' home.

I ain't had no fried chicken since I left old Alabam,
No pumpkin pie, no turnip greens, not even a smokehouse ham.
But I'll stuff myself with vittles rare, when I get back o'er the foam,
So get things ready for me, Ma, for I'm a-comin' home.

Again I'll swing the old front gate, open wide once more,
And run to greet the good old folks at the little cabin door.
I know I'll want to sit right there and never want to roam,
So get things ready for me, Ma, for I'm a-comin' home.

Go out to the old smoke house and get down that hickory ham.
I ain't had no red gravy since I left old Alabam.
Stir up plenty cornbread—I can eat a full-size pone,
And get things ready for me, Ma, for I'm a-comin' home.

Just catch a good young possum and cook him with some yams.
The best durn eatin's at my place just east of Birmingham.
So Ma, just grease the skillet and put on an old ham bone,
And get things ready for me, Ma, for I'm a-comin' home.

With a batch of sorghum 'lasses on biscuits buttered fine,
There ain't nothing half so tasty in the good old eatin' line,
With a glass of good cold buttermilk just as fresh as ocean foam.
Well, get things ready for me, Ma, for I'm a-comin' home.

When our AFN broadcasts started, I was singing with just my guitar; it was all I had. Then one morning on the show when I had finished a song, I remarked, "Boy, I'd like to sing that with a five-string banjo, but I can't find one anywhere." About a week later, a soldier came in from England, visiting the area; he stopped by the station and handed me this brand-spanking-new Vega "Little Wonder." "Here's a banjo for you," he said. "I stole it out of Special Services, but nobody there ever played it anyhow." I took it and began playing it more and more with the Mountaineers, and I brought it on home with me when I left Germany. In fact, it was with that banjo that I made my first hit record, "Old Rattler." You could say that I recorded my first hit with a hot banjo, but if the government ever wants to reclaim it, it sits today in the Country Music Hall of Fame.

Finally, I had enough points to go home. Those of us who were leaving were loaded on a 40-and-eight railroad car and started out with enough K-rations to do us till we got to the boat. We made a big kettle of coffee, and when the train started on the rough track we all nearly got scalded. Later we learned not to put quite so much in the kettle. As we went along, the K-rations went down, and when we got to the end of the line, there were very few left. One place on the way where we stopped to get out and stretch, there was a fellow on the platform playing a fiddle and another playing an accordion. I was very much surprised to hear them do an old tune that my pop played years ago—proof that a lot of the old fiddle tunes came from the old country.

We came home on a Liberty ship—one of a group of five—that took 19 days to get us here. The ship's screw was out of the water about half the time; we hit five storms on the Atlantic. One ship broke in two, and they had to tow the halves in. On another, two boys went out to empty the garbage, and a wave washed them overboard. Our ship was named the *James Monroe*. (I saw it on TV later when we gave some Liberty ships to England.) It was a rough trip; I couldn't eat anything for three days because I was so seasick. I'd start down the steps to the mess, and about halfway down I'd turn around and go back up on deck. The third day I was getting weak, so I gritted my teeth and forced myself to go down and eat all I could hold. I didn't have any trouble after that. One day I had my plate full of good food and was really ready to enjoy it. We had to stand at a high table to eat, and about the time I got my plate set on the table, the ship hit a big wave, and everything and everybody went on the floor. I ended up on my knees in blackberry jam. But I was better off than one poor fellow who lay in his bunk and didn't eat anything but an orange the entire trip.

Then we arrived, and I began wondering what had changed back home, and what the country music world of 1946 held for me.

Eight.

On February 9, 1946, I picked up a copy of *Billboard* and read about myself. "Grandpa Jones is back from overseas," it said, "and he was in Cincinnati a few days ago. His plans for radio are not known at present." That was putting it mildly, I thought. My plans for just about everything were not known. I had been discharged officially on January 6, but like many a returning service-man, I had found that things at home were not quite the same as when I left. Eulalia and I had decided to call it quits; we had both known it was coming for some time. Things weren't the same at WLW, either; the law said they had to give me my job back, and when I went to talk to them, they reminded me of the fact. That made me mad, and I told them I could get along without the job. But I didn't know how, really. All I knew was that things were changing awfully fast.

One good thing was that I found out I had become a modestly known recording artist while overseas. Though I had wanted to record throughout the 1930s, there were only three big record companies operating then, and it was tough to get an audition with any of them. I had pretty well given up—everyone said that you couldn't make much money at records, anyway, and that radio work was what counted—until one afternoon in the fall of 1943. There was a man named Syd Nathan who owned a record shop down the street from WLW. Syd was quite a character; he was a Cincinnati native, about 40 when I met him—a short, round man with thick, thick glasses and a case of asthma. He had been a jazz band drummer as a teenager, and then had done everything from promoting wrestling to running a chain of shooting galleries. He didn't really know much about country music, or care, but one day he bought out a radio store owned by Max Frank and found that most of the stock was what they then called "hillbilly" records, and that most of his customers wanted that kind of music. A lot of people from Kentucky and West Virginia were working in the war factories around Cincinnati then, and there was quite a market. One of the problems was that in 1943 there was a recording ban on, and it was hard to get records of any sort.

Syd got all hot to start his own record label, one that would feature hillbilly music, and he came up to WLW and talked to some of us about it. Everybody liked Syd's record shop because he had a lot of old records you couldn't get anywhere else. He didn't have much money, we knew, but finally Merle Travis and I said we would try to make some records for him. It turned out that there wasn't a suitable studio anywhere in Cincinnati, so we all three got into Syd's old DeSoto sedan and drove down to Dayton. There was a little studio there, a room over the Wurlitzer Piano Company, and that's where Merle and I made our first records. For one of them, we sang duets on "The Steppin' Out Kind" and "You'll Be Lonesome Too." On the other, Merle sang "Two-Time Annie" and a very forgettable effort called "When Mussolini Laid His Pistol Down." We weren't sure we wanted our names on those records, though: we didn't know how they'd turn out; we didn't know whether we ought to be doing it with the recording ban on; and we weren't sure that WLW, where we were under contract, would approve. So when Syd asked what we wanted to call ourselves on the records, we thought awhile. Merle and I both liked to draw little cartoons in those days, and one of my favorite characters was a little old man in long underwear with a kerosene lamp in his hand and a pipe in his mouth. I called him Mr. Shepherd because of the old man I had known as a boy. So Merle said, "Why don't we call ourselves the Shepherd Brothers?" I started laughing, but Syd said, "That's as good as any." Merle chose the name Bob McCarthy to cover his dirty work. I don't know where that one came from, but it got on the label. Driving back up to Cincinnati that afternoon, Syd asked us what he ought to call his new record company. We finally decided on King. "King of 'em all!" said Syd, and chortled.

Syd had trouble getting the records pressed, because back in 1943 there weren't many independent record companies, and it was hard to find someone to do custom pressing, especially someone to do it well. Some of those early King records came out warped so badly you could use them for bowls or ashtrays; as Merle said, watching a needle go around one was like watching a stock car on a banked race track. On November 15, 1943, our first two records were released; the Shepherd Brothers was King 500, and McCarthy was King 501. It was the start of a new company that was to become one of the country's biggest in the 1940s, but at the time we weren't worried about that. The records weren't exactly best sellers; in fact, for years I wondered if the Shepherd Brothers had ever been released to the public, because no one I knew had a copy. Finally, a few years ago, a fan found one and sent it to me in a special mahogany box, and that's still the only copy I've seen.

Sometime in January 1944, Syd set us up with a more serious recording session. I was due to leave for the Army at the end of the month, and Merle was planning to strike out for California, so we decided to do a good long session for Syd under our own names. (Syd never did issue any of Merle's first recordings, though, and a couple of years later Merle landed a contract with Capitol Records and had a string of big hits like "Divorce Me C.O.D." and "No Vacancy.") I recorded several of my own songs, including a prison song called "It's Raining Here This Morning" that I had been singing for several years. Syd put it out on King 502, and it really began selling pretty well—in fact, it sold over 50,000 copies during the time I was in the Army, and this got Syd's new company off to a pretty good start. Of course, I was only getting five-eights of a cent per side in royalties on it, but back in those days you had to take what you could get on records. The other side of my first real record under my own name was a love song called "I'll Be Around If You Need Me." I played standard guitar on these, and Merle played his electric guitar. (On some of them a young lady named Ramona Riggins played mandolin—but more about her later.)

All told, I cut six songs at that session, including the fine old badman ballad, "I've Been All Around This World," that I'd learned from Lenny Aleshire back in West Virginia. Syd didn't release many of these songs, though; he was still scurrying around trying to find a presser. He finally decided to borrow some money from his brother and start his own pressing plant to go along with his new record company. At first he knew so little about pressing that he went down to the library and checked out a book on the history of the phonograph.

Syd had me record another session when I was home on furlough later that year, but I hadn't heard much from any of these records while I was overseas. Now that I was back and getting royalty statements, I began to think maybe there was something to the record business after all. A few weeks after I got back, Syd wanted me to record again. I had the new songs I'd written while playing with the Munich Mountaineers (including "Get Things Ready For Me, Ma, I'm Coming Home"), and I also began polishing up a song I had written before I went overseas: "Eight More Miles to Louisville," which had been inspired by a big Delmore Brothers hit, Alton's "Fifteen Miles to Birmingham."

Before going overseas I had also begun singing with a gospel quartet over WLW. The Drifting Pioneers had sort of drifted away as the war heated up, and since they had had a daily half-hour show featuring old-time gospel singing, George Biggar (the program director) had told Alton Delmore that he would like to come up with a good country gospel group to fill that spot. Alton had learned to read shape notes and do real gospel singing as a boy in Alabama, so he went and got his brother Rabon, Merle Travis (who was about the only one of the Drifting Pioneers left), and me, and we marched up to the studio and stood out in the hall and tried out a couple of songs. They sounded okay, and we told Mr. Biggar that he had his country gospel group. "Good," he said, "start in the morning." Alton promised to help us learn to read shape notes—where the shape of the note rather than its place on the lines tells you your pitch. A lot of the good gospel songs of that day published by outfits like Stamps-Baxter and Vaughan and Albert Brumley were printed in little paperback books using these shaped notes. We felt that if we could learn to read those books, we would have no trouble making out 30 minutes of music a day.

After we got the job, someone asked what we would call ourselves. Alton and Rabon lived by the Brown's Ferry Road in Alabama and had written a famous song called "Brown's Ferry Blues," so we decided to call our quartet the Brown's Ferry Four. I liked to sing gospel about as well as any form of music, so I was glad when our versions of "Will the Circle Be Unbroken" and "Just a Little Talk With Jesus" and "Sweeping Through the Gates" won us a whole bunch of new fans. We all did our best at figuring out the harmony, and Merle did all the turn-arounds and accompaniment by himself on the guitar—even though Alton and Rabon were great guitar players in their own right. The hardest part of the whole thing was learning to read those shape notes. Merle caught on to it in a minute, but it took me a *long* time.

All these things came together in March of 1946, when Syd bundled the Delmores and me on a plane and took us to Hollywood to record with Merle, who had already moved to the coast. The ride was long and bumpy; we were on an old C-47, and after a really rough series of bumps, I said, "Tell that pilot if he sees a hole in the fence to get back on the road." The boys laughed, but Syd said, "That would make a great song title. Why don't you write a song about that?" I realized he was serious, and began thinking; before the flight was finished, I had the best part of a gospel song called "Get Back on the Glory Road." And before long we had recorded it.

Syd was wanting another hit record from me, something that would go as well as "It's Raining Here This Morning," and he thought "Eight More Miles" was it. Looking back on it, I can see he was right; it did become one of my big hits, and eventually became so associated with me that I use it as my theme song yet today. But we had quite a time making that original recording. Merle was to play his electric guitar behind me, and he had to capo it up pretty high, and the strings were ringing a lot. Electric guitars were still pretty new back then, but Merle's picking style—it was an old western Kentucky style where you picked rhythm with the thumb and did melody with the fingers—was so suited to the song that we really wanted it. I would do a clean take of the song, but Syd wasn't happy, and he'd shout from the control booth, "Pa, put some life into it!" And I'd do another one, and he'd say, "We need more life!" I finally got mad and stormed out of the studio.

Pretty soon Merle came after me. "That Syd makes me so mad," I said. "Yeah, he does kind of get you, doesn't he?" said Merle. We talked for a while, and then he said, "Come on back in and take a drink of this stuff." He had asked one of the studio men to go across the street for a bottle of whiskey. "I'm not much of a drinkin' man," I said. "How much should I drink?" Merle got a paper cup from the water cooler and filled it half full of whiskey. I drank it all down at once. "It stinks like the splatterboard of a gut-wagon," I said. Everyone laughed, but pretty soon I was feeling more ambitious. "All right, Syd," I shouted, "see if this has enough life," and Merle and I ripped into "Eight More Miles." When Merle started his solo, I shouted, "Play it, Merle!" Syd left the comment in, and Merle said later that he got more reaction and people commenting on that record than any other he played on.

Later on at that session, we did record "Get Things Ready for Me, Ma, I'm Coming Home," and the first two sides by the Brown's Ferry Four, but nothing caused as much stir as "Eight More Miles." Before long I was recording a session every five or six months for King, both under my own name and with the quartet. In fact, that first record by the Brown's Ferry Four was successful enough that later the same year Syd flew us to Hollywood to do a whole session, 12 tunes, of gospels. But he almost caused the whole thing to fall through. Syd was wanting to do something else in Los Angeles the day of the session, so he brought in some local bald-headed guy who had worked a lot with pop music and dance bands but didn't know beans about country music. We didn't know him and he didn't know us, but we started recording, and regardless of how we did on a take—we could tell at times that we had made a mistake—he would gloss over it and say, "Okay, let's go on to the next one." Alton and I were getting madder and madder—I had sort of a reputation for having a short fuse in those days—and we finally called a halt and took off for the hall. Alton said, "That guy won't even look at us. He doesn't care a thing about our music." We all agreed, and finally Merle went and phoned Syd and told him he'd better get over to the studio.

Syd arrived and went into the control room. The four of us and the bald-headed producer stood in the studio. "Let's take a vote on all this," came

Syd's voice over the intercom. "Rabon, what do you say about this guy?" Rabon always held his head at a little angle and had a habit of grunting before he spoke. "Mmmm, well," he said. "I don't think he understands our music." The bald-headed man just stared at us. "What about you, Merle?" said Syd. Merle walked up to the microphone and said, "Syd, he's not paying attention to anything we're doing, and he doesn't know anything about gospel music." "What about you, Pa?" Syd asked me. Merle said later that when I was this mad I looked like the devil on a lye can. I walked up to the mike: "Well, I just don't like the poor so-and-so." This time the bald-headed man really flinched, but the best was yet to come. "Alton?" said Syd. Alton had a nasal voice, and took little quick steps across the studio to the mike. "Well, I tell you, Syd, he acts like a man with all the pores of his skin stopped up." This finally did it; the bald-headed producer left, and Syd took over the session himself. We started in on "I'll Fly Away," and the Brown's Ferry Four stayed in business.

Hardly anybody knew it at the time, but the Brown's Ferry Four that recorded was not the same group being heard on WLW in 1946. Merle and I had actually left the station by the time we made our first Brown's Ferry Four records, and Alton and Rabon Delmore left soon after. A whole bunch of different people appeared in the radio versions of the quartet, including Roy Lanham and Dolly Good, one of the former Girls of the Golden West, and later on we even had quite a few personnel changes on the records. Either the Delmores or I did about every record, though; after Merle dropped out because of his new Capitol contract, we replaced him with Red Foley for a time; later on, Clyde Moody and Red Turner sang with us as well. But in spite of all the confusion, the quartet became one of the most popular old-time country gospel groups, and some of the old records we did then are still in print today, more than 30 years later.

So I was finally making records right and left and selling them—or Syd was—even though I still didn't have a regular radio job. But other changes were happening during those hectic months. One of them involved Ramona Riggins. Back before the war at WLW a bunch of us had crowded into a studio one day to listen to a new group coming in for an audition; the manager wanted our opinion about how it would fit in. Sunshine Sue and her Rock

Creek Rangers were from WRVA in Richmond; Sue's real name was Sue Workman, and she was originally from Iowa, but had been on radio in Chicago and Louisville. Sunshine Sue was very popular—she played the accordion, a sort of unusual instrument for country music back then—and she was one of the first women bandleaders in country music. She's another unsung pioneer from early days that the historians seem to have forgotten. That afternoon at WLW we all liked what we heard, and especially the trio that Sue formed with Jane Allen Workman, her guitar player, and Ramona Riggins, her fiddle player. We all thought they were mighty pretty girls, and later we were glad to hear they had been hired by the station. We had a lot of fun on the Galloping Goose singing trios and playing fiddles, guitars, and mandolins on the way to and from appearances.

I struck up a special friendship with Ramona Riggins. She had grown up in Daviess County, Indiana, around a little mining town called Raglesville. Her father was a part-time coal miner and a part-time farmer, but he was a good old-time fiddler, and he saw to it that his daughter learned to play fiddle when she was just out of her teens. In fact, Ramona's oldest brother took her aside when she was 16 and told her, "If you learn to play a tune on that fiddle by spring, I'll take you down to Evansville to play in that big contest." She not only learned the tune; she won the contest. Before long she was entering the talent shows that Sunshine Sue used to run over WHAS in Louisville, and about the time she was due to graduate from high school, she got an offer to go to Richmond and work with Sunshine Sue and her band.

She told us stories about how people reacted to a woman fiddler. "In high school, the teachers would ask, 'What are you going to do when you grow up?' The other girls would say they wanted to be a nurse, or to do this or that, but I'd just say, 'I don't know what I want to do.' I did know, but I knew they'd laugh; I knew they'd make fun of me if I said 'I want to play the fiddle.' " People stared at her when she got on a bus with her fiddle case, too. Cousin Emmy and the Coon Creek Girls were about the only women radio stars then playing stringed instruments, so it was a little unusual. But when Ramona took off on "Ragtime Annie" or "The Gal I Left Behind," people perked up and took note, and nobody worried much about whether it was man, woman, fish, or whatever.

Ramona and I hit it off great and even performed together some. As I said, Ramona played mandolin on some of my early King records, and I thought about her a lot when I was overseas. So the day my divorce from Eulalia became final, I went over to the King offices and was talking about it all to Syd. He insisted I find Ramona and give her a call. She had left WLW; she and two of Sunshine Sue's brothers-in-law and Jane had formed up a new band and were working up at WKNE in Keene, New Hampshire, with Yodeling Slim Clark. Syd told me where they were and insisted I get to her. I was not really in the mood to do that, but he kept insisting. So I went up there early in the year. It was 28 below zero when I pulled in, but I was glad to see Ramona. I didn't quite know what to say, so I told her that I was going for a job audition at WSM in Nashville, and would she like to come down and work there if I got it. Well, I didn't get an affirmative answer then, but I did finish a song I was writing. I felt a lot better when I got back to Cincinnati.

Bradley Kincaid had come to my rescue again and had lined up an audition for me with Pee Wee King's band on WSM's *Grand Ole Opry.* Pee Wee had not yet recorded his "Tennessee Waltz," which was to make him a household name, but he had been a star of the Opry for almost ten years, and as a member of the Camel Caravan had toured military bases all over the world. Though he grew up in Wisconsin, he had spent a lot of time playing on Louisville radio, and for a while had been with Frankie More's Log Cabin Boys, the same group that Cousin Emmy had worked with. Pee Wee's father-in-law was J. L. Frank, the famous promoter, and Eddy Arnold and Pete Pyle had been vocalists with him. Just before my audition, my old friend Cowboy Copas had joined him. I passed my audition, and on March 16, 1946, I gave my friends a big surprise when I made my debut on the stage of the Grand Ole Opry as a member of Pee Wee's group. The first song I did was "I Like Molasses," and though *Billboard* billed me as the "Old Man of the Mountains" and said that I "went topside" with the song, I don't remember quite knocking the audience out with it. And I sure didn't have any idea at the time that I would be working off and on at the Opry for the next 37-odd years.

Bradley had been working in Cincinnati, and before long he decided to come down, join the Opry, and start booking out with a tent show. Tent shows were a big thing then, and several Opry people had started them during the war. You didn't have to worry about renting a hall or an auditorium that way; you just pulled into a town, set up a big tent, and ran your own operation. Bradley wanted me to start booking out with him, and he decided he wanted Ramona to come down and play fiddle on the show. So I called her long distance and asked her again what I had asked her earlier in New Hampshire. This time she said she would come down if she could work for Bradley. Meanwhile, my former wife Eulalia had married Rusty Gabbard, so I could be open about wanting Ramona to come down.

We worked several months that spring with Bradley, but I could tell he wasn't really happy on the Opry. He felt that he didn't get as good a hand as some of the other stars on the show, even though I thought he did as well. But the audience in Nashville was different from audiences in New England. Bradley was doing songs like "The Legend of the Robin's Red Breast" and "Footprints in the Snow" and "The Gypsy's Warning," songs that you've really got to listen to because they are slow and tell a story. The Opry audiences were into a lot of noise and hand-slapping, and more of the band sound was taking over. By then the Opry even had electric instruments, steel guitars and electric guitars, and even though Bradley with his "Hound Dog" guitar was popular with many of the older fans, he was almost swallowed up. So we weren't too surprised when he decided to leave the Opry and go back up to Springfield, Ohio, to help run a radio station he had helped build.

After this the Bailes Brothers asked Ramona to join their act; they did some tent shows, but they were really big on the Opry then, with their hit "Dust on the Bible" and "The Pale Horse and His Rider." Ramona played both fiddle and bass fiddle with them. One day Johnny Bailes told her, "You're so versatile, you ought to do more than play," and so she started singing harmony in their gospel trios. After a while they wanted me to join them, too, and this was fine with me, since I was wanting to be around Ramona as much as I could.

Ramona finally said yes, and we were married on October 14, 1946. Though we had been working in Nashville, we decided to get married up in Henderson, Kentucky, since I still had a lot of relatives around there and a lot of them wanted to come. The minister who married us was the local Baptist preacher, E. Keevile Judy, and the couple that stood up with us were friends named Estes who came up with us from Nashville, where we all boarded at the same boardinghouse. I never will forget what Mr. Estes said just before the ceremony: "I don't know about this—you're getting a new car and a new wife in the same week." The new car I had just bought wasn't really so new: it was an Oldsmobile and definitely a pre-war car. Sometimes it acted like a pre–Civil War car.

On our wedding night we went to Owensboro, Kentucky, and started our one-day honeymoon. I remember that after I went to sign the register at the motel, I came back and told Ramona I was so nervous I had written everybody's name down but my own and, Johnny Bailes's. The next morning we took a bus to join the Bailes Brothers on tour and went right back to work. It wasn't exactly a honeymoon cruise to Bermuda, but we were as happy as if it had been.

We continued to work for the Bailes Brothers for a while; then we decided to go out on our own. We got a spot on the Grand Ole Opry, and for a time we hooked up with Lonzo and Oscar, the comedy team who had had the hit "I'm My Own Grandpa"; they hired us for their road show. One night we were playing a courthouse (yes, we worked courthouses, too) in Harlan, Kentucky, and I was on stage finishing up my part of the show. I finished, and introduced Lonzo and Oscar with a big buildup, but they didn't come out. I stared out of the lights into the shadows offstage but couldn't see a thing. They must be there, I thought, and wound up and made a big pitch of an introduction again. They still didn't come out. What in blazes, I thought, and took off back to their dressing room. There they were, down on the floor, counting picture money.

Later on, times got a little rougher for Lonzo and Oscar, and they came to us and said they would have to let us go as they weren't making ends meet. My records had started taking hold by this time, especially "Eight More Miles to Louisville" and "East Bound Freight Train," and that was having a real effect on my personal appearances. So I told Lonzo and Oscar, "Well, why don't you boys just work for me, and I'll pay you." It sounded kind of funny, but they thought it over and agreed, and so we worked that way for a while.

I was exposed to some great comedy teachers in those days with the

WSM tent shows. That's where I first met Minnie Pearl. But one of my favorites that a lot of people today don't remember was Lazy Jim Day, who traveled with Cowboy Copas on all his road shows. He used to do a lot of talking blues numbers, and also what he called the Singing News, where he would make up little songs about the news events of the day.

Jim was about as clean as anybody I've ever seen. He would stay an hour in the bathroom every morning just getting ready for the day. He wore bib overalls, but they were spotless. When we stayed in a hotel, he would hire the maid to take his underwear home at night and wash it and bring it back in the morning; that way he didn't have to carry so many changes of clothes. In fact, all he took with him was a little bag he called his "getaway satchel." In one little town one night when he wanted some beer, he found out that he was in a dry county. Then somebody told him where he could get bootleg beer, and when he pulled up in the driveway of the house, there hung his longhandles on the clothesline. The hotel maid's husband supplied the beer for the county.

I remember how popular Jim Day was at WLW in Cincinnati. He made money there and always carried four or five $100 bills around with him. Once they went into a fine restaurant to eat; to the waitress, Jim in his bib overalls looked like he didn't have a cent. When he ordered a big steak, she informed him that it would cost $4.50. He said, "I don't give a damn if it's $10; bring it on." When he went to pay her, he gave her one of those $100 bills, and she had to go out and get change. He wouldn't have done that if she hadn't said what she did. Jim would lend money to a lot of people on the show, writing their names in a little black book. I've borrowed money from him myself.

Copas used to get aggravated at Lazy Jim; once he said, "If I was your wife, I'd shoot you." Jim said in his slow drawl, "Well, if you were my wife, I'd shoot myself." One afternoon the group was traveling close to Beaver Dam, Kentucky, and Jim said, "Now right around that curve there'll be a sign that says, Short Creek 3 miles." When they rounded the curve, the sign said Short Creek 5 miles. Jim said, "Well, they've moved it two miles."

Travel was rough back in those days. It was pretty much all by car, and you had to get back in on Saturday nights to make your appearance on the Grand Ole Opry. Whenever musicians got together, they would swap tales about life on the road. Two of my favorites involve two of the all-time greats of bluegrass music, Bill Monroe and Lester Flatt. For a time Bill Monroe hired a duet act, Mel and Stan, the Kentucky Twins, to work the road with him. One night late when Mel was driving, Bill told him to pull over, that he had to go to the bathroom, that he just couldn't wait. Mel pulled off the road somewhere up in the hills of Kentucky, and Bill opened the door and stepped out into the dark. And just kept stepping—down and down some steep bank, about 15 feet. He crawled back up covered with leaves an dirt, climbed back in the car, and fired Mel and Stan, the Kentucky Twins, on the spot. Now somebody told me that story, and I don't know for sure that it's true. I know people are always telling tales on me, and some are true and some are not.

Another time Lester Flatt was playing two dates in Texas and then had to go back to Nashville to make some commercials for Martha White flour; then he had to go all the way back to Texas for two more dates. Some old Texas coot heard about this and went up to Lester's fiddler and said, "Why don't you boys just stay here and play the other days instead of going back to Nashville?" The fiddler didn't feel like going into a long explanation, so he told the old boy that the banjo picker in the band had a potato patch and that the bugs were eating up his crop, and they had to go back and dust the potatoes. The old man drew in his lips and nodded and said, "Well, they are workin' on mine too; they are bad this time of year."

But as long as we are telling stories, let me tell you the official version of one of the favorites they tell on me. I've heard this from dozens of different people, and here's my chance to set the record straight. It was in February 1948, and we were playing a little high school in Kentucky right up on the Ohio River. Before the show the local booker had helped set us up on stage, but just before we went on, he took us aside and pointed to a trapdoor just offstage. "Now don't think that's a dressing room or anything, 'cause it ain't," he said. "Don't go down there at all. Just keep it shut." So I didn't think too much more about it, and the show went on. It came time for me to do my bit, and I went out and told my jokes and then started to sing. All of a sudden I heard this burst of laughter from backstage. I looked down to make sure they weren't laughing at me, and looked offstage, but couldn't see anything. In a couple of minutes the laughter in the wings was loud enough for the audience to hear. What in blue blazes, I thought, and I quickly called up one of the other performers and bowed out and stalked off to find out just what was going on. One of the boys in the band, it seems, had decided he just had to find out what was under that trapdoor. He had opened it and found a flight of steep steps leading into the dark, so he jumped down there real fast and fell right into the Ohio River! It seems the flood had backed up water into the school basement—it was a common enough thing around there—and this poor soul (who shall remain nameless) came sputtering up, drenched to the bone and cursing under his breath. The rest of the group backstage tried to hold it in but couldn't, and burst out laughing, show or no show. And I couldn't blame them; when I got a look at him standing there dripping water, I joined in. I told a newspaper reporter later that night, "Next week, we're going to add to our billing—'Radio's Only Musical Hillbilly Seal.' "

'Nine.

THE DOG AND THE DEW

Sunday, July 27, 1947: I am in Oxford, Pennsylvania—no, make that *West Oxford*—at Sunset Park, one of those country music parks that they used to have all up through there. Sunday afternoon crowds are usually good, and we've pulled in several hours ahead of schedule. The rest of the troupe hasn't arrived yet, so I walk onstage to look things over. A huge roar goes up and I look out to see the place filled. I duck back offstage, and start to leave to go get some lunch, but the clapping keeps up. I've heard of good crowds, but this one is really up, I think. I stick my head out again—more applause. All right, I shrug; I'll give you a little preview of the show. I unlock my banjo case and tune up and wander out, me and myself, and do a quick number. They keep clamoring, so I go back out again. And again. Three, four, five times. By the time the rest of my act arrives, I'm already tired and glad to see them take over. I'm sitting backstage shaking my head and wondering, when did all this start? When did I become a full-time country music star?

One big step took place on March 28, 1947, when Ramona and I did another King recording session with Cowboy Copas. Looking back on it, I can see how it was a first on several counts. It was the first time we had ever recorded in Nashville, though modern country singers had been doing that for about a year, and record companies were starting to get the idea that Nashville was the place to go to record. But it was also the first time I had gotten up enough courage to record with the banjo. I had been playing the banjo on the radio since the war but had never recorded with it. A lot of producers thought the banjo was out of style on records, and throughout most of the late 1930s and 1940s you just never heard it. The greats who played old-time banjo, like Uncle Dave Macon, couldn't get recorded during those years—the sound wasn't "modern" enough. But I knew from my mail and from my fans at shows that they did like my old-time frailing banjo style, especially on fast numbers; back in Wheeling and elsewhere in West Virginia, we had always used the banjo in our opening number, what we called our "shout" tune, where the whole cast sang to open the show. So I felt it might go over pretty well on records, too. About that same time Earl Scruggs had been playing his new bluegrass banjo with Bill Monroe, and they were going over well on the Opry and on records, so I thought that I might try recording a little old-time banjo playing.

The song I chose to try it out on was "Mountain Dew." This was one I had learned from my old friend Scott Wiseman, of Lulu Belle and Scotty, who for years had been on radio in Chicago and Cincinnati. Scotty told me later that he got it from Bascom Lamar Lunsford, "the minstrel of the Appalachians," a famous folk song collector and singer from Asheville, North Carolina. Lunsford was a lawyer, and had written the song in 1920 or thereabouts; it originally had a courtroom setting, where a moonshiner is hauled before the judge and has to try to talk his way out of a stiff sentence. I found out later that there's an even older Irish song called "The Real Old Mountain Dew," about a judge who tricks a moonshiner into giving him his secret recipe for the brew, and that this might have inspired Lunsford's song. Anyway, Scotty said that Lunsford had recorded his original version in the 1920s, and Scotty had picked it up in the late 1930s. Since Scotty wasn't a lawyer, he rewrote the song and took it out of the courtroom, starting off with the famous line, "There's a big hollow tree, down the road here from me." This went over so well that Lulu Belle and Scotty recorded their version in 1939, and Scotty got to singing it at personal appearances a lot. He tried to use it on his show on WLS, but the managers wouldn't let him sing it on the air because the subject matter was illegal. About that time I learned it and begin singing it with my banjo. Merle Travis and I used to fun around with it a lot when we were in Cincinnati and even added some verses. I came up with this:

> Well, my old aunt June
> Bought some brand new perfume,
> It had such a sweet smellin' phew.
> But to her surprise,
> When she had it analyzed,
> It was nothing but good old mountain dew.

So on that Friday afternoon in Nashville, Ramona got her mandolin, Cowboy Copas played the guitar, and we put on wax our version of "Mountain Dew." It was only one of eight songs we recorded that day, but we felt pretty good about it.

So did Syd Nathan. It was the first thing he released from that session, and he had it out by May. Right away it started selling, and my quarterly royalty statement through June of that year showed me that it had already sold 20,000 copies—not bad for those days. The next quarter showed another 20,000. All of a sudden I had a hit that was a lot bigger than anything I'd had before, and I began to see how a hit record could really have an effect on your bookings and radio work; over the years "Mountain Dew" has become associated with me by almost everyone. After that, I started using my banjo more and more, and doing more up-tempo songs with an old-time flavor. Even today, "Mountain Dew" is the song that I use to start off all my personal appearances. If I don't, someone will ask why not.

Naturally, Syd was anxious to get out a follow-up to "Mountain Dew," and he got after me to find another "banjo song." In September 1947, Syd sat up a session in the old WSM studios at Seventh and Union in Nashville, and Copas, Ramona, and I walked up those stairs to cut just two sides. One was a version of "Move It On Over" that Copas and I did. The song had just come out on a new label called MGM by a young singer from Alabama named Hank Williams; I guess Syd didn't think either the label or the singer would amount to much, and he wanted us to do him a version on King. In those days, when anyone got a hit of any size, four or five other companies would rush out what they called a "cover" version. We were wrong about the staying power of MGM and young Hank Williams, but fortunately, the other song we did at that session was more original. For that one, Copas played rhythm guitar, Ramona switched to bass, and I played banjo. It was a song about an old hound dog named Rattler.

Nobody knows who actually wrote "Old Rattler," and on the King record we deliberately left the composer credits blank. The idea of a good hunting dog named Rattler goes way back; one of Davy Crockett's hounds was named Rattler. But after all these years, I'm still not sure just where I learned the song about that dog. I remember singing it back in Wheeling, where we used it as one of our shout tunes to open the show. I vaguely remember hearing somebody from East Tennessee do it, and a lot of the boys on the old *National Barn Dance* used to sing it. In fact, although Bradley Kincaid recently told somebody that he had learned it from me, he had it in one of his song books that was published before I even met him. The Cumberland Ridge Runners, with Slim Miller and Karl and Harty, used to do it and even recorded it back in the early 1930s. Then my friends Cap, Andy, and Flip had a version in their 1934 song book, and a man named Frank Dudgeon, who used to sing on West Virginia radio, also did it a lot and even made an early record. I've never been able to straighten it all out; I only know it was an old song that I adapted to fit my style and that I had been singing long before I recorded it. It was something I grabbed for when Syd said he wanted me to do another "Mountain Dew."

Syd had "Old Rattler" out in a couple of months, and it took off like a one-eyed cat in a dog pound. It was selling double what "Mountain Dew" did, and it kept the pressing plants in Cincinnati working overtime. By Christmas time it had sold over 40,000 copies, and was the fastest-selling record I had ever had. When I played our big New Year's Eve show that year at Thompson's Hall in Indianapolis, "Rattler" was the big hit, the one that brought the house down. Everywhere we played, hunters would come up and want to know if I really hunted (yes, I did) and tell me they had named their pups after

Yes, I really did have a dog named Old Rattler, and he wasn't a bad little coon dog. This picture dates from 1948 or so.

Rattler. I sometimes wonder how many dogs named Rattler there are running around the country as a result of that song.

So by 1948 I had pretty much become the Grandpa that I am today. I had my mustache, my boots, my suspenders, my banjo, and my old-time songs. "Rattler" had got me to playing the banjo more than the guitar, and people seemed to like the old-time songs the way I did them. Syd rushed me back to the studio again and again in those next few months, trying to get more hits but also trying to beat the recording ban that was about to start under the musicians' union leader, Joe Petrillo. It was my hard luck that this year-long ban took hold just as my records were starting to hit. So we went in and did a bunch of traditional songs like "Come Be My Rainbow" and "Kitty Clyde"; "Daisy Dean," an old murder ballad my mother used to sing; "How Many Biscuits Can You Eat?" the tune Dr. Humphrey Bate used to open the Opry with back in the early days; "The Bald Headed End of the Broom," "Going Down Town," "Jesse James," "Stay in the Wagon Yard," "Uncle Eph's Got the Coon," and lots more. For years I had been saving up any old song books I could get from other singers on stations where I'd worked, and Ramona had her own collection of stuff, so we had a good file of old songs to draw on. I also tried to write some "new" songs that sounded like old-time ones, since I would get composer royalties on these. I wrote several answer songs to "Rattler," like "Old Rattler's Pup," but they never did do anything. For a while I got into the boogie-woogie craze that was going around and recorded "Grandpa's Boogie" and "Five String Banjo Boogie" and one or two others, but they didn't exactly bring down the house, either.

And I had my first song censored. "Due to the Shortage" was intended as a sort of topical song about how there was a shortage of everything in those days right after the war—housing, tires, and so on—and how we could not do or have this or that "due to the shortage." One of the lines said something about how you could get married but couldn't have kids, "due to the shortage." Boy, that fixed it. The engineers started giggling when they heard it, and Syd said to me later, "Grandpa, that one's a keeper. We'll put it in the vaults. We don't want to be hauled into court over it." And that's how I wrote my first and only dirty song.

On a makeshift stage in Korea, 1951, with Ramona (to my right) and Mary Klick playing the bass fiddle.

DUE TO THE SHORTAGE

Now that the conflict's over
And has been for two years,
We should not go into a store
And find the things so "dear."
But when you ask them what they have,
They give you this old line:
Due to the shortage
I just don't have that kind.

Chorus:
Due to the shortage
You cannot have one now,
And where we'll ever get one
I don't know when or how.
Now if you wait a month or two,
You'll find one I allow,
But due to the shortage
You cannot have one now.

I went to buy a suit of clothes
To try to dress up neat.
I wanted to look spic and span
From my head down to my feet.
I wear a thirty-four, I said.
He didn't pay no mind.
I looked like P.T. Barnum's tent—
He sold me a "forty-nine."

Chorus:
He said—Due to the shortage
I cannot fit you snug.
I look like I was wrapped up in
A ten-year-old rag rug.
Some day I hope they'll get ahead
And make my size again,

*Me and my banjo with
Gordie Tapp on Main Street
Jamboree in Toronto about 1957.
Ramona is tuning up, and Harry
Smith is holding his big electric
guitar. Photo by Joseph Bochsler.*

Cause due to the shortage
I've nearly gone insane.

One day last week I told my wife
That a certain little thing
Would make the household brighter
When we heard its laughter ring.
I said we had some money now,
And might feed two or three.
She knocked me down; when I got up
She shouted this at me:

Chorus:
Due to the shortage
We cannot have one now,
And if we ever get one
I don't know when or how.
Maybe in a year or two
If adoption laws allow,
But due to the shortage
We cannot have one now.

The Grand Ole Opry in the late forties, when I started there, was a pretty different place from what it is now. We did the shows in the old Ryman Auditorium in downtown Nashville—hot in the summer, and cold and drafty in the winter. Some of the acts that were on the show then are still there, like Bill Monroe, Ernest Tubb, Roy Acuff, Minnie Pearl, and the Crook Brothers. But a lot of the people who were really popular back then aren't around now, and a lot of young people today haven't even heard of them. Oh, they will have heard of Red Foley, who was about as big a star as Roy Acuff during this time, but you don't hear much about Smilin' Eddie Hill, a big easygoing guitar player and songwriter who later moved to Memphis and helped get the Louvin Brothers started; Eddie still lives near Nashville, though he's not in good health. Then there was Milton Estes, who won his fame by doing some of the fanciest and best square dance calls around; he was also from Kentucky and had spent a lot of time traveling around listening to the old-time dance callers up there and learning his trade. He later had a

I spent a lot of time bouncing over two-lane roads with Jackie Phelps (center); the big guy is Harry Smith.

popular noon radio show in Nashville, and a band called the Musical Millers. Wally Fowler and his Oak Ridge Quartet—the *original* Oak Ridge boys—were popular. They started off doing country music and later switched to gospel, and Wally was very active in publishing and promotion. Paul Howard was there, the man who really brought western swing to the Opry, and Johnny and Jack with Kitty Wells, and Robert Lunn, the original talking blues man, and comedian Rod Brasfield, who used to work so much with Minnie Pearl.

For a while I had a guitar player from western Kentucky named Mose Rager working for me; he was one of the inventors of the "modern" thumb-and-finger picking style that Merle and Chet Atkins were using. I had happened to ask Merle Travis one day, "Merle, where can I find a guitar picker that picks like you, cause that's the kind I really need on my personal appearances." And he said, "Well, why don't you try Mose Rager? He taught me to pick." So I got in touch with Mose, and he said, "Why, yes, I'll come down and pick with you," and he started playing out with me around Nashville. He was a fine picker, and could do great solos—his specialty was a hot version of "Tiger Rag" that really stunned audiences. He was also a funny man on stage in a quiet sort of way; he would make funny little comments that broke up an audience. Mose stayed in professional music only a couple of years; then he went back to Kentucky, but everyone who heard him agreed that he was one of the best. Come to think of it, I've had the pleasure of working with more than a few of the great guitar players; Merle Travis, Mose Rager, and later in Washington one of my guitar players was a young man named Roy Clark. Chet Atkins even played on some of my Victor records.

In August of 1947 they told us that the Grand Ole Opry network show, which was heard nationwide, had a rating of seventh best in the country—and not just in country music, but all kinds of music shows. But they didn't need to tell us that we were doing all right with the fans. In September I had some pictures of myself printed up and offered them free; the first week I got over 5,000 requests. Of course, I don't know what people were doing with all those photos; they may have been using them to hang in the chicken house, but I sent out a lot of them. That same fall I brought out my biggest song book yet, done by Lois Publishing Company, which was an arm of Syd Nathan's business. Unfortunately, it had been put together before I got my big hits on

"Mountain Dew" and "Rattler", so it didn't include those, but it did have most of my earlier so-called hits, such as "My Darling's Not My Darling Anymore" and "East Bound Freight Train" and "It's Raining Here This Morning." I think the cover of that book was the first one that showed me with my Grandpa mustache and my banjo.

One of the favorite characters on the Opry back then was Uncle Dave Macon, the old banjo player and singer who had been with the show ever since it had started. When I knew him, Uncle Dave was over 75, but he still did a lot of tent shows and tours with people like Curly Fox and Texas Ruby, Bill Monroe, and others. A lot of people think I learned my banjo playing and old-time songs from Uncle Dave, and a lot of people today tell me, "I remember hearing you on the Opry back there in the 1930s," but of course they are remembering Uncle Dave; they confuse me with him. I did do a couple of show dates with Uncle Dave, and we did travel some together, but I had already learned the banjo and a lot of my songs long before I met him. So I can't really say he was an influence on my style, but I did enjoy watching him and hearing his jokes. He liked to do imitations of "serious" love songs of the day, and I can still remember his takeoff on Floyd Tillman's song "I Love You So Much It Hurts." He would sing the first line in a strong clear voice, "I love you so much it hurts," and then go, "OOOOF!" One night Floyd Tillman himself watched Uncle Dave do this and got so mad he was steaming.

Most of the time I was on the Opry, I toured out into Georgia and Alabama and Tennessee, and managed to keep pretty busy; we worked with Bill Monroe on occasion, and Wally Fowler on occasion, and fine musicians like Vic Willis and Brownie Reynolds and Ernest Ferguson. It was about this time that a disc jockey and promoter named Connie B. Gay started helping us get bookings up around Maryland and Washington, D.C., and Pennsylvania, where they had all those music parks. By the middle of 1948 he was getting us more and more dates up there, and we enjoyed working with him. So we weren't too surprised when he asked us to go to work for him at station WARL near Arlington, Virginia, just across the river from the capital. He was really starting to promote country music in Washington and finding out that there was a lot of interest in it up there. He also asked Chubby Wise, the great fiddler who had worked with Bill Monroe, and Clyde Moody, a good bluegrass singer, to come up. There was a lot of excitement about country music in Washington; in fact, at the same time that Harry Truman had his formal inaugural ball in 1949, Connie staged a "Hillbilly Inaugural Ball" at Turner's Arena up there and brought in a lot of big stars.

So Connie kept after us, and we finally agreed to meet him halfway at Salem, Virginia, and talk about it. We drove up there and met Connie and his secretary Jane Trimmer, and he talked us into the move. "There's only one thing I demand," I told him. "You've got to find me a farm. I'm not going to live in town." And sure enough, he called back in a couple of weeks and had found us an 18-acre farm at Lorton, Virginia; it had a big old house, a lawn, a garden spot, and even a place to have a few chickens. So we agreed to take the plunge and in the summer of 1948 moved north.

Connie B. Gay was born in 1915 or thereabouts in a place he called Lizard Lick, North Carolina, and had been the conductor for the *National Farm and Home Hour*, which was one of the oldest and longest-running national programs aimed at rural audiences. He had branched out into a number of shows and enterprises, starting off as a disc jockey on WARL with a morning record show called *Let's Be Gay;* then he did a big afternoon show that mixed records and live acts called *Town and Country Time*. Next he had a big three-hour television show called *Gaytime*, which was broadcast every week from "beautiful and historic" Constitution Hall in Washington; he would have acts like Eddy Arnold, Hawkshaw Hawkins, the Sons of the Pioneers, Hank Williams, Elton Britt, and his own band called the Radio Ranchmen; Clyde Moody, Chubby Wise, and accordion player Pat Patterson. He staged big country shows that he called "Whing Dings" on special occasions like New Year's Eve, and on top of all this, he had Club Hillbilly, about a mile out of Washington over near Seat Pleasant, Maryland. This was quite a place, too: each Monday night there was a songwriters' contest; Tuesday night, a talent hunt run by Clyde Moody; Wednesday night, a square dance; Thursday night, a beauty contest. It was a different kind of club and a different kind of work, but we enjoyed it. We kept up the old banjo and fiddle tunes, and "Rattler" and "Mountain Dew", but we also did a lot of hymns that were popular, like "Building on the Sand." The fan magazines were calling me "the old man of the mountains" and "old leather britches" and "the most popular man about town," and I had to pinch myself every now and then to remind me that I was still just 36 years old and that I was once again playing country music in a part of the country where they weren't supposed to like country music. It would be another 30 years before country music would be welcome at the big white house on Pennsylvania Avenue, but the working people in and around Washington sure were accepting it. But what did we expect from a town where you could get fried okra in the federal workers' cafeteria?

Connie kept on getting us good bookings, and set up trips into Canada and even Nova Scotia. We also got some bookings through Jolly Joyce, which was then about the biggest agency for country talent around; it handled movie stars like Tex Ritter as well as country music stars. We did a lot of work in Maryland for International Harvester, the farm equipment company; in those days the company would go into farm communities and set up big tents to have tractor shows, and we would provide the entertainment, even out on the Eastern Shore. One of the people we worked with a lot was "Smitty" Smith. His full name was Bascom Doyle Smith, and he was from Georgia originally but was already working for Connie when we got there. He was not only a guitar player and a singer but a great comedian; in fact, I owe a lot of the jokes I use on stage today to "Smitty" Smith. He's dead now; he never made any records, and he's been pretty much forgotten, but I learned a lot from him.

Lenny Aleshire also rejoined us in Washington. I hadn't worked with him since 1941 in Fairmont; he'd been on the *Ozark Jubilee* in Springfield, Missouri, but he called me before we left for Washington and said, "I don't care how far I have to go, just so I get to work." Well, it turned out that his first date with me took us almost 2,000 miles—all the way to Nova Scotia—and his words came back to haunt him. Billy Grammer, the famous guitar player who is still on the Opry today and who later had the big hit record with "Gotta Travel On," was on Connie's shows then, too, and often flew into Cincinnati to work on Syd's King recordings.

We also began doing stints at the *Old Dominion Barn Dance* down the road a few miles in Richmond; the emcee was Sunshine Sue, the singer Ramona had started with. This show, though relatively new, was really popular in the 1950s, and when some of Connie Gay's programs began to drop off in Washington, Ramona and I became regulars. It had a CBS network hookup by mid-1950, and the performers were getting good exposure. Some familiar modern Nashville faces were working there: Jackie Phelps, who is known for his work on *Hee Haw* with the late Jimmie Riddle and is also an excellent guitar soloist; Joe Maphis, another famous guitar player I had known since Cincinnati, who later helped discover Barbara Mandrell; and Joe Wheeler. Others included Chick Stripling and Leon "Hank" Silby, who did the comedy; Buddy Allen; Benny Kissinger and Curly Collins; Roy Parks and accordion player Buster Puffenburger, who used to play backup to Sunshine Sue's vocals; Toby Stroud; John Workman (Sue's husband); Quincy Snodgrass; and Slim Roberts.

Meanwhile, times kept changing; we had hardly gotten over all the postwar shortages before we were in another war, this time in Korea. They called it a "police action," but to the boys who went over there, it was a war just like the other one. Connie B. Gay wanted us to go to Korea and got a tour set up through the Pentagon in March of 1951, just about the time the United Nations forces were recapturing Seoul and President Truman was getting ready to fire General MacArthur. Just three of us were to go; me, Ramona, and Mary Klick, a bass and guitar player and singer from Washington County, Tennessee. We were eager to go, to see the boys in action and to see what the war looked like up close. We started out in Richmond and got everything ready, and we got all the way to Washington when I suddenly stopped and hit my head and looked at Ramona and said, "I forgot Grandpa!" I had left behind the little suitcase that held my Grandpa costume—suspenders, baggy trousers, spectacles, old hat, striped shirt, makeup, banjo strings, and all the rest. (I was forever forgetting it, and we were always having to go back and "get Grandpa.") We were all supposed to go to a big dinner that the Pentagon was having for us, which Connie had helped set up, but the two girls had to turn around and go back to Richmond and get the Grandpa case, while Connie and I went on to the dinner. That's how forgetful I was, and that's the kind of start the Korean trip got off to.

We got on an old four-engine propeller plane, and it took us 13 hours to get to Hawaii. I remember how beautiful it was—it was the first time I had been there—and the hotel where we ate didn't have any doors because the climate was so nice they didn't need any, and it never closed. It took another 12 hours to get to Tokyo; but we hit the ground running: the second day there we'd played 15 shows in hospitals and other places. We played for some soldiers who were wounded so badly they couldn't leave their beds, and we went right into their hospital rooms. We were exhausted that night, but we felt good. And it was only a preview of things to come.

When we went on into Korea from Tokyo, the plane we used had bullet holes in it where enemy fighters had strafed it. We were starting to feel close to the war—and in fact, the fighting wasn't too far away. During the next few days we played little makeshift theaters in rice paddies, but those were some of the best audiences we had ever played to; many of them hadn't seen any entertainment or anybody from the States in nine months. We went in three jeeps, each one with the names on it. One time the weapons carrier that was bringing our equipment didn't get there, and we had to borrow instruments from different boys in the audience who happened to have them. They were some of the worst I've ever played, but we put on a show with them anyway. We went on for two weeks, playing three shows a day at hospitals, combat divisions, corps headquarters, and service commands; after we were finished, they guessed that we had played to over 38,000 soldiers. We played almost to the 38th Parallel—they wouldn't let us go right up to it—and in sight of Seoul. Connie started out the tour with us, but a while into it, he said, "I can't take this, I'm heading home." But we played on. One of the favorite songs I did then was "Rotation Blues," about the method of assigning troops to front-line duty in rotation. It was written by Lieutenant Stewart Powell, and later on I recorded it. Part of it went: "Rain in Korea sure gets cold and wet, and the rotation papers are sure hard to get." As the old-timers used to say, it was a true song. Korea was surely cold and wet, and a lot of the boys surely did feel that when their turn was up, the rotation papers had "set them free."

The following winter—on January 10, 1952—we drove to Nashville for another recording session. This one was a little different, though: it was my very first for RCA Victor, which was then about the country's biggest record company. I had been unhappy with King for some time; we kept recording, but nothing really took off the way some of the early releases had. Some of us had gotten to thinking that King was becoming more interested in its rhythm-and-blues than its country line, and the company was full of people I didn't really know, or who didn't know our type of old-time music. So Roy Starkey, who had once worked a lot with King himself, managed to talk to Steve Sholes, who was the new head of country and western recording at Victor.

For that first session Chet Atkins had organized a band of some of the better Nashville musicians: himself, Smilin' Eddie Hill on guitar, and Tommy Jackson on fiddle. We did a couple of old-time songs, such as "Mountain Laurel" with Ramona singing harmony and playing mandolin, and "Stop That Ticklin' Me," a comedy song in the old-time vein that Joe Maphis had done. Then we did one called "T.V. Blues" by Ruby Wheeler; television sets were still pretty new then, but I already had a couple of kids and knew what kind of trouble was down the road. The song started off:

> We've got a brand new television in our home,
> I didn't know to leave well enough alone.
> It just doesn't matter if it's rain or shine,
> The thing keeps a-ravin' on all the time.

At the end I sang about how the kids were "as white as a sheet" and I couldn't get them to the table to eat, and said if things didn't change, I'd get so mean that I'd "shoot out the glass of the TV screen."

Steve Sholes liked the idea of songs that had a topical or current events twist. He thought that was the way to go and wanted me to do more of them. I had to admit that the last several numbers I had recorded for King hadn't done too well; they had been good old-time songs, or new ones—like Merle's "Dark as a Dungeon"—with an old-time flavor. So I thought that maybe it was time for a change, and during the next couple of years I put out on Victor a string of songs about everything under the sun that was the current topic of conversation. Right away I did that "Rotation Blues" about Korea; then I did "I'm No Communist," which was written by my friend Scott Wiseman. This came out during the McCarthy hearings and was very popular for a couple of years; a lot of different country singers did versions of it. I wrote a song called "You Ain't

Seen Nothing Yet," which was a sort of science fiction country song about what life would be like in 1995. I had supersonic highways running up to Mars, and men taking rocket ships to the moon, and eating a full-course meal in one little pill—that is "if the new Hydrogen bomb hasn't blown us all away." Then there was another one by Scotty called "That New Vitamine," which was all about the wonderful effects of vitamin B-12, which had just been discovered.

I kept doing these kinds of songs for RCA records, but none of them sold very well. My older-style songs, like "Mountain Laurel" and "Sass-a-Frass" and "The Closer to the Bone the Sweeter is the Meat," sold a lot better. Steve was hoping I could appeal to a big pop audience, and he tried all kinds of things. He even had Minnie Pearl and me cut a version of "Papa Loves Mambo," but it didn't do very well, either. Steve didn't really understand the kind of thing I ought to do. He'd bring in songs I couldn't sing at all; one time he brought me one called "Hey Liberace," which was downright ridiculous. "I can't do this stuff," I told him, and I don't think he liked that. After a time, I sort of lost interest in the record-making, and he lost interest in me, and RCA Victor and I parted ways. And that was about the end of my efforts to be a big pop star. I decided I was best at old-time country music; that's all I had ever wanted to do, and if I couldn't make it doing that, then I wouldn't make it.

Ten.

Sometimes when I am reading biographies of other singers, I get the impres-
sion that all they ever talked about was their music and their careers, because
that's all we read about. Or they go to the other extreme and talk about
nothing but the scandals in their lives. I can't do the latter sort of book,
because we've never really had any juicy scandals: no problems with alcohol
or dope, or getting married two dozen times, or doing a stretch in jail. But
there was a personal side to all this music-making; Ramona and I were like lots
of other young couples back in the 1940s, starting our families, taking care of
the day-to-day chores of getting food on the table, finding a place to live, and
paying taxes.

When I first went to Nashville in 1946, I had boarded at a roominghouse
run by Ma and Pa Upchurch, two fine people who were well known to the
musicians in Nashville then. A lot of the Opry pickers boarded with them and
had for years; they were an institution, and their good meals soothed a lot of
bruised egos and homesickness. After Ramona and I were married, we moved
to a house on Boscobel Street; it was just a few doors away from the little white
house where the son of Jesse James—Jesse, Jr.—was born. I always meant to
take a picture of that house, but somehow I never got around to it. Since then

they've torn it down; now a freeway runs through there, and that little bit of history is gone.

Next we bought a house and 16 acres out around Donelson close to the airport. We had a fine garden there, and I had a few whiteface cattle. My mother was living with us then, and also Marsha, my daughter from my first marriage. Eloise was born there in 1948. In fact, just before she was born, we decided we needed to insulate the house, and the company we called came out and used a then-new method of blowing the insulation into the walls. This was fine, except that there were a few cracks in the walls, and the insulation came through the cracks and got all over the house. And they had taken the windows out, and it was cold inside. All this, with Ramona about to have a baby. She got a little upset about it, and I guess I could understand why. But we didn't know they were going to insulate in that fashion.

Everywhere we've lived I've tried to raise peaches, because I love peaches above all else. It seems I'm destined, though not to have peaches anywhere. Bugs, worms, cold weather, or something gets them every year. I remember one time the peaches were just beautiful on the tree, and here came the June bugs; they just covered them up. I was so mad. There was this one peach in particular I had been eying, a perfect peach, and when I went out that morning, it was jut a solid ball of June bugs. I stalked into the house and got my shotgun. Ramona looked at me in a funny way, and said, "What are you going to shoot, Grandpa?" But I stalked out, getting hotter all the time, and walked up to the tree where that peach was. And I took good aim at that poor miserable peach and pulled the trigger; I blew that peach and those June bugs all to pieces. I knew it was like taking a drop of water out of the ocean, but it made me feel better.

We had an electric fence around the garden, and my mother would forget about it and get shocked every time she went out there. One day she had some kind of tin bucket with her, and she thought, "Well, I'll hold that wire down with that bucket." And of course the shock was worse than ever. She never did learn about that fence.

One time Merle Travis landed at the airport, which wasn't very far from our house, so he walked out there to surprise us—only we weren't at home. He waited around and waited around and finally started walking back. He met us coming down the road; we saw this familiar-looking figure walking toward us, and then all of a sudden it broke into a buck dance. Then we knew who it was. We picked him up and took him on back to the house, and he said, "I know where every bird's nest is on your place."

After our excursion into Washington and Richmond, we came back to Nashville in the summer of 1952, and at first we moved into a little place just off Eastland Avenue. We hated that place worse than anything, I guess because it was in the city. One day Ken Marvin and I had been fishing, and coming back down the Ashland City Highway north of Nashville, I saw this little stone house way up the hill with a For Sale sign in front of it. We went up there and looked at it, and it was a pretty nice place, with about 16 acres. I got Ramona to come out there; we liked it, and we bought it. Eloise was in the second grade by then, and the school at Bordeaux was right back of the house, and she could get there by crossing a field. She had to go over a fence, so I built her a stile, a set of wooden steps. This worked fine until one morning when the snow was about knee-deep; she waded to that fence and went over, and when she got to school, she found there was no school—it had been canceled because of the snow. She came back as mad as a hornet.

The people up there were country people, even though it was close to Nashville. Back in those days, you weren't afraid to pick up hitchhikers, and one day Ramona and I saw an old fellow trudging along with a sack over his shoulder. I said, "Let's pick him up—he looks like he can't hardly go." He crawled in the back and put his sack on the seat, and when I turned around to say howdy, I saw that the sack was moving. I looked at Ramona, and she shrugged. I said, "What you got in the sack?" "Pig," he said, and pulled down the sack to show us. It was a pig all right, a live one. I didn't want to appear rude, and we had offered him a ride, but the farther we drove, the stronger the smell got from the back seat. It was cold, and we had the windows up; after a few more miles, though, I decided that there were some things worse than being cold, and rolled mine down. It became a sort of contest: his pig against my good will. But I was determined to see my good deed through, and by the time we let the stranger and his sack off, neither Ramona nor I was breathing any more than we had to. We aired the car out the rest of that trip, and washed the back seat the next day.

Merle Travis was not only a great guitar player and singer but a fine cartoonist. When our son was born, Merle designed this announcement for us.

That was a good house, and I remember it because our son, Mark, was born there in 1955. Eloise was seven at that time, and Marsha was seventeen; the family was growing, but the country music business was not. Rock-and-roll was starting to come in, and that meant hard times for a lot of us who didn't want to rock-and-roll. I remember about this time that all of us went to Oregon with Merle Travis to play at the big centennial out there, along with Hank Snow and Hank Thompson and Boob Brasfield and even Liberace. Times were so tough that we all piled into a camper to go. We stayed over a day in Minneapolis, and Eloise and Ramona went shopping. I remember telling them, "Go shopping, but only buy one thing." That's how tight it was then. And even after we got to Oregon and played the date, things were still tight, and booking fees were down, and I told them the same thing in Oregon: "Go shopping but only buy one thing."

But if American audiences were turning away from real country to rock-and-roll, we found that the people in Canada were only too glad to pick up the slack. I had played Canadian tours as early as 1950, but by 1954 I was getting more and more work up there. Connie B. Gay did a lot of the early booking, but later we began working with a Canadian booker and entertainer named J. B. Hamm, and by the mid-1950s we were keeping mighty busy north of the border. Hamm booked one tour for a guaranteed $130 a show, not bad for that day and time, and in 1955, while Elvis was sweeping the lower forty-eight, I actually did most of my performing in Canada—five long tours. Canadians always seemed to like their country music pure, without the electric instruments, and they really liked my yodeling. Sometimes I toured just with Ramona, and then after Mark was born, with Jackie Phelps, and other times with Howard White, Billy Grammer, Red Murphy, and Red Herron. Later on, a man named Norm Riley booked us a lot up there.

Another way of surviving rock-and-roll took us by surprise: the rise of folk and bluegrass festivals. In the early 1950s I had been working a lot with Kirk McGee as our fiddler; Kirk went way back into the early days of the Opry. He had worked medicine shows and played a lot with Uncle Dave Macon; he had made records back in 1927 and 1928 with his brother Sam, a fine old-time guitar player and one of the first to pick melody on the guitar.

As I recall, this was some sort of early TV show in Nashville. That's Lew Childre (Doctor Lew) getting ready to fix me up, and Carl Smith in the fancy suit. Announcer Louie Buck stoically endures the nonsense.

Kirk was not all that used to doing the darting in and out behind a mike you have to do in a modern act. He'd be standing off to the rear of the stage, so far away that the mike could only pick up a few notes of his fiddling. He and Sam were still on the Opry, but had not toured much. Kirk was working in real estate, and Sam worked on his farm, and they felt their music was so old-timey that no one would want them on tour. But in May of 1955 I took them with me to play a date at New River Ranch in Maryland, and after they walked on stage and picked a little, people in the audience began shouting out requests for the old songs they had not done in years.

Both Kirk and Sam were amazed at these young people that knew their old music, and I was surprised, too. But we began to learn in the next few years that more and more young people—especially from the North and especially on college campuses—were starting to look at our old-time country songs as "folk" music. Which, of course, it was, though we had never called it that. I noticed the same thing when we began to play Bill Monroe's festival up at Bean Blossom, Indiana, in 1955. I'm no bluegrass banjo player and never have pretended to be; but I discovered that the audience that liked bluegrass at Bean Blossom also had a lot of interest in the old-time drop-thumb banjo songs and tunes that I did.

I had moved from RCA Victor to Decca records and then back for a while to Syd Nathan; I remember he recorded my version of a then-popular "folk" song, "Rock Island Line," but it never went anywhere. Then Billy Grammer, whom I had known since my Washington days, came up with a big hit on an old folk song called "Gotta Travel On" in 1959. He recorded it for a new label, Monument, headed by a man named Fred Foster. One day Billy introduced me to Fred, and before I knew it, I was recording for him, too. A lot of my early albums for that label were filled with old songs that I hadn't sung or played in years, songs that the new folk audience liked. I actually had a hit with my version of Jimmie Rodgers's old "T for Texas" song in 1961, and in the next couple of years I did several Monument LPs, including one called *Grandpa Jones Sings Real Folk Songs*, which featured old ballads like "Willis Mayberry" ("The Hills of Roane County"), "Oh Captain, Captain," "Devilish Mary," and my own "Tragic Romance." Fred always let me pick the best

I grew a real beard for a while in the mid-1950s, but I think I was the only country singer then who did—I was just ahead of the times. Backing me up are (from left) Jimmie Selph, Don Helms on steel guitar, Ramona (well, her dress anyway), Shorty Lavender, and bass player Lightning Chance.

Nashville sidemen for my sessions, people like Jerry Byrd and Floyd Cramer and Ray Edenton and Harold Bradley—the men who really created the so-called Nashville sound. And Fred wasn't afraid to use the old songs, or put my banjo up front, and to this day I think the records I made for him are the best I ever made for anybody.

But I'm getting ahead of myself. I was working all this time on the Opry; I had rejoined it on August 16, 1952 (I wrote it down in capital letters in my notebook), and stayed on steadily except for one six-month furlough in 1957, when I left to take over Jimmy Dean's television show in Washington, another project of Connie B. Gay's. I wasn't used to live television, especially doing those commercials, and rock-and-roll was still killing country music all over, so that show only lasted a few months. Soon I was back on the Opry, and have been ever since.

When we came back to Nashville that time, we located near the northern suburb of Goodlettsville. We got 90 acres very reasonably and settled in for a stay. We wanted to build a house on a hill; I walked over the land with the owner, and I said, "Right here is where I want my house built." He told me later on that he thought I was crazy, because it was right on top of a knoll. We did build there, though, and later we paid for it: the driveway was steep and faced north, and when it snowed we really felt it. One winter we couldn't get the car up to the house for 31 days; we had to walk up and carry every can of beans, every sack of dog food, and every instrument—day in and day out. The ice would stay on that driveway even after every road in the county was clean and dry.

We had trouble with the water there, too. We dug a well before we built the house, but it wasn't until afterward that we found the water had sulfur in it. It was just terrible, with that constant smell of rotten eggs. Even the change in your pocket would turn blue, and the silverware—we were the only people in the country who had blue silverware. It was black sulfur, too. So for the next well, we got an old man who claimed to be a water witch; he used a forked stick, and he said, "Now here it is, here's the water and it'll be 35 feet deep and that's all." So we drilled, and we went 250 feet deep, and got sulfur again. I hated that sulfur so badly that I even wrote a song about it; it was a parody on Bob Nolan's cowboy song called "Cool Water."

In California in the mid-1950s, one of the shows we liked a lot was Town Hall Party. *That's Ramona with the fiddle, and our good friend Joe Maphis with his famous double-neck guitar.*

SULFUR WATER

All day I've drilled on this old hill with not a swill
Of water—just sulfur water.
Ray and I are powerful dry and the kids all cry
For water, not sulfur water.
The well digger says that he can't guess, where is that mess
Called water, that cool clear water.
Sometimes I think I'll go get a drink, but it sure does stink,
That water, that sulfur water.

Keep a-diggin', John, it wont' be very long, till we reach Hong Kong
With our money all gone for water.
I've just got a note from Mao on a boat; he wants to cut my throat
Cause I've drained his favorite moat
Huntin' water, cool clear water.

The digger's hands are red, he's ready for bed, and I heard him when he said,
Sulfur water, buzzard bait water.
So I'll tell him to load, and I'll go on the road 'cause my last cent I've blowed
For water, but got sulfur water.

Think I'll dance a jig, for he's loading his rig, and his bill will be big
For water, sulfur water.
But 'twas a big sacrifice to sink his device till we smelled Chinese rice
Not water, just sulfur water.

There's a personal side to the Grand Ole Opry, too. The show is sort of like a repertory theater company, and the cast doesn't change much from year to year; some will hit it big for a while and then kind of fall back, and others just keep going along at the same steady pace year after year. Some of the old-timers have been around the Opry for over 50 years, and people like the Crook Brothers and Kirk McGee have been there since the very beginning. Kirk played with the Fruit Jar Drinkers (his brother Sam died several years ago), and was one of the best storytellers on the show. He'd spin yarn after yarn about Uncle Dave Macon, since he worked with him for years, and about growing up in the backwoods. Kirk knew what he was talking about

On tour in the Northwest about 1957: Hank Thompson is seated at the far left; then comes "Brother George" Liberace, Phil and Don Everly (who were just starting to hit big), Hank Snow, and Merle Travis. I'm standing in the back with Boob Brasfield, Rose Lee, and Joe Maphis. Photo by Photo-Art Commercial Studios, Portland, Oregon.

there. He came from an area near Franklin called Little Texas; it was called that because of all the shooting that went on in the early days. One time Kirk went to a little movie there; a traveling drummer had set up a projector and was showing a western picture with a lot of action and shooting. Some old guy from the hills wandered in, and Kirk said he didn't think the fellow had seen too many movies before, because he got so excited at what was happening that toward the end, when the bad guy came on again, the old-timer jerked out a big pistol and shot at the picture, right through the screen—and uttered some choice words to boot!

But a lot of us have more in common than music. Many of us like to hunt, and the Opry itself sponsors an official Annual Opry Duck Hunt up on Reelfoot Lake in northwestern Tennessee. This started about 1969 when Bud Wendell (who was then the manager of the Opry) and Tex Ritter (who had moved back to Nashville from Hollywood) and I got together; we all three loved to hunt, and we knew a lot of the boys on the show did too, so we cooked up the idea. I don't recall just who went on that very first duck hunt, but over the years regulars have been Jimmy C. Newman, Charlie Walker, Tom T. Hall, Roy Clark, Brent Burkett (one of The Four Guys), Stu Phillips, Tennessee Ernie Ford, the late Bob Luman, Julio Pierpaoli (the manager of Opryland), Les Leverett (our official photographer), and Neal Craig (the president of National Life and Accident Insurance Company, the group that started and still owns the Opry). We have official Opry caps, and shirts with the official patch, and we always have a good couple of days' hunting. I generally don't like to hunt anything I won't eat, and that's why I won't hunt deer; I like to hunt birds and grouse and goose. I'm not too awfully fond of the ducks we get, but I notice I have never had much trouble giving them away to Jimmy C. or Charlie Walker.

For years, of course, the Opry was in the old Ryman Auditorium in downtown Nashville, and it had all the shortcomings everybody has already talked about. It was hot in the summer: there was no air conditioning, and people would sit on the old wooden pews and try to keep cool with these paper fans they used to sell with entertainers' pictures on them; and the people in the balcony would buy Cokes and drop them, and the Coke would run through the cracks between the old slats and drip on the people under the

Merle Travis shows Billy Grammer a new lick in my dressing room at the Opry.

balcony. In the wintertime it was cold and drafty, and backstage was the biggest crowded mess you ever saw. But in rain or snow or heat, there would be long lines of people waiting to buy tickets or to get in, usually stretching all the way down Fifth Street, around the corner and down Broadway, by Tootsie's Orchid Lounge, and on toward the Cumberland River.

There were some nice things about the old Ryman. I remember, for instance, some tables to the left of the stage where we used to sit and talk and laugh and relax. In earlier days, Robert Lunn used to hold court there. He was the "talkin' blues" man on the Opry and one of our favorite comedians. He used to get a lot of laughs by telling all these guys who managed to sneak backstage and try to get on the show that he was the one in charge of giving them auditions. A lot of times he would take them out in the alley and make them dance or juggle or some such thing that had nothing at all to do with their singing.

But on March 15, 1974, we played our last show at the old Ryman and got ready to move to the big new Opry House out near the big new amusement park called Opryland. It's about a half-hour drive from downtown Nashville, on the Cumberland River near Madison. There is air conditioning for the audience, and the entertainers, and more seats—4,400 of them—though some in the second balcony are so high up you might need oxygen. There's a dressing room for each major act, something we sure didn't have at the Ryman. But no one except Roy Acuff has a permanent dressing room, so you never know from night to night where your room will be. And some of them are a little small; I've only got four people in my band, and we can hardly get in some of them to rehearse. They also promised us a lounge where we could get coffee and sandwiches, a private lounge away from the public, and we got the lounge, but it is usually so full of people who have managed to get in backstage that you can't even find a place to sit down.

It seems to me something was lost in the move—some closeness among the entertainers. But this may be simply changing times, the changing of the guard, with the new entertainers coming on to replace the older ones. Some of us worry about whether or not real old-time country music on the Opry will survive after our generation is gone. David (Stringbean) Akeman once said to me, "Grandpa, you and I are about the last of the real old-timers. When we are gone, that'll be it." Well, String is gone now, and there aren't too many who play the old-style music—the kind we played even before bluegrass came along. The Crook Brothers and the Fruit Jar Drinkers both have leaders in their seventies; Wilma Lee Cooper, Roy Acuff, Billy Grammer all do the older forms of country music yet; and once a year there's an "Old-Timer's Night" when former stars like Curly Fox, the Duke of Paducah, Paul Howard, Pee Wee King, Sid Harkreader, and others come back and do one or two numbers. But I don't see many younger bands playing in this style; as Billy Grammer says, there're some sets out there when all you can hear is rock-and-roll. And he's right. That's one of the reasons he unplugged his electric guitar and went back to his acoustic—to give the people at least three minutes a night of unamplified music.

And the staff band at the new Opry house is different; in earlier days we didn't have a staff band. It's very convenient, and the musicians are among the best; when a guest star shows up, it's useful to have a band that's versatile enough to back him up. But we have also had people complain to us on tours that the background is too much the same for every entertainer, that the staff band doesn't give them enough individuality. I remember that when the WLS *National Barn Dance* put a staff band—a sort of pop orchestra—behind everybody, it killed the show in a hurry. But things aren't that bad with the Opry staff band; it's loud, but it's still plenty country.

Still, with all of this, there's a lot of friendship and bantering backstage at the new Opry house—though not very much of it is about music. Most of the backstage talk is about ballgames (Roy Acuff is a great basketball fan, and a lot of the boys like to go out and see Nashville's minor league team, the Nashville Sounds) or fishing. Almost all the boys have fine fishing boats, and they mostly fish for bass. They can hardly wait until the water is right at Centerhill, Old Hickory, Cordell Hull, Percy Priest, or Kentucky Lake; all are within easy driving distance of Nashville, and I've spent more than a few hours trolling those waters myself.

Rosie is always backstage with a big coffeemaker, and although sometimes the coffee will take the enamel off the kitchen sink, the boys are glad to get it. And people are always putting up funny things on the bulletin board. For a while George Morgan posted what he called the Ugly List, where everyone could vote for the ugliest person. Every week someone would win first place; one time my boy Mark and Paul Russell tied for the honor. And when George passed away, Little Roy Wiggins, the great steel guitar player, took over the traditiona nd ran the Ugly List for a long time. Someone even started a little backstage newspaper called the *Herald Weekly*. This doesn't make sense until you know that one of the staff drummers at the Opry, one who laughs at all our jokes and chews nine packs of gum a night, is named Harold Weakley.

There are a lot of practical jokes backstage, since a lot of the Opry players have known each other for years, and some of these jokes have become classics—people tell them and retell them to newer musicians. One was a famous bit between Marshall Barnes and Bill Carlisle. Marshall is an expert watchmaker, a good bass fiddle player (he now works with the Carlisles), and a "dressing room comedian"—always good for a laugh, even though he seldom laughs himself. His biggest worrier is Bill Carlisle, "Jumpin' Bill," one of the great veterans of the business and one of the liveliest entertainers around. Bill is always pestering Marshall, even though they are the best of friends. Marshall keeps repaired watches and watches to be repaired in his locker, and Mr. Bell, who sits by the door to the backstage entrance and sees that the wrong people don't come in, has the only other key to Marshall's locker. One Saturday night they talked Mr. Bell into unlocking it, and Bill hunched over and climbed in and shut the door. Then one of Bill's henchmen went to Marshall and pretended to want to look at some of the watches Marshall had repaired. So Marshall took his key and proudly unlocked his locker—and there sat Bill Carlisle in his red wig, grinning like a lizard. Marshall stared for a minute, then shut the door again, shook his head, and walked off. This kind of thing keeps a ring of laughter going on in the Opry halls most of the time.

In fact, they got me with those lockers one time. Here's how it happened. One day at home I was taking a nap, and when I nap, I do like to snore quite a bit. I guess that day I was in extra good form, because Ramona went and got the tape recorder and put it right up next to me and taped my snoring for about 15 minutes. The next night at the Opry she told Vic Willis about it. Vic is one of the best sports around; he and the Willis Brothers (they used to

Bill Carlisle (left), who has been in the business about as long as I have, shares a joke with me and George McCormick backstage at the Opry. Photo by Les Leverett.

be called the Oklahoma Wranglers) have been on the Opry since the late 1940s, and what a lot of people don't know is that they backed Hank Williams on his first records. When Ramona told him about the recording, his eyes lit up, and he said, "Get me that tape." So she brought it to him, and he took it home and recorded over it, playing "Rock-a-bye Baby" on the piano between the snores. The next Saturday night he brought the tape down to the Opry, put it on a portable tape machine, turned up the volume, and put it in his locker with the tape running. Then he locked the locker and walked off to do his show. So snoring and piano music boomed out of this locker, and people would walk by and stop and look and wonder what was going on. Finally, the word got out that it was me. They told that on me for a good long time.

During all this time my producer, Fred Foster, who founded and owned Monument, kept doing everything he could to get me a hit single on the charts. We could do and did do great albums, but the name of the game was hit singles, and even though I explained to Fred that I had *never* had any really big hit single, we kept trying. When we finally got one, it came about in a way none of us would ever have imagined. Sometime in 1969 Ramona was looking through one of those old "gift books" of poems and came across a beautiful one about an old man named Conrad who hears the Lord speak to him in a dream and say that He will visit the old man the next day, which was Christmas. She asked me to read it, and I was really moved by its beauty and simplicity; I found out later that the story of the poem was based on an old mountain folktale, but the author of this poem was listed simply as "Anonymous."

A lot of radio entertainers back in the old days had performed poems and recitations on the air as part of their shows, and while I had never done much of that, I had always liked poetry. I remember in high school I had to memorize the last section of William Cullen Bryant's poem "Thanatopsis." I didn't know what a lot of it meant, but when I was older, I got interested in it and learned the entire poem. I did it in a night or two (I was pretty used to learning song lyrics) just for my own enjoyment, and I can still recite most of it today. I read a lot of poetry, and especially liked Eddie Guest and John Greenleaf Whittier and the older poets. I have written a lot of poetry myself

Good pals keep you smiling: on the left is Merle Travis (who helped make a lot of my records sound good enough to keep); on the right a mutual friend, Mr. Sweet.

and like to recite it aloud, so when I read the poem Ramona had found, I took it to Fred Foster and asked if we couldn't try it as a record.

Fred and I looked over the poem and decided it might go if we had a better ending, so we sat down and rewrote that part. Then Fred got Bill Walker, one of the best Nashville arrangers, to write some background music for it, and in September we went into the old Monument studios in Nashville, and I found myself looking at a small symphony orchestra that had assembled. There were more musicians than I had ever seen at a session before, and Bill had written out the arrangements for the violin players and singers. Even though it was a hot September afternoon (in Tennessee, September is as hot as August) and we were all in shirt sleeves, we managed to get into the Christmas spirit. I began my recitation:

It happened one day near December's end,
Two neighbors called on an old-time friend,
And they found his shop, so meager and mean,
Made gay with a thousand boughs of green,
And Conrad was sitting with face a-shine—
When he suddenly stopped as he stitched a twine
And said, "Old friends, at dawn today
When the cock was crowing the night away,
The Lord appeared in a dream to me
And said, 'I am coming your guest to be,'
So I've been busy with feet astir,
Strewing my shop with branches of fir.
The table is spread and the kettle is shined
And over the rafters the holly is twined—
And now I will wait for my Lord to appear
And listen closely so I will hear
His step as he nears my humble place,
And I open the door and look on his face."
So his friends went home and left Conrad alone,
For this was the happiest day he had known.
For long since his family had passed away *(pause)*
And Conrad had spent many a sad Christmas day.
But he knew with the Lord as his Christmas guest,

I love hunting and have collected quite a few guns over the years. This is a sample of my collection in 1958.

This Christmas would be the dearest and best.
So he listened with only joy in his heart,
And with every sound he would rise with a start
And look for the Lord to be at the door
Like the vision he had a few hours before.
So he ran to the window after hearing a sound,
But all he could see on the snow-covered ground
Was a shabby beggar whose shoes were torn
And all of his clothes were ragged and worn.
But Conrad was touched and went to the door,
And he said, "Your feet must be frozen and sore—
I have some shoes in my shop for you,
And a coat that will keep you warmer, too."
So with grateful heart the man went away—
But Conrad noticed the time of day;
He wondered what made the dear Lord so late
And how much longer he'd have to wait—
When he heard a knock and ran to the door,
But it was only a stranger once more,
A bent old lady with a shawl of black,
With a bundle of kindling piled on her back.
She asked for only a place to rest,
But that was reserved for Conrad's great guest,
But her voice seemed to plead, "Don't send me away,
Let me rest for a while on Christmas Day."
So Conrad brewed her a steaming cup
And told her to sit at the table and sup.
But after she left, he was filled with dismay,
For he saw that the hours were slipping away,
And the Lord had not come as he said he would,
And Conrad felt sure he had misunderstood,
When out of the stillness he heard a cry,
"Please help me and tell me where am I."
So again he opened his friendly door
And stood disappointed as twice before.
It was only a child who had wandered away
And was lost from her family on Christmas Day.

Hugh Benner, 1961 national champion pistol marksman, gives me a few pointers.

Again Conrad's heart was heavy and sad,
But he knew he could make this little girl glad,
So he called her in and wiped her tears
And quieted all her childish fears,
Then he led her back to her home once more.
But as he entered his own darkened door,
He knew that the Lord was not coming today
For the hours of Christmas had passed away.
So he went to his room and knelt down to pray,
And he said, "Lord, why did you delay?
What kept you from coming to call on me,
For I wanted so much your face to see."
When soft in the silence, a voice he heard,
"Lift up your head for I kept my word.
Three times my shadow crossed your floor;
Three times I came to your lowly door;
For I was the beggar with bruised cold feet;
I was the woman you gave something to eat,
And I was the child on the homeless street;
Three times I knocked, three times I came in,
And each time I found the warmth of a friend.
Of all the gifts, love is the best;
I was honored to be your Christmas Guest."*

*© 1969 Loray El Marlee Publishing Company.

A few weeks later "A Christmas Guest" was released as a single, and right away radio stations began picking it up and playing it as the Christmas season started. The story seemed to catch everybody's attention, and before I knew it I was being asked for the recitation at concerts. I had gotten my big hit single, and it has continued to be a seasonal hit every year since then.

I never have done anything else like "Christmas Guest," but I have kept writing poems and developing recitations. Some day I hope to be able to do an entire album of recitations, and Bill Walker has said he would like to do the music for one. I don't suppose that such combinations of poetry and music are all that commercial, but I would sure like the chance to find out. Maybe someday I'll get it.

Would you believe a 6-3/4-pound bass? Ramona took this one.

As I have said, most of the entertainers on the Opry are really devoted to trying to keep country music country, and sometimes that's quite a battle. In 1974 we had quite a commotion about this issue, and a bunch of us got fed up with pop singers and rock-and-roll singers trying to call their music country. For some time a lot of us had been upset at so-called country stations not playing real country records, but instead playing stuff by Olivia Newton-John and John Denver and others. So we formed an organization called ACE, Association of Country Entertainers, designed to promote more authentic country music. George Jones and Tammy Wynette started it at their house one night with a meeting of a bunch of us country singers in Nashville. George was upset because he wasn't getting his records played—he sure is now, but back then they thought he was "too country." But the people who really pushed and got the thing together were Jean Shepherd and Vic Willis. A lot of people joined, including Roy Acuff and even, for a time, Dolly Parton.

Things looked pretty good for a while, and Vic and Jean came to me and asked if I wanted to be president of ACE. I said that I wasn't much for making speeches and didn't really know anything about doing publicity and being president of any public organization, but they kept after me and argued that my name would lend prestige to the organization and help it get attention, so I finally agreed. I said, "Okay, if it'll do any good, I'll come to the meetings and do what I can." But before long, after the first couple of years of action, people began to drift out of the organization. The Country Music Association (which some of us at that time thought had gotten too much into pop and rock) looked on us as a threat or a rival, and the big record companies didn't like it, and the WSM management told us not to do any fund-raising shows in Nashville and hinted that they might fire those of us who did. Then, to top it all off, just when we were having the most trouble, a stenographer who worked for us ran off with $7,000 of our money, and that sure didn't help any. We had such a run of bad luck with ACE for several months that a couple of the singers even wrote me sour letters, saying that this was all my fault as president. One of them never has forgiven me for what happened.

Even during all our troubles, though, we managed to keep up our sense of humor. We held our ACE meetings downtown in Nashville in Faron Young's building. Now there is a stairway in the main hall, and there's a little

Music always goes along taking a picking break during a 1979 bear hunt near Arlington, Virginia.

compartment under it with a little door about two and a half feet high. It looks like a real door, with nice paneling and even a knob on it. One night Vic Willis got a sign painted on that little door saying *Little Jimmie Dickens Enterprises.* Faron saw it the next day, and never one to spoil a good gag, he sent Jimmie a bill for $1.86 for "office rent." This got around the Opry pretty well, and more than a few laughs were on Jimmie, but he got the last laugh: he actually sent Faron a check marked "Office Rent," something that would make his taxes a little more interesting than normal. But Faron struck back—he held onto the check and didn't cash it. He held it and held it, and finally Jimmie gave in and wrote asking him to please cash the check so he could balance his books.

ACE has had an effect, though; country stations are sure back to playing country today, and people like George Jones and Ricky Skaggs and Merle Haggard are getting airplay and recognition. I don't think there's too much danger of their voting "Oliver Newton John," as Roy Acuff called her, into the Hall of Fame. But there's still the problem of the radio stations playing only the Top Ten or the Top Twenty or whatever; nobody has solved that yet, because the disc jockeys and station managers are going for the money. My old friend Merle Travis wrote an unpublished song about this problem; it tells how he fell asleep listening to a Top Forty radio station and dreamed he was in a supermarket that carried nothing but the Top Forty foods. People who wanted anything different to eat were flat out of luck. Well, I don't reckon Merle's song will ever make it to the Top Forty—it may not even get recorded—but I'm glad somebody said what he said. And with that, I rest my case. But if talk about food has made you hungry, get some peanuts, and we'll get on to a chapter about *Hee Haw.*

This was our home near Goodlettsville, Tennessee, in the hills north of Nashville. We still own the property.

Eleven.

WHAT'S FOR SUPPER?

In October 1968 I flew up to Canada to do a new television show that would feature country comedy. It was called *Hot Diggity*, and it was produced by Stan Jacobson; the regular stars were Gordie Tapp and Don Harron, and the show I was to be on also featured Minnie Pearl and singer Tommy Common.

Hot Diggity was a 60-minute program with a lot of one-liner jokes, some songs, and a long skit that was a takeoff on the old *Mission Impossible*, in which I played Minnie's father and tried to get her to stop seeing a character called Loverboy. But one of the most popular segments was made up of quick one-shot jokes; the set was made up to look like a barn, and different ones of us would sit around on hay bales or barrels. A string band would play "May the Bird of Paradise Fly Up Your Nose," and they would cut to me, and I'd say something like, "Twenty years ago the girls wore bathing suits that looked like Mother Hubbards; now they wear ones that look more like her cupboard." Then the music would go on for another chorus, and they would cut to Minnie for a joke. And Gordie would tell a gag at the end of every segment and slap his leg and say, "Hot diggity!" That's where the name came from. At the end they had a series of what they called "hillbilly" drawings to run the credits over. It was a popular show up there and different from anything that

*Here I am on Joey Bishop's
ABC-TV talk show about 1969.*

had been done on American television; it was comedy with music thrown in, whereas American shows had always been the other way around—mostly music with a few jokes thrown in or a short bit by a comedian like Speck Rhodes or Rod Brasfield or the Duke of Paducah.

I went on back to Nashville after my appearance on *Hot Diggity* and didn't think much more about it until a year later. I was with the Moeller Talent Agency then, and one day Lucky Moeller's son, who was doing a lot of my booking, called me into his office and asked, "How would you like to be on a show that they're starting here in Nashville, called *Hee Haw?* They want you as a comedian." It turned out that some of the people who had done *Hot Diggity* had decided to try an American show, and it was to be a summer replacement on CBS. Sam Lovullo, Bill Davis, and some of the others had already had a meeting in Los Angeles with Gordie Tapp and Archie Campbell, and Gordie and Archie told them about my comedy. So I went home that day and told Ramona about it and said, "*Hee Haw.* Whoever heard of a name like that for a show? That'll be enough to kill it right there." But when I talked it over with Stringbean Akeman, who had also been approached, we agreed that our acts were getting a little stale and that our records weren't getting played much on the radio. Maybe a little TV exposure was what we needed, so we agreed to sign on.

It was quite a group that assembled in Nashville in the spring of 1969 to start work on this new show. (The TV critics were calling the idea a "cornball version of *Laugh-In,*" which was then a big hit and used a lot of quick jokes and bits rather than long skits.) Buck Owens and Roy Clark were on the show from the first, along with Archie Campbell, Gordie Tapp, Minnie Pearl, Don Harron, Junior Samples, Lulu Roman, Jeannie C. Riley, Gunilla Hutton, Cathy Baker, the Hager twins, and Don Rich, plus Buck's band, the Buckaroos. And, of course, Stringbean and me. When we started our second season, we brought in Lisa Todd, a tall, lovely girl who was going to provide a romantic lead for Junior. There were seven staff writers originally, to turn out the weekly scripts for the show. In addition to picking and singing and doing comedy ourselves, we had a lot of big Nashville guest stars during our first year, which was as a summer replacement. We had Roy Rogers and Dale

"What's for supper, Grandpa?" I write my own rhyming menus for these Hee Haw *spots.*

Evans, Waylon Jennings, Charley Pride, Dolly Parton, Mel Tillis, George Jones, Porter Wagoner, Tom T. Hall, Lynn Anderson, and others. In December 1969 the show joined the regular season lineup on CBS, and in September 1970 it started its second full season.

One of the great surprises of the second season was the discovery of the eephing and hamboning of Jimmie Riddle and Jackie Phelps. Eephing is a sort of hiccupping and gasping music that Jimmie had learned up in his hometown of Dyersburg, Tennessee, where they used to do it at old-time dances. Later on, Jimmie became a great harmonica player in Roy Acuff's band, and he used to do a backstage comedy act with Jackie that kept everyone in stitches. Jackie had worked with me for years, playing everything from banjo to lead guitar and steel guitar, and was known as one of the great backup men in Nashville. Somewhere he picked up hamboning—slapping the hands against the legs in rhythm. It is an old, old art, even mentioned in Mark Twain's *Huckleberry Finn*. Archie Campbell knew how well Jimmie and Jackie worked together, and suggested them for the show. It worked out fine. The first time the boys did a series of short bits for the camera, Jackie walked off and said, "I couldn't pick up a pencil right now, my arm's so tired. But I wouldn't trade places with anyone in the world right this minute." Jimmie Riddle told me he had thought he would never get on network TV because he didn't think his harmonica playing was all that good, but "now here I am on *Hee Haw*, and I got here by doing something that I've been doing since I was four years old." Jackie and Jimmy continued their act on every episode of *Hee Haw* until Jimmy's death in 1982—over 12 years.

Hee Haw went pretty well for a couple of seasons more and we began to get some idea of just how much television could help our bookings. We could go out and ask a decent price for our road shows and concerts, and get it. But then in 1972 the network canceled *Hee Haw*—not because our ratings were bad but because the network had decided to get rid of nearly all the shows that appealed to rural audiences. It seems the country folks weren't buying as much as the city folks, or older folks as much as younger folks, and this was bothering the advertisers. We were all pretty downhearted at first, but right away the producers announced that they felt the audience was still out there,

You might call this the top of my form.

and that they were going to try to syndicate the show and distribute it independently. So Youngstreet Productions took over, and we went on with the show pretty much as it had been. It worked, and soon *Hee Haw* was going strong again, as it still is today, and was attracting a larger audience than any other syndicated show.

One day somebody—I don't remember who—came up with the idea of my doing the "What's for supper?" routine. They would shout out, "What's for supper?" and I would make up these old-time menus. Once again, I went home sort of disgusted and told Ramona, "I can't see what's the slightest bit funny about that," but I started writing up some menus anyway. One of the first ones I used has been one of the most popular:

> Cornbread, turnip greens,
> Candied yams and butterbeans,
> Blackberry cobbler and all things rare,
> And the more to eat, the more to spare.

Since then we've used "What's for supper?" on just about every show, and I write all the menus myself. It's gotten so popular that when I go out on tour, someone from the audience always hollers, "What's for supper, Grandpa?" I always have to have a couple of the menus ready. A lot of people think I invented the routine or used it before *Hee Haw*, but I didn't do either. It keeps me on my toes to think up different menus that have real old-time dishes in them, but it's fun. Here's another favorite:

> Venison roast with onion and taters,
> With a good-size bowl of okra and tomatoes,
> Homemade light bread a golden brown,
> And the strongest coffee there is around.

Or sometimes I use:

> I boiled a ham and cooked some corn,
> Got a cucumber salad as sure as you're born,
> With cold milk and pie, the kind you desire,
> Why, you can eat this meal with one foot in the fire.

Dueling jokers: the Hager twins corner me on the Hee Haw *set.*

And one time, for variety, I fixed up a sort of non-menu:

> Beauregard slipped in and ate the meat,
> And walked in the pudding with his muddy feet,
> No wood in the kitchen and the stove is cold,
> So you better eat this baloney before it gets old.

Since so many people are involved in *Hee Haw* and there are so many different schedules to work around, nowadays we tape a whole bunch of shows at one time. In fact, we do enough material for 13 shows in one three-week taping session; we do one of these sessions in June and another in October, and that gives us our year's supply of 26 one-hour shows. Everybody gathers in Nashville during those weeks, and we shoot from early to late; the rest of the work is done in the editing rooms. At first we shot the show at the WLAC studios in downtown Nashville, but in 1981 we moved to Opryland's new television studios.

From my diary of June 1981, I can reconstruct a typical day's shooting to give you an idea of just what goes on with the making of the show.

June 15, 1981. I woke up at six-thirty, my usual time, took a shower, and shaved. I had to be at the Opry house for makeup at eight-thirty and had to go by the Checkerboard restaurant to get breakfast. I keep an apartment up near Goodlettsville for when I am working in Nashville, either on *Hee Haw* or the Opry, and it is about a 20-minute drive down to Opryland. I had one egg, bacon, toast, and some coffee, and went on down.

We park in a special lot behind the Opry house, and there is a guard station there that is manned whenever there's something going on. The guard waved me on in, and I parked and went into my dressing room. I share the dressing room with Gordie Tapp, Archie Campbell, Roy Clark, and Don Harron. The girls start their makeup call at seven-thirty, and the makeup people do three or four of them every 15 minutes or so, and usually by eight-thirty they are ready for some of us menfolk in the cast. Elizabeth Linneman usually makes me up and does a good job of it.

On the schedule was the entire cast for Buck's songs; "Moonshiners"; "Gloom, Despair, and Agony on Me"; and then some "wild lines" for a few of

Kenny Price (left), Grandpa Jones, Roy Clark, and Buck Owens—we're the Hee Haw Gospel Quartet, which specializes in the straightforward old-time gospel music we all grew up with.

us, and some expressions (shots of us reacting to things off camera). We would do as many of each of these as we could that day. Buck had picked out some pretty easy songs, and we were glad of that because we all had to sing the chorus along with him; the first one was "You All Come." After we finished off Buck's songs, we went into "Moonshiners," which consists of two of us lying on some sacks at the still with the old hound between us. One says something like this: "Grandpa, did your wife raise any poultry this year?" And the other replies: "Yeah, Archie, she planted some, but the chickens scratched them up." Another exchange goes: "Sometimes I can't go to sleep." "What do you do for it, Grandpa?" "I take me a big swig of whiskey every half-hour." "Does it make you sleep?" "No, but it makes me more satisfied to stay awake." Today we got off about 10 or 12 of these, and then it was time for lunch.

Some of us headed for the dressing room to change shoes or hat or whatever, but others decided to go as we were and took out to one of the nearby eating places. Sam Lovullo reminded us to be back in one hour. I went with Archie and Jackie Phelps to a place on Gallatin Road that serves fine food cooked the old-fashioned way. Everyone in the restaurant recognized us, as we were all in costume.

When we got back to the studio, it was set up for "Gloom, Despair, and Agony on Me." There were about 10 or 15 of these numbers, and it took quite a while, since they involve some singing and groaning as well as jokes. Usually Archie, Roy, Gordie, and I do them. They are written by Bud Wingard, one of the full-time writers for the show, and he writes some dillies; some are hard to get with the music and finish with it. There was just time left after the "Gloom, Despair" bits for a few wild lines by some of the cast. Then they yelled, "That's a wrap," and everybody headed for the dressing room to get ready to go home.

As I said—it was a typical day.

During the Bicentennial celebration in 1976, the *Hee Haw* writers outdid themselves in takeoffs of the "Bicentennial Minutes" that the major television networks were running. I recently found two of the old scripts in my files. On one of them, I appeared on camera and said: "This is Grandpa Jones. Some 200 years ago, George Washington threw a silver dollar across

When Ernie Ford is in town, he often comes by the Hee Haw *set to sing bass in a few gospel numbers. Here he poses with Ramona and me.*

the Potomac. If that was today, he'd only have to throw 14 cents. I'm Grandpa Jones, and this is the way it was 200 years ago, more or less." But a couple of shows later, they topped even that: "This is Grandpa Jones. Some 200 years ago Benedict Arnold decided to join the British 'cause he thought they would win. Twenty years ago his great-great-grandson bought the first Edsel. I'm Grandpa Jones, and this is the way it was 200 years ago, more or less."

Besides composing my menus, I hand in some general jokes for the show at large, and they give me credit for being a writer. A lot of the show is written by Archie and Gordie; then they have some writers in California, and Don Harron does all of his own material. But when the cast gets to taping, there's such a relaxed atmosphere and so much fun that a lot of ad libs stay in. And a lot of times someone reading a line will change it and say, "I think it might be better this way," and they'll take his judgment on it. After all, there are a lot of years of comedy experience represented by this cast. But sometimes things happen on stage that nobody plans, and sometimes the stuff can't even be used. Maybe they're saving it for more lenient times on TV. For example, the "old dog" that Roy and I use in the "Moonshiners" bits is actually a young dog, because he can be trained easier. This day something on my big old boot got him excited, and he tried to mount my boot. And then he went over and mounted Roy's boot. We hollered, "Somebody get an older dog!" And a voice from the control booth came over the loudspeaker, "That's a keeper!"

One of my favorite parts of *Hee Haw* is the Gospel Quartet. I had always liked to sing gospel quartet music, even before I worked with the Brown's Ferry Four, and I knew how popular it was with country fans. I mentioned this one day to Sam, and he decided to try it. It turned out that Roy Clark liked it, too, and Tennessee Ernie, who was down for that taping, always likes to sing gospel. So we taped four songs, for four different shows, by the Hee Haw Gospel Quartet, and at the next taping session we did four more. That was just four gospel numbers out of 13 shows, and people liked them. But then John Aylesworthy and Frank Pepiot, the coproducers, seemed to think it was slowing the show down. I told them, "You all don't go out in front of these people like we do, and you don't know what they want. There's so many people that tell us the thing they like best about the show is that gospel stuff,

Billy Carter's brother still had a job in Washington when Billy was a guest on Hee Haw. Here a bunch of us gang up on him backstage, including the Hagers (in straw hats), Archie Campbell, and me.

and I don't think we ought to take it off." But they took the quartet off anyway, for six months. Then Frank came around to me one day and said, "You were right." They had started to get mail wondering where the quartet was and complaining that it hadn't been on. So it was put back in the show.

Now, the quartet is made up of Roy and Buck and me and Kenny Price, who sings bass—except when Tennessee Ernie comes in, and then he sings bass. We've made a record album that's done well, and in 1981 we were lucky enough to win Best Gospel Group in the *Music City News* annual awards. But the quartet adds another dimension to *Hee Haw's* old-time country humor, and the picking and singing. The fans don't seem to like to let the show get too risqué; every so often the producers get letters from people complaining about the girls' short shorts or low-cut blouses, and sure enough, the next taping session they'll raise the necklines and lower the hemlines. But gradually things start creeping back to where they were—until another bunch of letters comes in.

Hee Haw is where I really get a chance to do my comedy. Of course, I get to do some on personals, but there isn't much time to do any on my Opry appearances. My work on *Hee Haw* is pretty much all comedy, though, and a lot of the routines I use go back through my career. Country comedians don't usually hire gag writers, or write much themselves, or even get things out of books. Much of what I do I learned firsthand from people I worked with over the years. Most country comedians develop this way, and their jokes are passed on by word of mouth from one generation to another. Good jokes are like good songs; you can even remember who you got them from, and every time you use one it's like paying a little tribute to one of your teachers. And that's good, for the old comedians have never been given their due, and there are no really good young ones coming up in country circles.

I guess I started doing comedy skits when I was with Bradley, and I can still do one of the first I learned with him. Bradley would say, "Grandpa, do you know the difference between prose and poetry?" And I'd say, "No," and he'd say, "Well, prose is 'There was an old woman who lived by the mill, and last week she moved to town.' That's prose, 'cause it doesn't rhyme. Then look at 'There was an old woman who lived by the mill, and if she's not dead, she's living there still.' That's poetry, 'cause it does rhyme." And I said, "I

Loretta Lynn (right) joins Jackie Phelps (left), me, and Buck Owens in a "Moonshiners" sketch.

understand that all right." And Bradley said, "All right, then, let's see you do it." So I said, "There was an old woman who lived by the well, and when she died she went to—what do you want, prose or poetry?"

Another one of Bradley's jokes that I still use occasionally involves a professor who has invented a big machine that will let you tell whether or not a chicken egg will hatch a rooster or a hen. "That's nothing," I say, "I know a quicker way." "What's that?" Bradley would say. "Wait until the egg hatches," I say, "and then sprinkle some bread crumbs down in front of the chick. If he eats it, it's a rooster; if she eats it, it's a hen."

Back before I went in the Army, I didn't tell many stories on stage, but we did use a lot of little skits with two or more people. In West Virginia, when four or five of us would drive out to put on a two-hour show, we'd fill in with comedy skits. Some of the old ones were five minutes or so long. Take "The Buzzing of the Bees." They'd get the group's comedian out, and someone would tell him, "You be the queen bee. We really feel like we've been making fun of you all night tonight, and we want to make it up, so you be the queen bee and we'll be the workers. Now you stand here in the middle of the stage, and we'll come out and buzz around you." So he would stand there, and the rest of us would run into the wings and then run out and run around him going "buzzzz" all together. Then we'd tell him, "Now it's time to bring you the honey," and buzz offstage. Back there we would each get a mouthful of water and then rush out again. "Give me the honey," he'd say, and we'd all let him have it. We'd blow him plumb full of water. I don't know how old those skits were, but everyone used them; they were handed down, probably from vaudeville.

One of my big comedy sources was Hank Penny; I worked with him in the early 1940s at WLW. People today remember Hank as a bandleader and western swing musician, but he was one of the funniest comics around back then. I copied nearly everything he used to do. One that I still use is his old sweet potato gag. "I took my old aunt to town and she got in a hotel lobby and came upon a full-length mirror. She never had seen one before, and she didn't know what it was. So she walked up to it and saw her own reflection and said, 'Well, poor old thing, you look bad. I believe I'll go get you a sweet potato to eat.' So she went out and got a sweet potato and walked back into the hotel

Even the Reverend Billy Graham relishes a joke now and then.

and over to the mirror. She held the sweet potato out to the mirror, and then said, 'Oh, I see you got one already. I'll just eat this one myself.' "

Someone once asked me how my comedy was different from Bob Hope's. Bob Hope does mostly one-liners, and he does a lot of political jokes. I never do much with politics; I don't know enough about it. I'm kind of like the absent-minded professor who put a sign on his door saying "back in thirty minutes" and then sat down and waited for himself. But my best stuff is in the form of stories. I've even tried to record some of my better stories.

One of my favorites is about a Texan who came up to Arkansas and was talking to an old farmer he met at a gas station. The Texan had a big car and was as rich as cream, but those old boys down in Arkansas don't pay too much attention to that. So the Texan asked him, "How big is your place," and the Arkansas boy said, "It's 31 acres." The Texan laughed; "Why, I get in my pickup at six in the morning and drive until twelve noon, get out of my pickup and eat my lunch, get back in my pickup and drive until six that night, and there's my line." "Yeah," said the old man, "I had one of them pickups once." That's the kind of humor I like; it's real and honest and puts down blowhards. I don't like smutty things; they're not funny to me at all. Sometimes the mirth will override the filth, but not very often.

Another thing about country humor that makes it different is that a lot of times you can tell a story "on" somebody. That means you can take an old story that's been around for years but make believe that it happened to one of the band members or one of the sidemen. It's a form of kidding, but it makes the joke somehow seem new and fresh, and more personal. And there's another thing about country humor, or the subjects of country humor. I have always told jokes on myself or my family, and found that this is really important. If an audience ever thinks you think you're above them, they don't like you as well. But if you can poke fun at yourself or your family, they like you; that's why a lot of my jokes center on my kinfolks—even though the stories may be as old as the hills and my kinfolks never heard of them. There's also a strong streak of nostalgia in my stories; when I play middle-size or large towns, a lot of my audience is made up of former rural people who have had to move to the city, and who see in my music and my jokes a chance to be carried

Musicians and politicians sometimes get along; here in a 1974 picture are Barbara Mandrell, George "Goober" Linsey (right), and me with Alabama's Governor George Wallace.

back to their childhood. And this is fine with me, since I never have liked the city myself and have tried to live in the country as much as possible.

Every now and then we use a story that really did happen to us. One time I was up north on tour with Mel Tillis and Billy Grammer. Now everybody knows that Mel stutters a little bit, and most people know that I'm getting a little hard of hearing, and some people know that Billy has eye trouble—and a lot of fans know all three things. This night we were riding along in a little Nash Rambler that Billy had; we were somewhere out in North Dakota, and we were plenty lost. Finally we came to a crossroads, and began to debate which way to go. I said without thinking, "Well, I can't hear, and Billy can't see, and Mel can't talk, so it will take all three of us to get out of here." Sometimes Mel will tell that as one of his gags, and sometimes I do. Sometimes I think our adventures on the road make up the best joke book of all—and I never have trouble remembering the punch lines.

I know there's a lot of tales told about me, and some of them have more to them than others. By the time they get around and back to me, some of them have changed so much that they are right interesting again. I heard one the other day about Copas and me when we were working down in West Virginia. We had asked the local booker to call ahead and get us some rooms at this little hotel out in the middle of nowhere, and he said he had. So Copas and I dragged in about midnight, tired, sleepy, dirty, been driving all night in the rain, and limp up to the desk. "Room for Copas and Jones?" I asked. "Yes, sir," said the clerk, turning his register around. "Proud to have you here. Now that's Grandpa Copas and Cowboy Jones, right?" "Close enough," I said. "Give me the key."

Working with Minnie Pearl is always a delight.

Twelve.

FAN MAIL

Augsburg, Germany
July 24, 1945

Hyda folks, How is you all:

    We enjoy listening to your program each morning, to the extent that we carry our own radio to our motor pool each morning to listen. We don't start work until 8:31 in the morning; the reason is we hear the news from 8 to 8:15, and 8:15 to 8:30 we listen to your program.

    This is my second letter to you all. I haven't heard you play my first request yet. I know you all are kind of busy each day, trying to play as many songs as the boys request. There is nine of us mechanics and we all come from the South. They call us hill-billys and ridge runners, so you can see what we put up with all day.

    Well, here is a little request from the 3810 O.M. motor pool: "There's a Star-Spangled Banner Waving Somewhere."

Sincerely,

Tent City
Mainburg, Germany
July 23, 1945

Dear Grandpa Jones,

Your program is enjoyed by all of Headquarters Company each morning. We wish that you were on the air for a longer period of time, though, as fifteen minutes seems so short.

The "Dirty Dozen" of Hqs. Co. has a request for you to sing two songs for us. They are—"The Lonesome Pine," and "Whiskey Made Me What I am Today." Please dedicate these songs to Hqs. Co. of the 602 Tank Destroyer Batalion.

We like your Saturday Night Jamboree very much, too.

Thank you very much,

Hq. Co. 51st Armed Inf. Bat.
APO 254, US Army
July 25, 1945

Dear Buddies:

I am from Kentucky, the same place you are from, the place where they carry 38 Smith and Western revolvers. Wish you would play "When My Blue Moon Has Turned to Gray Again." I have hoboed all over Kentucky and think it is a great country; drank plenty of Budweiser beer there. Please play this song for me, as I like it.

Your buddy,

Toging, Germany
27 July 1945

Dear Grandpappy,

We uns up here shore do like yer programme and shore would be appreciative effen you would give usuns your rendition of "Good Ole Mountain Dew" jest as sune as possible. We ain't got many points, so you better sing'er quick.

Sined,
"Luger Packin" Ivan
"Thirty-Two" Willie
25th Tank Bn.

July 26, 1945

Hello Grandpa,

I have been fortunate enough to hear your program about twice. I mean I really enjoyed it, too, and I am speaking for all the rest of the boys in my company. I have found that the complaints of all the boys are (1) You come on at a time when most of us are unable to hear your program, and (2) there is such a few minutes devoted to us hill-billies. I don't know if all C.O.'s are like ours or not, but we aren't allowed to play the radio after eight o'clock. It would be greatly appreciated if you could arrange it so you could come on an hour earlier and stay on for at least a half hour. I think if you would try the City Slickers wouldn't mind too much. I think if you would look around you would find that most of the boys go to work at eight o'clock. If you could do this, you would have lots more boys able to hear your program, and I know you would get more requests for numbers. We would like to hear "Crash on the Highway."

A radio friend,

Elchingen, Germany
July 12, 1945

Hi Grandpa:

Just got a radio and being a fan of yours for a very long time, thought I'd write and ask for a few songs. Just one question, Did you sing over the WWVA Midnight Jamboree?

Here's a few songs I'd like to hear. Not all at once, but when you come to them. I'm really a hillbilly myself, from the Blue Ridge Mountains in Tennessee. Harriman. Ever hear of it? Anyway, some of the songs I'd like to hear

1—When the world has turned you down
2—Low and Lonely
3—I'll Get Back, But I'm Wondering How
4—Mule Skinner Blues

These are just a few. Every song is sweet music to my ears. Thanks a lot.

An old fan,

Cincinnati, Ohio
Feb. 13, 1948

Dear Grandpa Jones:

Would you please do a favor and settle an argument between a friend and me? My friend said you are at least eighty or eighty-five years of age, and I say you're not

Hee Haw's hospitality is far-ranging; Roy Clark (left), Minnie Pearl, and I welcome Lorne Greene, known around the world as the head of Bonanza's Cartwright clan.

over half that, as I saw your picture in a Cincinnati Post paper about a year ago and you didn't appear to be eighty or 85 years old. So, if it isn't asking too much, would you please answer this letter and tell me just how old you are? It's the only way we will know.

Sincerely,

New Albany, Ind.
Jan. 26, 1948

Dear Grandpa,
     I listen to you every Saturday night. I think you are swell. You are my favorite singer. I even play your records over about 5 times every ½ hour. Grandpa, I'd like for you to send me your life story and a picture of you.

Sincerely,
A listener

Seattle, Washington
January 13, 1948

Dear Grandpa,
     I seldom, if ever, write a fan letter, but our family enjoys your singing so much that I thought I'd like to tell you so. As a matter of fact, you are a great favorite of a lot of people up here in the Northwest, and maybe you'd be interested to know that one of your recordings started a controversy that almost amounted to a feud among the radio listeners of one of our local stations. I mean the recording of "Old Rattler". Our station KVI plays a lot of old ballads and western tunes every day, and "Old Rattler" was so popular that a few people started complaining, and, of course, others who liked it resented anyone who didn't want to hear it. When a vote was finally taken, though, we "Rattler" fans won, 100 to 1.

Respectfully,
     P.S. I've never been east of the Mississippi, but my father was from Tennessee.

Another Hee Haw guest was "Grandpa Walton"—Will Geer—who shared a bit of philosophy (or a long joke) with Buck Owens and me.

South Wellington,
British Columbia
May 20, 1948

Dear "Grandpa,"

I sure enjoy your singing very much. I get a bang out of the way you do those old hillbilly numbers such as "Mountain Dew" and "Old Rattler." That "Old Rattler" is quite a favorite with radio listeners up this way. Not a week goes by without that recording being heard two or three times. You really put a zip in those old numbers.

I've got it on good authority that you are just a young fellow with jet black hair; and on the stage you wear a wig, an old battered straw hat with hay sticking out here and there, and you make yourself look like an old hayseed. Am I right? Have you any pictures of yourself you could send me?

Yours sincerely,

Salisbury, N.C.
July 31, 1948

Why hello there, Grandpa,

How's banjo picking these days? Fine, I guess. Well, Grandpa, I want to get something straight with you now.

If you don't stay out of the country and leave my woman alone, I'll sic Old Rattler on you, and run you about eight miles to Louisville, and Maw don't get things ready for you I will.

Well, so much for that. I sure would like to have a picture of you. You are my favorite radio star.

Your friend,

Independence, Iowa
Feb. 6, 1948

Dear Grandpa Jones,

I was born in Kentucky but I now live in Iowa. I listen to the Grand Ole Opera every Saturday night. It makes me a little homesick, but I love Southern songs and voices.

Say, I think we should have a song about us housewives who still long to go out once in awhile even tho we love our family and our home. So many husbands just think because we are married, we never care to have them take us out. I am 35 years

☞ "As we drop in on the Culhanes tonight, they sit watching their gas-powered TV": it's Hee Haw's version of soap opera, featuring (from left) Gordie Tapp, Junior Samples, me, and Lulu Roman.

On the road again, in my van. Touring wears out a lot of cars.

old and have 9 children and I don't feel a bit old yet. (Ha ha.) Anyway, I still like my husband to take me places as well as ever. I am sending you a few words to give you an idea of what I mean. I wish you would write a song and just put the words right and put it to some snappy music, and I believe it would make a very pretty song, and also one that would make a hit.

Yours truly,

Indianapolis, Ind.
March 29, 1948

Dear Mr. Jones,

Will you please send me your picture? I am trying to collect all the hillbilly singers' pictures. My mom is a Hillbilly too, and I sure wish I was either from Kentucky or Tennessee. I really do.

Yours truly,

Grasonville, Md.
Jan. 21, 1948

Dear Grandpappy Jones:

I just enjoy hearing you come on in the mornings with that yodel. Always try to get your program although we sometimes experience difficulty in getting WSM.

Isn't there some way that I can get a picture of you to show friends who have not seen you? I journeyed from Eastern Shore, Md. over to Washington, D.C. last September to take the excursion on which you were entertaining. I sat and waited on third deck for your appearance for two and a half hours, and finally decided that I would not get as much as a peep before docking.

Then I rushed down on second deck and with much effort, I succeeded in getting your autograph. With the surrounding mob, intense heat, and probably writer's cramp, I felt assured that you wanted no further disturbance so I left. On the radio the next morning, I got a few facts on your career and a few more from Connie B. Gay, but no picture.

Musically yours,

Mobile, Ala.
Nov. 19, 1948

(Sent in an envelope marked "Please rush before the next broadcast" to WSM, and written on the back of a check on The First National Bank of Dallas, Georgia, made out to Grandpa Jones for the sum of $25,000.94.)

Please accept this and go off the air or blow your nose on it before you try to sing again.

Signed, Z.Q. Kilroy and
129,999,999 other people.

Springville, Oregon
October 24, 1982

Dear Grandpa and Ramona Jones,

I am writing you to ask a favor of you and that is I know that every year you leave *Hee-Haw* to go and be on your own. There is something I would like you to do for me, and that is, if you hear of someone who has a bass fiddle to sell and will tell you how much they want for it, and what it would cost you to send it to me, I'll send you the money and you can mail it to me.

Your friend,

Wichita Falls, Tex.
Jan. 30, 1948

Dear Grandpa and Chillun,

Folks, have you seen any of those rose bushes and gardenia plants you are advertising? Oh boy. I ordered the ones that you had on in December, and I received them yesterday, and what dried up, pitiful looking things they were. We came very near to throwing them in the garbage can, but I am an optomistic person so we crossed our fingers, pruned them as directed, and set them out. Two of them were labelled "Golden Dawn," but one poinsettia and the other no one will know what it is until it blooms. That poor little scrawny gardenia bush! It is every bit as big as a match stem, and about four inches long—but oh yes, it was rooted, about a half dozen little roots. As I said before, I am optomistic and fairly good humored. I'm just telling you I was aggravated, and I can't keep from laughing every time I look at my

Our dinner theater near our home in Mountain View, Arkansas.

gardenia—the one I am going to use to grow my own corsages. Well, it's all planted with tender care in a pretty red coffee can, and it's in the house until warm weather. I can look at it and mentally kick myself! Better looking bushes (from the same farm) here cost me 29¢ each.

I'm not saying they won't grow, 'cause I hope they do. If they don't, I'm just out $1.35 because I'm a sucker about flowers and music. I'm not sore, and I'm going to keep listening to you and all the barn dance gang.

Didn't I hear something about you passing cigars around? That can only mean one thing, and you must not be such an "old man." Anyway, I never did think you were, as you are too full of pep at 5:45 A.M. to be a grandpa!

Please sing for me, "Turn Your Radio On."

Thank you,

Jackson, Miss.
May 5, 1981

Dear Grandpa,

It's taken me two weeks to get up the nerve to write you and I pray you will not think that I am stupid. I am a Christian and through voices and guidance I get my prayers for the grace period of my Eastern Star chapter of which I am chaplin. Recently these same voices gave me a beautiful song and told me to allow Tennessee Ernie Ford to hear them first, that he could have a gold record with them. I don't know how to reach him but I knew you are his friend. At first I tried to ignore all this, and felt foolish, but something keeps tugging at me. Please tell him for me that it's really a beautiful song about country music, God, and America. I am enclosing a self-addressed, envelope and pray you will find out when I can contact Mister Ford and at his convenience.

Sincerely,

---

13 September 1982
Detroit, Michigan

Dear Grandpa Jones,

I miss the country, our country, the United States. . . . The flag is ours, but its colors aren't primary, arent' red, yellow, and blue. . . . I am open to Dixie as I am the

It always tickles me when people ask for autographs.

Promised Land. The blessing I have in the name of Daniel is of "empathy, love, and joy" wished upon mankind by the dervish, sufi philosopher-poet Sam Lewis; but it's a curse at present. . . . I'm a detective to find the humility of it.

"Pancakes"
one cup of white flour
one teaspoon of iodized salt
one cup of cold water

"Bisquits"
one cup of white flour
one teaspoon of iodized salt
one-third cup of cooking oil
one cup of cold water

Thank you,
Sincerely yours,

OLD GRANPA JONES

I have been a dirt farmer for fifty years
I have toiled in the cold and the heat
Raised seven children by the sweat of my brow
While raising the corn and the wheat
I have plowed level fields and steep ones too
Many acres of loose and tight stones
But I have tossed up the sponge and quitting the job
Since listening to old Gran Pa Jones.

••

Old Gran Pa Jones is a fine singer his voice is so sweet
With his guitar and banjo in tune
His daily two programs 8:20 A.M.
And a program at 3 P.M. afternoon
When its time for Gran Pa's programs
My blood pressure is high I feel it all over my bones

I leave my team standing on top of the hill
And run down to hear old Gran Pa Jones.

• • •

My farm is a thicket all gone to seed
A farm that no one admires
It is all covered over with all kinds of filth
And a sprinkled of sticking old briars
I often get lost while hunting the cows
And fall over stumps and large stones
And I just lay my troubles on one old man
And that man is old Gran Pa Jones..

• • • •

When time for the programs I quit work
And run to the old radio
If working in hay or fighting a fire
I just stop and let the work go
The poor house is open for me on the hill
I swear as I rub my stiff bones
My misfortunes I blame on one old man
And his name it is old Gran Pa Jones.

Composed by Newton T. Fluharty
Fairview, W. Va.

Thirteen.

STRING

Back during those first years of *Hee Haw,* in those warm fall afternoons in the early seventies, I would be puttering around the farm, keeping an eye on the clock, thinking that it was getting to be about time to start down to the Opry or the studio, and the phone would ring. I would answer it, and say, "Hello," and then I would hear myself talking back. It was like an echo, only it wasn't an echo. I could hear myself, or something that sounded just so much like me that it wasn't funny, saying, "All right, I'll come by and get you, String." As many times as it happened, I never got used to it: it was Stringbean's way of letting me know that he would like to ride in with me.

There were other phone gags. String and I used to like to pick on an old song I recorded for Syd in the 1940s called "Going Down the Country." It took the melody from an even older song the Carter Family used to do that began:

> Jeff Davis knew, when the cruel war begun,
> That he wouldn't be a Union man,
> Or carry the Union gun.

String and I were probably the only two people in Nashville that knew or cared about this older song. Sometimes he'd call, and as soon as I answered, without any preamble or anything he'd ask in a forceful voice, "Now *what* was it old Jeff Davis knew?" And then *we* knew who was calling; it was a wry, funny, shy, gentle man who was born David Akeman but whom the world called Stringbean and we called String.

I met String right after I came to the Opry in 1946, and we hit it off right away. Though String was, like me, from Kentucky, we had never met before and had followed different careers. String was a tall, skinny boy who grew up knowing what hard times were and working in a government-sponsored CCC camp to get a little money to share with his family. In the late 1930s he entered an amateur contest playing the banjo, and pretty soon he was working on the stage with Asa Martin, a fine old-time singer from up in that area. String picked the banjo and gradually started doing some comedy (including even a little blackface), copying his getup—a long shirt and little short pants, with the belt about at his knees—from an old Renfro Valley fiddler and comic named Slim Miller. The way String told it, he wasn't called Stringbean until one night when Asa forgot his name, looked over into the wings, and saw this long, tall, skinny character who looked like a string bean, and made up the name on the spot. As it turned out, String loved to eat those beans about as much as anything, so the name stuck, though in the early days he was called String Beans—two words. When I first met String, he was working a duet with another famous Opry comic, Lew Childre.

I guess the reason we hit it off so well was that we both liked to hunt and fish; we talked hunting and fishing all the time and did a lot of it, too. String never liked to get up at four in the morning to fish. He said if he had to work at it, he'd just stay home. But he'd get out there about nine o'clock and fish all day and have as many fish as any of them. He went for the joy of fishing and being out in the open air on a beautiful stream or lake. String and I started floating the Stones and Harpeth Rivers, staying all day and cooking the fish on the bank. I had a box rigged up that had everything to cook fish with, everything to season them with, and everything to wash the dirty dishes with. We had some good times on those rivers. As we floated along we would gather wood here and there to build the fire with later. I had a grill that stuck in the ground and you could build a fire under it. We had a coffeepot that you boiled the coffee in. String would say, "Make me some of that Agrifortus coffee." He meant very strong, and I did, and it was.

We would take two cars with boat racks on them and two boats. We would unload both boats at the starting place, drive both cars to the finishing place, leave one car, and all go back to the boats and leave the other car there. Then we would float all day and end up at the other car. One river bend was so long that we could float all day and be only about a quarter-mile from where we put in the river. String was a funny man. He kept me laughing on all the floats. Those floats were much, much fun. He always cleaned the fish, and I did the cooking and fire building.

When we returned to Nashville in 1952, the hunting and fishing started all over again. While String was living in town and we had bought our place on Ashland City Highway, String wanted to get out in the country; he found a 143-acre farm on Hyde's Ferry Road outside of Nashville with two houses on it, for $10,000. He didn't have that kind of money at the time and neither did I, so he suggested we go in together and buy it. We did, and those were some of the best years of my life. Many an evening Ramona and Estelle (String's wife) would cook up a lot of food, and we would eat out on the picnic table that sat between the two houses. I remember once we were having corn on the cob. String would eat all the corn off, throw the cob back over his shoulder, and say, "This is a handy old place." Once after I went up to Washington to work, I got a letter from him, and at the top of the letter was written, "THE PRODUCING OLD FARM." Estelle said that I better consider myself lucky because, as far as she knew, that was the only letter he ever wrote to anybody.

Estelle's brother (his name was Innis Stanfield, but we called him "Big") was a painter and carpenter, so we hired him to repair the two old houses. String was a little close with his money; he used to say that every time he went out on a tour, when he got back he just handed over the money for repairs on those old houses. I was doing the same thing. However, we did move in after a while, and had a lot of fun on the old place. We had a big garden, and we picked a lot of blackberries and made jam. It goes so well with biscuits in the morning. And I don't think there was a morning that String missed having biscuits for breakfast. All through the winter, he would take a little jam out of

Stringbean (David Akeman) and I warm up our "fives" for a show up in Kentucky. Photo by Sonny Brown, The Courier, Evansville, Indiana.

the jar and heat it up before he ate it. Said it made the jam taste like it was just made. And by golly, it does.

We bought a tractor together. String never would drive a car, so he said he couldn't drive the tractor. I told him that I wasn't going to do all the driving, and he would have to learn. So he got on one day and put the tractor in gear, and when he let out the clutch, it jumped about three feet. But he finally caught on and did a lot of work with it.

After it got too cold to fish, we started quail hunting. Neither of us had a bird dog, so String would just whistle like a female quail, and the bobwhite would call back. Then we would go to where the call came from and nearly always get up a covey. String was a good wing shot, and he never used anything but a little Stevens 20-gage double with the barrel cut off about an inch. Sometimes he'd get two birds on the rise. A lot of our quail hunting was done on the railroad that ran in front of the farm we lived on. The trains would come along with loads of corn or wheat, and some of it would spill out along the track. The birds came there to eat, and they stayed around the track a lot. Once we parked the jeep at the crossing and walked four or five miles and didn't get a shot. We came back and unloaded our guns and were getting in the jeep when a covey flew up right in front of us. We just stood there and watched them fly off. We killed lots of quail along that railroad, though.

There was a cave behind the little house that String lived in on the farm. I went back in the cave three times, but it was a little scary, as you had to crawl about 30 feet on your stomach. But there were some nice rooms and a beautiful waterfall in there; it went back about 360 feet. String would never go into it. If a bad cloud came up, though, he and Estelle would go sit in the mouth of the cave until the storm was over. There were a lot of spotted lizards in the cave, and a lot of the boys at the Opry, especially Gene Martin, liked to fish with those lizards. He told Alisa, my daughter, he would give her 50 cents apiece for all the lizards she would bring him. So she made a deal with String and me for her to catch lizards out of the cave. She did pretty well until she saw a little snake in there.

At one time String and I both had small Nash cars, and one of their features was that the back of the front seat would let down and make a bed. He always was telling me about the "Blue Holes" that he used to fish when he was a boy in Kentucky, so we planned to go up there and try them. We took off, the four of us, in the two cars. About halfway there it started to pour, and when we got there, the place was nothing but a mud hole. We told him they were yellow holes instead of blue holes. We slept in the cars that night and never wet a hook the whole trip. We kidded him for years after that. I think we got a fish sandwich on the way home.

String didn't like to own up to the fact that Estelle could almost beat him throwing a plug. She could really put a plug right where she wanted it. Estelle's brother Big fished with us a lot. String would get excited and say, "Throw right over here, Big," and Big would say, "You throw where you want to, and I'll throw where I want to." Big used a jitterbug nearly all the time, and he would come up with about as many fish as anybody who changed plugs often. Once we had been fishing on the Stones River all day without any luck. We were really getting hungry. Finally, about dusk, I caught a 6¼-pound bass. It didn't take Big long to get that fish ready for the skillet, and when it was cooked he ate half of it. He really liked bass.

String, Estelle, Ramona, and I were on Indian Lake fishing one day, and Ramona hung a big bass on a hoola popper. She was struggling with it, yelling, "Oh, I know I'm gonna lose him." But she finally got him in where we could net him, and he weighed 6¾ pounds. That was another fine fish.

At the farm there was a groundhog's hole about 150 yards from the house. Every day at noon he would come out and sun by the hole. I had a 22/250-caliber rifle, and one day when Big was there, I shot the groundhog. It turned out to be a fat one, and Big said he wanted it for supper. My daughter was small then, and she said, "If you eat that groundhog, you'll be sick." But he took it home, anyway. The next day he didn't show up for work; he had eaten too much groundhog.

In 1957, when Connie B. Gay called and asked us to take over Jimmy Dean's television show in Washington, we had to get ready to leave Nashville again. I called String to tell him the bad news (or good news, whichever way you looked at it), and to sell him my part of the old farm. He bought it, but the day we met to sign the papers, he said, "You'll be back in a year." We were optimistic, though, and while I ran off to do a tour of Europe, Ramona took over the job of finding us a house in Virginia and moving from the old farm.

To this day she likes to tell how she watched our moving truck leave for Virginia from Nashville, while she followed along in a little car with 35 guns, a German Shepherd dog, and Eloise and Mark.

But String was right, in the end. I was back in 11 months. We had hardly gotten started on the TV show when a boy named Elvis came out with his rock-and-roll and almost killed off country music. Or maybe it was my trying to do TV commercials on the air; I had never done them before, and since they were live, you didn't get a second chance. At any rate, the show was soon off the air. The only compensation was that I got to do some hunting up in Virginia with Joe Wheeler, who was working with Connie then. Joe was and is one of the finest sportsmen I've seen, and he and I both hunted everything from groundhog to bear. And we both liked to shoot pistols—especially 44 Magnums. Without ear plugs. And I regret that now, since I've developed hearing trouble and date a lot of it to those Magnums.

When I got back to Nashville in 1958, the 90 acres I bought on the edge of Davidson County was not far from the old farm that String and I had. Right away String and I got back together again, and I found out that he had gotten interested in hunting ginseng. He had done this since he was a kid back in Kentucky, but now he had discovered that you could get good money for it in Nashville. He taught me how to spot ginseng 30 yards away, and we spent many a day hunting it together; of course, it was a good excuse to just get out and walk the woods, which we both liked to do. Later on, when we built a cabin up on Center Hill Lake, String would come up and fish all day until we were all tired, then tie his boat up in the willows and go into the woods and hunt ginseng for a few more hours. We got to carrying small pistols for snakes, since copperheads and rattlers like the same sorts of places ginseng does. String got a big kick out of selling "sang," and the night before he died, he showed us a check for $27.50 he had gotten for some.

Though String and I were closest buddies, we never actually performed much together on tours or personal appearances. We were too much alike, and most people didn't want *two* banjo players on one show, both of them telling jokes. Actually, come to think of it, we didn't even really pick all that much together. String had this old hard hat, an African safari hat, and he wore it walking the woods and everywhere, and everyone could recognize him for a mile off with his lanky body and that hat. (He always said it was cooler than a fishing hat, and you couldn't argue with him about it—or about anything else: when he first bought a motor for his boat up on Center Hill, he got a little Mighty Mite; he said it didn't burn any gas at all, but you could hardly see his boat moving either.) Anyway, though we didn't pick the banjo much together, String would take that safari hat and put it in his lap as I was driving along in the car, and he would sit there and play on that hat like a banjo and sing to me for hours—every old song you can imagine, and then some.

I never did know of String driving a car for a single mile; he would have Estelle do the driving if they had to get somewhere. Lew Childre, who used to partner with String, claimed that he got him to drive for about 30 miles once somewhere down in Alabama; Doctor Lew just said he was tired, crawled into the back seat, and went to sleep. String wanted to get on home, so he drove. At least that's what I've heard; I'm still not sure I believe it.

String wasn't a drinking man. He would drink a little beer, but never Canadian beer; he thought it tasted too much like home brew, and he had gotten sick on home brew once when he was a kid up in Kentucky. We used to get some Old Tankard and take that on our fishing trips; Estelle said String could drink one can of beer and get high, and that when he did get tight, he would talk, talk, talk until she thought she would go nuts. Because String was not a talking man, either. Many times on our trips, we would go for hours without either saying a word.

String was not your world's greatest optimist. He and I watched as they dammed up a lot of the rivers around middle Tennessee and made them bad for fishing, and one day we were out in one of the areas the government had purchased to make a lake. "Boy, just look at this land," he said, waving his arm at the rich fields and woods. "They're going to fill it up with water; they're going to flood it." "Yep," I said. He said, "They're paying a lot of money for it, I hear. And I could have bought it a year ago for little or nothing." I said, "String, what do you want with more money? You got all you want." "Yeah," he nodded, "but still. . . ." I quoted a couplet from Pope that I had learned years before: "Hope springs eternal in the human breast: / Man never is, but always to be, blessed." String looked sidewise at me, stared off across the field, and said, "Yeah, and he's a turkey all the way."

Ramona, Estelle, String, and I used to go down to Theda, Tennessee—Estelle's hometown—to hunt squirrels. We always ate lunch with Estelle's mother; she served some fine old country meals. Once Ramona had a squirrel up a tree and was trying to get a shot at it. String said he could go on the other side of the tree and scare the squirrel around. While he was over there, he shot it, and Ramona accused him of shooting her squirrel. She always kidded him about that.

Sometimes String would ride with us down to the Opry (when it was at the Ryman Auditorium). I remember one night he went with us when the roads were just a sheet of ice, and Estelle didn't want to drive. When we got out of the car in the parking lot, String was all bent over, carrying his banjo. I asked him why he was bent over, and he said that way he didn't have as far to fall.

In 1969, when String and I joined *Hee Haw,* people all over the country got to share in this droll humor of String's. We both found ourselves with plenty of bookings, and neither one of us really felt it could last. During the first year of the show, String and I found some little store up in the country that had a bunch of the big-collared plaid shirts we wore on the show. They were on sale at a good price, so we each got several and marched out of the store feeling proud of ourselves. On down the road, String got to studying and thinking, and I waited until he got ready to come out with it. Finally he said, "You know, that show's not going to last forever, and if it goes off next year, we're going to be stuck with a lot of these old shirts with these big collars." I reassured him, and sure enough, the show continued. String and his "Cornfield Crow" became one of the hit attractions.

String learned a lot of his banjo tunes from Uncle Dave Macon, and he really loved the old songs and played them well. He traveled a lot more with Uncle Dave than I did, and even got one of Uncle Dave's original banjos. He was really devoted to old-time music and old-time ways. He was a fireplace man, and he lived a simple life. He used to say, "A man who plays the banjo has got it made. It never interferes with any of his pleasures in life."

On November 10, 1973, Ramona, String, Estelle, and I were sitting at a table backstage at the Opry House between shows, and String was eating his egg sandwich and banana, and we were talking of a hunting trip up in Virginia with Joe Wheeler the next morning. String said that when he promised to go it was warm; now it was getting cold out in those mountains, and he wished he hadn't said he'd go. But he finally said he would, and I agreed to pick him up at six the next morning. So we played the last show at the Opry and went home. String had done two of his favorite songs on his last set: "You All Come" and "Green Corn."

The next morning I was all packed for hunting and went over to pick up String. As I drove up the lane, I thought I saw a coat lying about 75 yards out in front of the house; when I got closer I saw it was a person. I stopped the car and went over. It was Estelle; she had been shot in the back and in the head. I felt her, and she was cold. I rushed to their little house and hollered for String. His banjo that he had played the night before was sitting on its side on the little front porch. I opened the screen; the other door was already open. String was lying in front of the fireplace, shot in the chest. I saw that the phone had been torn off the wall, so I jumped in the car and drove to my house and called Sergeant Nickens of the Metro Police homicide division. It took them about 25 minutes to get out to where I was to meet them and guide them to String's house. This was one of the worst things that I have ever witnessed.

String carried lots of money all the time, and a lot of us at the Opry warned him about it, but it didn't do much good. We were afraid someone would get him up in one of the coves at Center Hill Lake and rob him; we really didn't think about its happening at his house. The wrong people finally found out that he carried lots of money, but I don't think they got over $104. They missed about $2,500: as long as we knew them and as close as we were, String never said anything about Estelle carrying any money, but she had about $2,500 on her.

This terrible thing was a blow to everyone on the Opry and *Hee Haw,* because everyone loved String. Sam Lovullo, the current producer of *Hee Haw* and one of the finest men I know, came to me and asked if I thought they should use the film that String had already made. I told him I thought they should, as folks would still like to see String and remember him as he was on the show; they would still like to hear him read his letter from home. So *Hee Haw* and the Opry are still going and are still missing Stringbean a lot. I know I am.

In my travels since String's death, I've been asked thousands of questions about him. Each person always tells me how much they miss him. There's no way I can tell them what it feels like to lose a friend like String.

Fourteen.

HOME IN ARKANSAS

Thursday, March 17, 1983: Our plane began its approach to the Nashville airport about noon, and I put down the Washington paper and glanced out of the window at the familiar scenery. There was I-65 heading up by our old place at Goodlettsville, and a little south was I-40, Tennessee's major east-west road linking Memphis and Knoxville. Down below was Percy Priest Lake, where Stringbean and I had spent so many afternoons fishing, and on the other side of it was Donelson and the little farm where I had shotgunned the June bugs off the peaches. I knew it as well as the back of my hand, and only a few years before I would have been relaxing about now, knowing that I was home. But this time I had another eight-hour drive ahead of me, all the way from Nashville across half of Tennessee and Arkansas to a little town called Mountain View. I wasn't quite home yet.

We had moved to Arkansas in 1979, right after Alisa had graduated from high school. We still loved our ranch house up by Goodlettsville, but it was remote and out of the way, and after the murder of Stringbean and Estelle, that pretty countryside never seemed as nice anymore. String and Estelle had lived just over the ridge from us, and even with our big fence and a guard dog, we couldn't help feeling uneasy.

I had heard a lot about Arkansas from my old friend Lenny Aleshire. It was Lenny who had taught me the old song "Happy Little Home in Arkansas" that I had recorded for King years ago, and Lenny used to tell a tale about Arkansas and Missouri. It seems that there were these two old people who lived right on the line between Missouri and Arkansas. They were happy there, but one day the surveyors showed up to resurvey that part of the state line, and they moved it so that it ran a few feet to the north of their house. The old woman came out, took a look at the new line, and put her hands on her hips. "Look at that," she said "We're gonna have to move. I'm not gonna stay down here in Arkansas and die of malaria fever!"

People have been joking about Arkansas for years, even with songs about the Arkansas Traveler, and about hard times in Arkansas and the bad climate and all, but when we started visiting my brother Gordon, who lived in Mountain View, we learned it was not like that at all. Mountain View was way up in the mountains, on the White River in Stone County, and it was as remote and unspoiled as it was pretty. Stone County hadn't had a paved road until about 20 years before, and when we first visited there, Mountain View was just starting to become a center for folk festivals and programs. In fact, when my brother got sick, we bought a five-acre plot for him in town, just a short distance from where the big Ozark Folk Center was later built. The hunting and fishing were fine in those hills, and we spent a lot of time visiting Jimmy Driftwood, the singer and songwriter who wrote "The Battle of New Orleans" and "Tennessee Stud." He was a native of the area, and the more we visited him, the better we liked it. Ramona and I were also wanting more and more to get back to the older type of old-time country music we both loved, and the people in Stone County really appreciated that and promoted it in their folk festivals.

So when we found 40 acres and an old house high on a ridge overlooking the river north of town, we bought it and packed up our trunks of song books and records and memories and made the move. I was an Arkansan now, and I had never really thought that old song about a "Happy Little Home in Arkansas" would be so true. I was anxious to get onto the highway and get home, and as the plane taxied up to the gate, I picked up my case and got in line to get off.

As I made my way through the Nashville airport, I saw several other musicians and singers lining up to get their luggage and their instruments. A lot of us had gone up to Washington for a very special television show and concert celebrating the twenty-fifth anniversary of the Country Music Association. My old boss and booker Connie B. Gay had been one of the founders of the CMA, and it was decided to celebrate the anniversary on Connie's home ground of Washington. We had gotten a letter early in the year naming the place and the date: the old Constitution Hall on March 16. They wanted all of the living Hall of Famers to be there, along with a bunch of other big names in country music, from Willie Nelson to Gene Autry to Charley Pride to Roy Acuff, and about anybody else. The show was going to be shown nationwide over CBS, and there were rumors that we might meet the President himself. For some of us, the show was extra special, though; we had worked in Washington, and with Connie B. Gay, before. In fact, Minnie Pearl, Roy Acuff, Kitty Wells, and I were all on that first show broadcast from Constitution Hall way back in 1948, and I had spent quite a few years trying to sing our music in what Billy Grammer called "the largest city in North Carolina."

So Ramona and I had made our plans to go up there again on March 13; I had been working the Opry, so it was decided that I would leave my car in Nashville and fly up, while she would drive to Memphis (the nearest big airport to Stone County) and fly in from there. We met at the Washington airport and were picked up by our old pal Joe Wheeler, who had worked for Connie in the 1950s. Joe and his brother Buddy used to sing close-harmony duets back then, and later on he worked with us. Joe and I spent many weekends fishing, shooting, and hunting together, and it was good to see him again. He used to be a mapmaker for the government, and as we drove to his home in Herndon, he told us he had started up a little recording studio and was keeping busy. We spent the afternoon and most of the evening just talking, and the next day he drove us downtown to our hotel, and I got out the schedule the CMA had sent me and started figuring out how to get down to business.

I was due to rehearse at four to five that afternoon, and from five to seven, we were all to go to the White House. Each of us had a limousine and driver assigned to us, to take us wherever we wanted to go, so about three o'clock we went down to the old Constitution Hall to see what was up. There we found an interesting group of fiddlers and pickers milling around and trying out tunes: Ricky Skaggs, the young bluegrass picker who had just hit it big in the record business; Bill Monroe, the father of bluegrass music; and Senator Robert Byrd, the West Virginian who had become the Minority Leader of the Senate for the Democrats and who was getting a national reputation as a mean man with a fiddle bow. Roy Acuff walked in carrying his fiddle, too; a lot of people don't know that Roy started out as a fiddler, or that in recent years he has picked up his fiddle again and started doing a lot of the old fiddle breakdowns he learned as a boy back in East Tennessee. The show's producers, Chet Hagen and Sam Lovullo (the old *Hee Haw* producer), had decided that we would make up a great all-star bluegrass band; they had told me earlier to choose a tune, and we finally settled on "Lonesome Road Blues," with its famous chorus about "going down the road feeling bad." Everyone knew that one, and we began working out how it would go. Ricky and Bill started it off, singing a chorus and playing one, and then Roy and the Senator came out and sang and fiddled a chorus. Then I ran out and did my verse and thumped out a break on the banjo. It sounded all right, and the Senator was in top form; we had worked with him before on *Hee Haw* and respected his musicianship. We ran through the song again, and someone suggested that after the second chorus we go into a different key to give the performance a little extra goose. Bill and Ricky started the song in the key of G, then we stepped up to the key of A when I came on. This was fine for me, but rough on the fiddlers. "I just wish they'd stayed in G," the Senator whispered to me, as he worked away at the new key.

After we felt we had the piece down pretty well, we packed it in and got into regular suits for the White House reception (it wasn't black tie, though the show itself would be) and formed up our procession to drive over there. I don't know how many they had invited to the White House, but when we got there, we found an awful crowd. Someone later told me there were about 450 in attendance, maybe two-thirds musicians and the rest CMA executives and guests, but there seemed to be at least that many more photographers, and flashbulbs were popping every time you turned around. We didn't exactly

Roy Acuff (lower left) with me and Connie B. Gay (right) on the Hee Haw *set. That's my son Mark in the hat, beard, and T-shirt.*

have dinner, just *hors d'oeuvres* and drinks, but they had the biggest variety of foods I have ever seen—something for almost any taste. Pretty soon President and Mrs. Reagan came down and formally welcomed us. He started by saying that country music was one of the few art forms that we could claim as being truly American and that the music was known throughout the world for its commitment to country, freedom, and God. "You belong here," he said, and everyone applauded. Then he told us something we hadn't known. "I go back with this music a long way," he said, "long before the CMA was founded. I go back to station WHO in Des Moines." WHO had been one of the best country stations in the Midwest, and I had known several performers there. After this speech, Sam Marmaduke, the board chairman of the CMA, presented the president with autographed copies of albums by each one of us there that night. Then the President and First Lady came down into the audience; they didn't say much, but smiled as they shook our hands. A lot of country singers are conservative to start with and were big Reagan supporters; others are staunch Democrats, but everyone that night was impressed with the occasion and what it meant for our music. As the sun set, we all went out to the south portico to view the Washington Monument and listen to Bill Monroe and Charley Pride sing unaccompanied duets of "Footprints in the Snow," an old song that I had heard Bradley sing many times and that had become a big bluegrass favorite, and a hymn called "Mansions for Me." It was a good way to end the day.

The big show the next day went off well, too. The President and First Lady came, and when we got to the hall we saw fans lined up halfway around the block. With the President there, security was tight, and each person entering the hall had to go through a metal detector. It was a good show; there were film clips of the old Jimmie Rodgers I had listened to so often as a boy, and tributes to Hank Williams and Patsy Cline and Tex Ritter. It was like seeing a panorama of country music pass before your eyes. There were some surprises, too; a duet by Ronnie Milsap and Ray Charles, and another one by classical violinist Eugene Fodor and Charlie Daniels. Our "Lonesome Road Blues" came off all right, and at the end the President made some more remarks about our music. It was a far cry from the time we had spent entertaining at Constitution Hall in the 1950s. Back then, the DAR com-

When the Joneses get together, we can make up a pretty good family band. Alisa plays the hammered dulcimer, Mark the banjo, Ramona the fiddle, and Marsha the autoharp; Eloise helps out with the singing.

plained that the country show fans were carving their initials in the seats, and the Washington musicians' union made Ramona go down and play the fiddle for them to prove that a country musician was good enough to join. "You belong here," the President has said, but there was a time a few years back when that would have been hard to prove.

I loaded my banjo, my Grandpa case, and my suitcase into the trunk of the Lincoln and drove out of the Nashville airport. Flying was fine, but it was good to be on the road again, in a big comfortable car with the familiar sound of WSM on the radio. Traveling is part of the territory when you're in country music, and even though I enjoy it, I wonder sometimes. I've lost some good friends in accidents. Patsy Cline. Ira Louvin. Cowboy Copas. I think Copas's death hurt worst of all. Once before he got killed, we sat down and did some figuring. He figured he had gone two and a half million miles, and that I had gone two million in traveling to performances. But since then, I've probably done at least that much again; I really don't know, but I'd guess six or seven million miles over the years. Up until we got the camper and motor home, this was almost always by car; most country singers can't use planes much, because the planes don't land in the little places where you are playing. You would have to rent a car when you got there if you took a plane, and the instruments would get torn up. It's just better to go by car all the way, as we've been doing for 50 years. With some of the bigger acts, the leader flies and the band drives, and they pick him up, but I've never done that.

Travel depends on your booker; if he can book two or three dates just 200 miles apart, you're okay. But most of the time we have to go at least 500 miles for a date. This is rough, even with the new interstate highways and comfortable cars, but it was rougher back in the 1940s when the best road was a two-lane highway with low shoulders, narrow bridges, and potholes big enough to swallow a bus. A week before, I had played a date in Franklin, West Virginia; the next day I had to drive to Mariana, Florida, down below Dothan, Alabama; and then I drove back home—a solid 13 hours—the day after that. I did that by myself, and I guess I shouldn't, but as I said, this kind of travel goes with the job.

With all this, I've been lucky. I've had very few accidents—maybe an occasional fender-bender, but nothing much to worry about. Most of the

I was amazed at the amount of mail waiting for me when I got home after my first heart operation.

time, I do have someone drive with me; this motor home we have now will run 400 miles on a tank of gas. Three of us share the driving, and each takes 400 miles. Working for the regional radio stations years ago, you didn't go very far out of your listening area, not much more than 40 or 50 miles on a trip. But with *Hee Haw* on 226-or-so stations and the Opry heard all over the country, bookings are spread from Maine to California. The traveling was worst during World War II, with the old roads, the bad tires, the old cars, and the gas rationing—although a lot of times you could get extra ration cards if you could prove that the trip was necessary for your work.

We go through cars pretty fast, too. Since I got into the Lincoln and Cadillac class, I've worn out four Lincolns. I've also gone through a Packard and a Mercury, and we put at leat 100,000 on each one, and most of them 125,000.

Some trips are harder on cars than others. One time back in the 1950s, Ernest Ferguson, the mandolin player who worked with us for years, had booked us up in Kentucky, and we took off for a date up there. Clyde and Marie Dillehay were with us then, and we were all four in the car. We kept driving and kept driving, and the roads got worse and worse and worse yet, until at last we were actually driving up a creek bed. No one dared to say anything for a while, but finally Clyde said, "Ernest, how long was you a-missin' when you went and booked this?"

Well, Ernest is retired now and lives near Nashville, and Clyde manages a tobacco warehouse in Springfield, and they probably don't travel any more than they have to to see their grandchildren. And here I am, still traveling, coming into Memphis and hoping to be on the big bridge across the Mississippi before it gets too dark. I have to swing north of Memphis on the interstate because the I-40 link through town isn't finished yet, and I'm hoping to beat the worst of the rush hour. Finally I see the big bridge over Mud Island and get on it. Halfway across, the sign says "Welcome to Arkansas" and I figure I am about halfway home. On the other side of the bridge, the land levels off, and before I know it I'm off the interstate and heading west on the narrow two-lane blacktop.

You wear out a lot of things in 54 years of the music business. You wear out cars for sure, and costumes, and instruments. I've worn out my share of

Our group now (from left): *Mark Jones, me, George McCormick, and Joe Carroll. Photo by Les Leverett.*

I take the time to put on a little more Grandpa before we go onstage. Photo by Carl Fleischhauer.

banjos, and though I've never been a nut about collecting banjos just for the fun of it, I know that you can't do a good job without a good tool, and for me a banjo is a tool. I got my first one when I was at WWVA and developed such a love for Cousin Emmy's drop-thumb style of playing; I bought it in an Akron pawn shop. It was a Vega; I don't recall what model —I didn't pay attention at that time—but years later I gave it to Oswald Kirby, who works with Roy Acuff. He put another neck on it, and I think he still has it.

I got my second one when we had a booking up in Bangor, Maine. We wandered into a little music store up there, and I saw this Fairbanks White Lady banjo, a beautiful little instrument with a resonator on it that didn't reach out past the rim. When I asked about it, the man said, "The lady who owns it told me to sell it for $30." I didn't have much money with me, so I said, "Call her and tell her I'll give her $25 for it." He did, and she said okay, so I bought it for $25; now it's worth quite a bit of money. And that was my second banjo.

While I was at WLW in Cincinnati, the Williams boys were singing there—Andy Williams and his brothers and his dad (Andy was just a little fellow then). They showed me a banjo that their aunt had taken as payment for a board bill; it was a Bacon and Day Silver Bell, and they wanted $40 for it. I bought it, and later found a letter in the case indicating that the banjo had once been owned by Homer Davenport. Homer was one of the great Tennessee banjo players who recorded a strange bluegrass type of picking way back in the early 1920s when he was with a Chattanooga band called the Young Brothers. He hurt his arm in a train accident, and later moved to Iowa, where he was on radio for years (he played a famous version of "Sweet Bunch of Daisies"). I never learned what happened to Homer, but I do like to think I know what happened to his famous banjo. That was my banjo number three.

When I went overseas, I took my little green Gibson guitar but no banjo. After I had commented, on an Armed Forces Network broadcast, that one tune would sure sound good on a banjo, a boy from England brought me one he had liberated from Special Services. That was my fourth. In the next couple of years, someone from the Vega company, who saw a picture of me holding it, wrote and said, "We believe that you have one of our 'Little

Wonders,' and we would like to make you a better banjo." They did, and put my name in the neck of it. That was the fifth banjo I had.

I don't remember the model of the Vega with my name on it, but it was a better banjo than the Little Wonder. I played it so much in the late 1940s, when I had several banjo hits like "Mountain Dew" and "Rattler," that I wore it down in the neck; I sent it back to the company for repair, and while it was there, they had a robbery at the factory, and someone stole that banjo. I haven't seen it since, but it's got my name on it, and I don't suppose it would be all that easy to pawn.

The Vega company said, "Well, we'll make you another one." They did, and they shipped it, but while it was in the railroad station, the whole station burned down and the banjo went with it. I never even saw that one. So I told them to try again; I was beginning to think my connection with Vega was jinxed. When they finally did get one to me, I never did think too much of it; I figured I had better make my peace, though. Then one night I heard Sonny Osborne, and afterward he said, "Let me show you the banjo Vega sent me." It was one of the new Pro-Two's (I think that was the name), and that was a really good banjo. But the whole thing made me as mad as fire, and I called a fellow named Bill at the Vega factory in Boston and told him, "Why can't you send me a really good banjo, one of those Pro-Two banjos?" He said, "Okay, the next one that comes off the line is yours." I used that one a long time, then finally bought this one that I've got from Vega, and it's the best I've ever had for stage work. It's called a V.I.P. Later on, after Martin got to making it, I bought one for my boy Mark. Recently, Bill saw me playing the V.I.P. on *Hee Haw* and wrote me, "If you'll send that back to us, we'll gold-plate it free of charge." I did, and they did, and it still rings loud and clear; I can hear myself over the amplified bass or guitar or drummer or whatever else I do battle with.

OLD MAN BANJO

Look at Old Man Banjo a-restin' in his case.
It seems that I can see him smile,
But he ain't got no face,

I guess he's proud of what he's done
Throughout these many years,
For he's played through smiles,
Through joys and sorrows,
And he's played through bitter tears.
Why, I remember years ago
When he was in the store,
Every single time I passed,
I wanted him more and more.
Then came the time I had the price,
It was a happy day,
When I carried him from the store back home,
And he rared back to sound his A.
He even helped me court my gal—
Now that seems strange but true,
I think he helped an awful lot
To get her to say, "I do."
I've been with him to play for kids
Who laughed and danced with glee;
We've also played for some
Who had eyes but could not see,
Whose helpless arms and legs lay still,
But their little face was gay,
When Old Man Banjo came out of his case
And rared back to sound his A.
I've been with Old Man Banjo
To lands across the sea,
Where our boys were fighting bravely
For the cause of liberty.
Bullets whined up overhead
Beneath a sky of gray,
But there were smiles when Old Man Banjo
Rared back to sound his A.
Some of the boys didn't get back
Their mothers since told me so,
They said Old Man Banjo cheered them up
And that's sure good to know.

Said the tunes brought back home to them
From oh so far away
When Old Man Banjo, good and loud,
Rared back to sound his A.
Now I've been with Old Man Banjo
Since many years ago,
He helped find a nursing home
For a helpless old lady I know.
I guess Old Man Banjo has a right
To be proud as he can be,
For he's done a lot of good things
Since we joined up, him and me,
And I guess when old St. Peter calls,
And I walk in, what I'll see—
In the angel band, Old Man Banjo
Will rare back and sound his A.

If you don't watch it, you can even wear out not only your instruments
but *yourself* in the music business; I've known a few who did. You can replace
a car or a banjo, but it's not so easy to get a trade-in on a new heart or a new
kidney. I'm an expert on the heart matter, and I've got the scars of two
open-heart surgeries to prove it. My heart trouble started back around 1949 or
1950, when Connie B. Gay was booking us on a lot of dates, including that
whole string for International Harvester. We'd do an afternoon radio show
on WARL in Arlington with Connie, then take off for one of these dates on
the Eastern Shore of Maryland. We had to ride the ferry over, and after the
show we'd rush back, hoping to make the last ferry; if we didn't get there by
eleven o'clock, it would be closed down. Many and many a night we didn't
make it and had to sleep there on those benches, waiting for the ferry to start
up at five in the morning. That meant we wouldn't get home until nine
o'clock. We'd sleep a few hours, then get up and have to do that afternoon
show, and the whole cycle would start again.

The first time I ever knew anything was wrong with me was about this
time. I got to feeling rough, and a doctor up there told me, "You've got a little
heart trouble." I thought he was crazy, for I never had had any heart trouble,
and I was only a little over 40 at the time. "Well, I've got to play these dates,"

I said, and he said, "No, you don't play those dates. You stay at home. Get somebody else to play them." That sort of put us in a bind, but I got Jackie Phelps to do it, and he worked out fine. He said the show was so fast that if anybody missed a note or said the wrong word, somebody'd get killed. Jackie did so well, though, that we later worked together on the road.

I rested for a while and got better, and almost forgot about it until 1971. Then I got to feeling bad again and went to the hospital, and the doctor told me I needed to have an arteriogram. I didn't even know what that was, but I said okay, and they came in the next day and told me that two of the arteries around my heart were stopped up. The heart specialist at St. Thomas in Nashville was Dr. William S. Stoney, and he was recommended to do the open-heart surgery. He told me, "I'll have to take some veins out of your legs." I said, "What am I going to do without those veins?" "Well, you'll grow some more in no time." That was good to know, I thought. And he was right; it didn't hurt my legs any, and I can walk all day now. I came through the surgery fine, and I did all the exercises and diet they recommended—down to the last detail—and wore out the arm of a couch lying around and doing nothing for a while. But then I asked Dr. Stoney if I could do my shots on *Hee Haw,* and he said, "You can go down there for an hour and a half or two hours, and no more." It was the last day of the season's taping, and I drove down in the car alone (which I wasn't supposed to do) and stayed all day and did all of my material for the entire 13 shows.

I felt good again and was soon back on the road—until 1979. I was playing a date in Wisconsin when I started to get sick. Everybody in the band was worried about me, and said later they figured I would pass out right on the stage. I didn't, and I made it through that show, but I had to fly home while the rest of the band came down in the car. I went right to the hospital, since by then I was getting to know what this particular discomfort meant.

This time heart surgery was almost routine, and when they took the arteriogram, I watched it on TV. It's sort of sobering to watch that tube going up there and right into your heart; then they let loose this dye, and you can see where the arteries are stopped up. They found that the two they had put in were plugged and also two more, so I had to have a four-bypass surgery. I was a little nervous about this one, but I sailed through it again. It seems like the second one wasn't as bad as the first; I've watched my diet and followed orders and walked several miles a day, and I feel good.

You even wear out sidemen. If I were to have a reunion of all the boys who have played in my bands over the years, I'd be able to start my own Grand Ole Opry. And there'd be some good names in there, too, all the way from a young boy named Roy Clark to guitar greats Mose Rager and Billy Grammer; there'd be some of the people who have backed me on records: Merle, of course; Jethro Burns and his jazz mandolin; Tommy Jackson, the best of all the session fiddlers; Chet Atkins, who played guitar on all my Victor sessions; Ray Edenton, the best session rhythm guitar player around; and lots more.

My current band has been with me about as long as any, and they do the Opry shows as well as the road dates. Joe Carroll, who plays electric lead guitar, is a Virginia boy I've known since my Washington days. He replaced a boy named Doyle Dykes, a guitar player and singer who left us to devote full time to church work. Joe was a barber for years before he moved down to Nashville to work full time for me. (I have a theory that barbers, musicians, preachers, and crooks are all cut from the same mold but turned differently; I've known a lot of musicians who came from barbering, or went into barbering, or into preaching; I think there's just a hair's difference in the creative drive that separates the four.) My bass player is George McCormick, whom I met on the Opry several years back. George is an easygoing guy who likes to joke; he spent several years with Porter Wagoner, and before that he made records under his own name for several labels.

Some things don't wear out so easily, though. Take my old high-top boots—they were 50 years old when Bradley Kincaid gave them to me, and that was in 1935. I don't know how many times I've had them resoled, but they keep going on. And old songs—I still do songs that I did back when I first started out, and the people still seem to like them. Occasionally I will pick up a new one like "They Baptised Jessie Taylor" or "Neighbors" or "Applejack" (Dolly Parton's song; I first sang that one on her record of it). But I do a lot of traditional songs like "Pretty Little Pink" and "The Kicking Mule" and "Cindy" and "Rose Donelly" and "The Hills of Roane County," in addition to my old standbys "Rattler" and "Mountain Dew." In the 1970s I recorded four double albums for the CMH label in California, and nearly all the songs were old ones. I liked those albums especially because the whole family got involved: Ramona did several fiddle tunes as well as mandolin pieces; Mark did some old claw-hammer banjo tunes; Alisa sang and played hammered dulcimer; Marsha played the autoharp; and Eloise contributed some vocals. These albums are a long way from the slick, modern, pop-sounding albums coming out of Nashville today, but they represent what we call true old-time country music. Even though people continue to send me new songs every day—I have literally a bushel basket full of the cassettes—I still like to go back and find old songs and dress them up for a new audience to enjoy.

It was getting on toward eight o'clock, and I was coming into Mountain View. The all-night cafe was still open at the junction, but I decided to press on. I started up the hill by the Ozark Folk Center and looked up the road at our Dinner Theater. It was built in 1980 on the five acres I had bought for Gordon; Ramona had a gift shop there for a while, and then we decided to expand it to a theater. We can serve 300 people, feed them a good country meal, and give them a good music show to boot, all for one price. When I'm in town, I always perform there, and Mark and Alisa and Ramona hold down the fort when I'm gone. But tonight was the off season, and the theater looked peaceful and deserted.

A few minutes later I crossed the river and started up the ridge. I drove slowly, looking for my new road cut in through the trees, and finally saw it. The road was still a little rough, but more and more people were building down along it, including Mark and Alisa. I eased the big car on down and pulled into our back yard. The moon was out, and after I cut the motor I sat and listened to the wind through the trees. It was good to be home.

Biographical Notes

ALESHIRE, LENNY, although not recognized by many country fans today, enjoyed a long and successful career as a comedian, novelty musician, and songwriter. In 1917, when he was a teenager, he lost three fingers of his right hand in a saw accident but was still able to master a bewildering variety of traditional and novelty instruments. He made his show business reputation with the vaudeville team of the Weaver Brothers and Elviry, touring from coast to coast with them in the late 1920s. After his stint with Grandpa in West Virginia, he returned to his native Missouri, where he performed frequently on Springfield radio stations, often as part of the comedy team of Lenny and Goo-Goo. Today he is retired and lives in southwest Missouri.

THE BAILES BROTHERS, originally four brothers from West Virginia, developed into one of the most popular radio acts in postwar country music. They specialized in gospel or sentimental songs, such as "Dust on the Bible" and "The Drunkard's Grave," and were among the leading stars on the Opry from 1942 to 1948, when they moved to the *Louisiana Hayride.* The act broke up in 1949, when two of the brothers entered the ministry, although various combinations of the group are still active today.

CAMPBELL, ALEX and OLA BELL, pioneered the promotion of folk, bluegrass, and country music in Pennsylvania and the Northeast. Their Sunset Park establishment became one of the nation's leading forums for such music, and their own albums on the Starday label were well received by bluegrass and country fans. They are well thought of by musicians around the country, and still active in performing and promotion.

CAMPBELL, ARCHIE, is one of the major writers and stars of the television series *Hee Haw.* He began his career playing a radio character called "Grandpappy" on Knoxville, Tennessee stations, and moved into television and the Grand Ole Opry in the 1950s. His comedy hits have been in large part derived from his ability to use spoonerisms to retell old folk tales, such as "Rindercella" and "Beeping Sleauty."

CAPLINGER, WARREN, was a West Virginia native who came to Tennessee in the late 1920 to put together string bands; with Andy Patterson, he recorded widely, often using the name Caplinger's Cumberland Mountain Entertainers. In the 1930s, he turned to gospel music and renamed the group Cap, Andy, and Flip; this group was very popular on West Virginia radio, but is not widely known by modern fans because they tried to record on their own record label at a time when major companies ruled the market. Though he was a gifted singer and composer, Caplinger's reputation during his time was more that of a promoter.

COPAS, COWBOY, whose real name was Lloyd Copas, was an authentic Oklahoma cowboy who got his start in show business touring with an Indian fiddler named Natchee. He soon established himself as a radio star in his own right, working dozens of stations, as well as the *Boone County Jamboree* over WLW Cincinnati. By 1946 he was one of the biggest country stars in the nation, having hits with "Filipino Baby," "Gone and Left Me Blues," and Grandpa's "Tragic Romance." He was featured vocalist with Pee Wee King during the time King popularized "Tennessee Waltz," and he remained popular through the 1950s. His career was cut short in a plane crash in 1963, a crash which also took the lives of Patsy Cline and Hawkshaw Hawkins.

COUSIN EMMY, whose real name was Cynthia May Carver, was a skilled comedienne and instrumentalist whose work delighted radio fans across the country in the late 1930s and early 1940s. Though she could play as many as 15 instruments, including the handsaw, she was best known for her frailing banjo tunes and exuberant vocals on favorites like "Ruby" and "Bowling Green." She was one of the first commercial country stars to be documented by folklorists when she was recorded by Alan Lomax in 1947, and in the 1960s she made a brief comeback with a young folk revival group, the New Lost City Ramblers. Cousin Emmy died in Los Angeles in 1980 at the age of 77.

CROSS, HUGH, was a native of Oliver Springs, Tennessee, who first won fame on a series of sentimental records made for Columbia in the late 1920s; his duet with Riley Puckett on "Red River Valley" was the first popular recording of that classic. He also worked with the popular band, the Skillet Lickers, and for several years did duet work with his wife. He became a member of WLS Chicago's *National Barn Dance* in the early 1930s, and then teamed with Shug Fisher to form an enduring radio act called Hugh and Shug's Radio Pals. Singing in a light tenor voice, he continued to favor sentimental and novelty songs throughout his career. He later went into announcing and died in the mid-1960s.

THE DELMORE BROTHERS, Alton and Rabon, were two Alabama boys who had a substantial impact on country duet singing, guitar playing, and songwriting. Coming from a background that included rural church singing schools and gospel quartets, the brothers made their initial reputation on WSM's *Grand Ole Opry* in the 1930s, before moving on to other radio work that included WLW in Cincinnati, where they met Grandpa and Merle Travis and became part of the famed gospel quartet, the Brown's Ferry Four. After World War II, the quartet continued to make records, though not to perform together; the Delmores experienced a resurgence of their career with hit recordings like "Blues Stay Away from Me" and "Freight Train Boogie," which are today considered forerunners of rock-and-roll. Rabon, the younger brother, died in 1952, and Alton continued to work as a songwriter and to write his autobiography, as well as short stories, until his death in 1964. In 1971, on the strength of country music standards like "Brown's Ferry Blues," "Gonna Lay Down My Old Guitar," and "Southern Moon," the Delmores were elected to the Songwriters Hall of Fame.

GRAMMER, BILLY, a long-time friend of Grandpa's and member of the Grand Ole Opry since 1959, is recognized as one of the nation's premier guitar players and guitar designers. Son of an Illinois coal miner, he made his reputation in the late 1940s and early 1950s playing in and around the Washington, D.C., area, as well as doing extensive record work; he was a mainstay of the King studio staff, and would be flown from Washington to Cincinnati just to play on important recording sessions, including several of Grandpa's. For several years he was on national television programs with Jimmy Dean, but in 1958 he signed with Fred Foster's new Nashville label, Monument, and had a big hit record with "Gotta Travel On," which won him a gold record and a spot on the Opry. He has had several hit records since then, and in 1979 returned to playing the acoustic guitar, making him one of the few Opry regulars who prefer that instrument.

HALL, WENDELL, known as "the Red-Headed Music Maker," was a vaudeville entertainer from Kansas who was very popular on records and radio in the 1920s. Accompanying himself on the ukeleke and singing hit songs like "It Ain't Gonna Rain No More," he became nationally popular in 1923, and though he was not really a country singer, he appealed to a wide audience in the South and Midwest. He began directing and promoting shows in the 1930s and continued to be active in the music business until his death in Alabama in 1969.

KINCAID, BRADLEY, one of Grandpa's oldest friends and most important teachers, reigned for years as country music's most popular radio singer. Drawing on his genuine folk background in Kentucky, Kincaid used his trained tenor voice to develop a pleasant, nonnasal singing style that appealed not only to southerners but to midwesterners and even New Englanders as well; in fact, he spent much of his career working out of New

England and New York state, and became one of the first southern country singers to work successfully in the North. Though his audiences loved novelty songs like "The Little Shirt My Mother Made for Me," Bradley also popularized old folk ballads like "Barbara Allen," "Pearl Bryan," and "The House Carpenter." He recorded prolifically and was one of the first singers to issue his own songbooks. Later years saw him star on stations WLW (Cincinnati) and WSM (Nashville) before retiring to run a music store in Ohio.

KLICK, MARY, a singer and bass player who accompanied Grandpa and Ramona on their tour of Korea, was a native of east Tennessee and for several years a fixture on the Richmond *Old Dominion Barn Dance.* She enjoyed a brief career as a soloist for Columbia records in the early 1950s.

MAPHIS, JOE and ROSE, originally formed their husband and wife team in 1948 at Richmond's *Old Dominion Barn Dance* and found success as a duet act on the West Coast in the 1950s. Joe, a Virginia native who was an early and close friend of both Grandpa and Merle Travis, won fame as a superb guitarist (his work was heard on dozens of records by artists as divese as Ricky Nelson and Lefty Frizzell) as well as a songwriter ("Dim Lights, Thick Smoke, and Loud, Loud Music," a honky-tonk classic). Among his guitar pupils in the 1960s was (young) Barbara Mandrell. In later years Joe and Rose returned to Nashville, and appeared on several of Grandpa's CMH albums (see the discography).

NATHAN, SYD, the founder and owner of King Records in Cincinnati, is a major figure in the development of postwar popular music in America whose pioneering recording efforts overshadow the controversy that occasionally surrounded him. Born in Cincinnati in 1904, Nathan spent his youth as a dance band drummer and then drifted into a variety of jobs from radio to real estate. In 1939 he began a record distribution business in Cincinnati, and by 1943 he had decided to take advantage of the country talent that had gathered in the city to work on the popular *Boone County Jamboree.* After recording his initial sides by Grandpa Jones and Merle Travis, he set up his own pressing plant and was soon the leading independent record producer in the country. His country series was characterized by his willingness to let performers modernize the country sound by the use of electric instruments and drums; his "race" series was characterized by his willingness to record the newly developing rhythm-and-blues, which laid the cornerstone for rock-and-roll in the 1950s. All in all, Nathan was responsible for over 10,000 recordings of country, gospel, jazz, and rhythm-and-blues material, all during a time when American music was undergoing a crucial transition. He died in Florida in 1968.

PATTERSON, ANDY, was a Petros, Tennessee, native who is best known for his long partnership with Warren Caplinger, as part of the popular gospel team of Cap, Andy, and Flip. Primarily a guitar player, Andy could also hold his own with a fiddle, and performed with other east Tennessee musicians such as Luther McCartt (with whom he recorded the famous "Green Valley Waltz") and the Tennessee Ramblers, before he met Caplinger. Andy played an important role in preserving and transmitting the famous east Tennessee murder ballad, "The Hills of Roane County."

PHELPS, JACKIE, is another skilled Nashville guitarist, star of *Hee Haw* (especially in his classic eephing and hambone routines with the late Jimmie Riddle), and veteran studio sideman. He has been a regular with numerous Opry bands, including those of Roy Acuff and Bill Monroe, and has played both guitar and banjo on many of Grandpa's records.

STARCHER, BUDDY, a veteran West Virginia radio star, is best known today for such recitations as "Beyond the Sunset," "Day of Decision," and "History Repeats Itself." He won his reputation as a country balladeer and bandleader from 1933 to 1941, when he worked on several stations in his native West Virginia; after World War II he had several hit records, including "I'll Still Write Your Name in the Sand" and "Love Song of the Waterfall." His popularity hit one peak in 1949–51, when he recorded and worked out of Philadelphia for Columbia, and another in the mid-1960s, when his patriotic recitations struck a responsive chord with a Vietnam-weary audience.

SUNBROCK, LARRY, was a well-known promoter in the Midwest and Southeast who for years worked with Cowboy Copas and Natchee the Indian, as well as with fiddler Clayton McMichen. One of Sunbrock's favorite ploys was to go into a town, rent a hall, and stage a fake "fiddling contest" with Natchee or McMichen taking on all comers. By the 1940s he had graduated to more legitimate booking techniques and had become one of the nation's five leading bookers.

TROYAN, JOE, or "Bashful Harmonica Joe," is a Cleveland native who split his early efforts between harmonica playing and amateur baseball. He began working with Grandpa and Bradley Kincaid in the 1930s, then moved on to a partnership with a singer-guitarist named Pie Plant Pete. For years the pair was a fixture on Rochester, New York, radio and made dozens of records for the American Recording Company. A master of imitations and a fine raconteur as well as harmonica player, Joe today lives in Cleveland.

WISEMAN, LULU BELLE and SCOTTY, friends of Grandpa's since his Cincinnati days, were long-time stars of the WLS *National Barn Dance*. The Wisemans are remembered today as one of the country music's most popular husband-wife duos, and Scotty—a North Carolina native—as composer of country song standards like "Remember Me" and "Have I Told You Lately That I Love You," as well as cocomposer of Grandpa's famous "Mountain Dew." In the 1950s Scotty composed several other Grandpa Jones favorites, such as the topical "I'm No Communist." The Wisemans appeared in a number of Hollywood films and had their own TV show before they retired in 1958; then Scotty turned to college teaching, and Lulu Belle became a representative to the state legislature.

WORKMAN, SUNSHINE SUE, is best remembered by country fans for her early 1950s Decca recordings and her tenure as hostess of the *Old Dominion Barn Dance*. In reality, her career was much more complex and important than that. Coming from Iowa with her husband and manager, John Workman, Sunshine Sue became one of the first successful women bandleaders in country music; her instrument, the accordion, was unusual in country music, but she played it well, sang in a clear, high voice, and had a disarming personality that charmed listeners. Ramona, Grandpa's wife-to-be, joined Sunshine Sue in 1940, and in the next few years Sue's band, the Rock Creek Rangers, made its reputation over WLW in Cincinnati and WRVA in Richmond. Among the other sidemen in the band was guitarist Joe Maphis. Grandpa and Ramona worked with Sunshine Sue again in the early 1950s during their stint at the *Old Dominion Barn Dance*.

Grandpa Jones Discography

Compiled by Charles K. Wolfe

INTRODUCTION

The following discography attempts to chronicle all the commercial recordings made by Grandpa Jones from his recording debut in 1943 through 1983. Not included in this list are home recordings, radio air checks and transcriptions, tape recordings made by fans of concerts or radio shows, and recordings where Grandpa Jones performed only as a sideman. The discography lists only domestic recordings, not various reissued albums released in Canada, Germany, Japan, Sweden, Great Britain, Australia, and other countries. Many of the recordings listed here are out of print and unavailable except through rare record dealers.

Each entry follows a standard format. First, a headnote gives the place and date of the recording session, as well as the personnel and instrumentation. Next, the song entry starts with a number, this is the *master number* or *matrix number* (mx.) assigned by the record company at the time of the session to identify this particular recording within the company's archives (some are unknown). Next is listed the title of the recording, followed in parentheses by the composer credits (cc), as shown on the original label or in the record company's files. The numbers that follow are the various *release numbers* of the recording, or the catalogue numbers assigned to records or albums pressed by the company for commercial distribution. The first column of release numbers refers to *singles,* either 78 RPM or (after about 1952) 45 RPM. The second column (when present) refers to *EP releases:* "extended play" 45-RPM albums usually containing four songs. The third column (the numbers in italics) refers to *LP album releases;* any italic number denotes an LP issue. Popular recordings often appear on three, four, or even a dozen different LP editions. An LP released in 1982 might well contain recordings made as early as 1948 and originally issued on a 78- or 45-RPM record. A list of record label abbreviations used in the release numbers columns appears below.

This discography has been compiled from a variety of sources and with the help of a number of individuals. Dot Boyd, of RCA Victor's Nashville office, made heroic efforts to locate the original session sheets for Grandpa's recording on that label, assuring us that all personnel and dates are substantially accurate and complete. Sis Brewer did similar work for the sessions under the Monument Records label. The old King record files are inaccurate and incomplete; the material here was drawn from the King studio logbooks, and the personal recollections of Grandpa, Ramona, Merle Travis, Zeke Turner, Louis Innis, and Billy Grammer. Bob Pinson, Ronnie Pugh, and the staff at the Country Music Foundation Library in Nashville also helped in determining personnel, as did Robert K. Oermann, Ivan Tribe, and Rich Kienzle. Through the good offices of Richard Weize, I was also able to compare notes with German discographer Bernhard Vogt, who has independently been compiling a Grandpa discography that reflects the diverse international releases. To all of these people we are very grateful, as well as to the Faculty Research Committee at Middle Tennessee State University, which provided some of the funding necessary for this research.

Corrections and additions will be welcomed.

RECORD LABEL ABBREVIATIONS

ACE	Association of Country Entertainers (promotion record)
Cam	RCA Camden
CMH	CMH records
Col	Columbia
Dec	Decca

GJ	Grandpa Jones records
Gu	Gusto Records
Har	Harmony
HH	Hee Haw Records
Ki	King Records
MCA/C	MCA/Coral Records
Mon	Monument
Na	Nashville
PMR	Pine Mountain Records
PP	Power Pack
RCA	RCA Victor
RD	Reader's Digest
Sky	Skylite Records
St	Starday
Vi	RCA Victor
Voc	Vocalion
WBS	Warner Brothers

KING RECORDINGS

Dayton, Ohio, ca. Sept. 1943
Grandpa Jones, vocal and guitar; Merle Travis, vocal and guitar (as the Shepherd Brothers)

368-A	The Steppin' Out Kind (Merle Travis)	Ki 500
368-B	You'll Be Lonesome Too (Jones–Travis)	Ki 500

Cincinnati, ca. Feb. 1944
Grandpa Jones, vocal and guitar; Merle Travis, el. guitar; Ramona Jones, mandolin (-1)

1775	It's Raining Here This Morning (Jones)	Ki 502	Col 2668; PMR 214, St 3008; Ki 554, 1042.
1776	I'll Be Around If You Need Me (Jones)	Ki 502	
1780	Our Worlds Are Not the Same (Delmore)	Ki 524	Ki 967, 888
1781	Don't Sweet Talk Me (Jones)	Ki 517	
1782	Tears That Make Believe (Jones)	Ki 532	
1783	Why Did You Tell Me All Those Lies (Jones)	Unissued	

| 1785 | You Didn't Have to Leave Me All Alone (Jones) | | | Ki 888 |
| 1787 | I've Been All Around This World (-1) | Ki 524 | | Ki 1042 |

Cincinnati, ca. August 1944
Grandpa Jones, vocal and guitar; Billy Strickland, steel guitar

1900	Steppin' Out King (Travis)	Ki 513		
1901	You'll Be Lonesome Too (Jones–Travis)	Ki 513		Ki 554, 1042; St 3008
1902	East Bound Freight Train (Jones)	Ki 545		Ki 1042, 554; St 3008;
1903	I'll Never Lose That Loneliness for You (Jones)	Ki 508		Ki 888, 967
1906	There's a Grave in the Wave of the Ocean (Jones)	Ki 508		Ki 888
1907	You Done Me Mean and Dirty (Jones)	Ki 1301		Ki 967
1910	What Can I Do Without My Little Darling	Unissued		Ki 888, 994
1911	Maybe You'll Miss Me When I'm Gone (Delmore)	Ki 517		Ki 994

Hollywood, California, ca. March 1946   *Radio Recorders*
Grandpa Jones, Alton and Rabon Delmore, vocals; Merle Travis, vocal and guitar (as the Brown's Ferry Four)

| 1977 | Will the Circle Be Unbroken | Ki 530 | EP: Ki 320 | Ki 590, PMR 807, 943; 220, 250; St 3017 |
| 1978 | Just a Little Talk with Jesus (Derrick) | Ki 530 | EP: Ki 320 | Ki 590 PMR 250 |

Hollywood, California, ca. March 1946
Grandpa Jones, vocal and guitar; Merle Travis, el. guitar

1985	Eight More Miles to Louisville (Jones–Fine)	Ki 532		Ki 554, 1042; St 3008
1986	Darling Won't You Love Me Now (Jones)	Ki 575		Ki 888
1987	Are There Tears Behind Your Smiles (Jones)	Ki 587		Ki 888; Na 2069
1988	Get Things Ready for Me, Ma (Jones)	Ki 545		
1993	Ridin' on That Train (Jones)	Ki 587		Ki 967
1994	Heart Stealin' Mama (Jones–Travis)	Ki 575		Ki 967

Hollywood, California, ca. Sept. 1946
Grandpa Jones, vocal and guitar; Red Foley, vocal and bass; Alton and Rabon Delmore, vocal and guitars (as the Brown's Ferry Four)

| 2124 | Rockin' on the Waves (Sebren) | Ki 577 | EP Ki 320 | Ki 551; PMR |

				251, PMR 299
2125	If We Never Meet Again (Brumley)	Ki 577	EP Ki 237	*Ki 590; PMR 250; St SD-3017*
2126	I'll Fly Away (Brumley)	Ki 785	EP Ki 320	*Ki 551; PMR 251*
2127	The Lord is Watching Over Me (—)	Ki 631	EP Ki 238	*Ki 590, 943; PMR 220; St SD-3017; PMR 250, 299*
2128	Everybody Will Be Happy Over There (—)	Ki 631		*Ki 590, 943; PMR 220, 250, 299; St SD-3017*
2129	Hallelujah Morning (A. Delmore–Lanman)	Ki 750		*Ki 590, 943; PMR 220, PMR 250, PMR 299*
2130	Old Camp Meeting (L. M. Jones)	Ki 593	EP Ki 237	*Ki 551; PMR 251*
2131	There's a Light Guiding Me (Newton–Foley)	Ki 593	EP Ki 238	*Ki 943; PMR 220, PMR 251*
2132	Salvation Has Been Brought Down (—)	Ki 662	EP Ki 238	*Ki 551; PMR 251*
2133	When the Good Lord Cares (A. Delmore)	Ki 662		*Ki 590, Ki 943; St SD-3017; PMR 220, PMR 250*
2134	Over in Glory Land (Lou Ferden)	Ki 799		*Ki 590, Ki 943; St SD-3017; PMR 220, 250, 299*
2135	On the Jericho Road (D. McCrossan)	Ki 832		*Ki 832, Ki 943; PMR 220, 251*

Chicago, 2 Dec. 1946
Grandpa Jones, vocal and guitar; Zeb Turner, el. guitar, Red Foley, bass

2265	Call Me Darling Once Again (B. Stewart)	Ki 644		*Ki 888*

2266	Get Back on the Glory Road (Louis Jones)	Ki 601		Ki 822
2267	Alimony Trouble (Rex Griffin)	Ki 644		
2268	She's Gone and Left Another Broken Heart (Louis M. Jones)	Ki 601		Ki 888; Na 2069

Nashville, 28 March 1947
Grandpa Jones, vocal, guitar or banjo; Ramona Jones, bass; prob. Slim Idaho, steel guitar; Marshall Barnes, guitar; Red Herron, fiddle; Homer Haynes, guitar; Jethro Burns, mandolin; Hank Garland, guitar

2426	Weary Lonesome Me (Travis)	Ki 812		Ki 845
2427	My Darling's Not My Darling Any More (L. M. Jones–White)	Ki 624		Ki 888; Na 2069
2428	Mountain Maw (Fowler–Wilkins)	Ki 668		Ki 845, 1042

[NOTE: Mx. 2429–32 by Cowboy Copas.]

2433	There's a Hole in the Ground (Jones–Kinsey–Fowler)	Ki 1097		St 3008
2434	144 Thousand Were There (Fred Rose)	Ki 747		Ki 807, Ki 832, Ki 556
2435	Mountain Dew (Wiseman–Lunsford)	Ki 624, Ki 5867	EP Ki 223, St SEP 196	Ki 1027, KSD 1042; St 181, St SD-3017; Na 2069; St 452; Col CL-2668; St SD-3008, St SYS-6401; Col CS-9468; St SLP 164; PMR 214
2436	Going Down the Country (Jones–Scott)	Ki 685		Ki 845
2437	New Pins and Needles (Jones–Jenkins)	Ki 685		Ki 845

Nashville, ca. Sept. 1947
Grandpa Jones, vocal and banjo; Cowboy Copas, guitar and vocal effects; Ramona Jones, bass

2545	Old Rattler (—)	Ki 668	Ki 5867	Ki 537, Ki 554, Ki 1042,
			St 111	St 191, St 242; PMR 301,
			EP Ki 223	PP 301; Na 2097; St 3008;

Gu GT 001,
Gu 5028;
Na 2079

Grandpa Jones and Cowboy Copas, vocals; prob. Red Herron, fiddle; Marshall Barnes, bass;
Hank Garland, el. guitar; Slim Idaho, steel guitar

2546	Move It On Over	Ki 665	

Nashville, ca. Oct. 1947
Grandpa Jones, vocal; Alton and Rabon Delmore, vocals; Merle Travis, vocal and guitar (as
the Brown's Ferry Four)

2600	On the Jericho Road (McCrossan)	Unissued		
2601	His Boundless Love (Presley)	Ki 760		*Ki 551, 943;* *PMR 220,* *251*
2602	Rock of Ages Hide Thou Me (Hultsman)	Ki 700	EP Ki 238	*Ki 551, 943;* *PMR 220,* *251, 299*
2603	When He Blessed My Soul (Derricks)	Ki 780		*Ki 590, PMR* *250, 251*
2604	I've Got the Old Time Religion in My Heart (Milsap)	Ki 760		*Ki 551, PMR* *250*
2605	I'm Naturalized for Heaven (McCoy–Pace)	Ki 832		*Ki 590, PMR* *251*
2606	When He Calls His Reapers (Presley)	Ki 933		*Ki 590; PMR* *251*
2607	I've Made a Covenant with My Lord (Arnold)	Ki 738	Ki EP 237	*Ki 551; PMR* *250*
2608	Throne Eternal (Brumley)	Ki 933		*Ki 590; PMR* *250*
2609	After the Sunrise (Baxter–Wright)	Ki 799		*Ki 590; PMR* *251*
2610	I'll Meet You in the Morning (Brumley)	Ki 854		*Ki 590; PMR* *250*
2611	Jesus Hold My Hand (Brumley)	Ki 854		*Ki 590, 943;* *PMR 220, 251*
2612	Keep On The Firing Line (—)	Ki 700	Ki EP 237	*Ki 551, 943;* *PMR 220, 250*

Nashville, ca. Oct. 1947
Grandpa Jones, vocal and guitar; Merle Travis, ele. gtr.; Louis Innis, bass

2613	I'm On My Way Somewhere (Jones)	Ki 717	
2614	That Depot In The Sky (Jones)	Ki 747	*Ki 822, Ki 967*
2615	You'll Make Our Shack a Mansion (Jones–Marshall)	Ki 794	*Ki 967*
2616	I Ain't Got Much to Lose (McDuffee)	Ki 794	*Ki 845*

Cincinnati, ca. Nov. 1947
Grandpa Jones, vocal, guitar, and banjo; Alton and Rabon Delmore, vocal and guitars;
Wayne Raney and Lonnie Glosson, harmonica and vocal effects; Ernest Ferguson, mandolin;
Ramona Jones, vocal and bass; Zeke Turner, electric guitar

2645	Tragic Romance (Jones)		*Ki 888, Ki 994*
2646	Come Be My Rainbow (Jones)	*Ki 1301*	*Ki 967*
2647	I Guess You Don't Remember Me (Jones)	*Ki 733*	*Ki 845*
2648	You Never Can Be Mine (—)		*Ki 888*
2649	My Old Red River Home (—)	*Ki 740*	*Ki 809, 871, 969; Na 2069; St 3008; PP 301*
2650	Due to the Shortage (Louis Jones)	Unissued	
2651	Kitty Clyde (—)	*Ki 772*	*Ki 845*
2652	Old Rattler's Treed Again (Louis M. Jones)	*Ki 733*	*Ki 697; PP 301; Na 2097; St 3008*

[NOTE: Mx. 2653–56 by Delmore Brothers]

2657	Darby's Ram (—)	*Ki 708*	*Ki 809, 967*
2659	Take It On Out the Door (Neely–Jones–Kirby)	*Ki 708*	*Ki 809, 967*

Cincinnati, ca. Dec. 1947
Grandpa Jones, vocal, guitar, or banjo; Ramona Jones, harmony vocal and bass; Louis Innis,
rhythm guitar and harmony vocal; Jerry Byrd, steel guitar and harmony vocal

2793	Daisy Dean (Louis M. Jones)	*Ki 834*	*Ki 809, 967; St SR 200*
2794	How Many Biscuits Can You Eat? (trad.)	*Ki 740*	*Ki 809, 967; St SR 201; Na 2097; PP 301*
2795	You've Come Back to Me (trad.)	*Ki 5489*	*Ki 809, 909; St SR 202*
2796	Are You From Dixie? (Cobb–Yellen)	*Ki 847*	*Ki 554; St 3008; Ki 847*
2797	I Often Wonder Why You Changed Your Mind (Jones)	*Ki 694*	*Ki 809, 967*
2798	I'm My Own Grandpa (Lathan–Jaffe)	*Ki 694*	*Ki 554; St 3008*
2799	Going Down Town (Jones)	*Ki 772*	*Ki 809, 967; Na 2069*

2800	Our Fathers Had Religion (Jones–Miller)	Ki 875		Ki 822
2801	I'm Tying the Leaves So They Won't Come Down (Jones)			Ki 888, 967
2802	Jonah and the Whale (trad.)	Unissued		
2803	The Bald Headed End of the Broom (trad.)	Ki 717		Ki 809, 967; St 1042; PP 301
2804	Jesse James (arr. Jones)	Ki 847		Ki 845

Cincinnati, 15 April 1949
Grandpa Jones, vocal, guitar, and banjo; Ramona Jones, harmony vocal; Tommy Jackson, fiddle; Zeke Turner, el. lead guitar; Louis Innis, rhythm guitar or bass; Jerry Byrd, steel guitar

2884	Jonah and the Whale (trad.)	Ki 815		Ki 822; PMR 222; St 3008
2885	Light in His Soul (Miller–Jones)	Ki 1097		Ki 822
2886	My Little Nagging Wife (Kinsey–Jones)	Ki 834		Ki 809, 969; Na 2069
2887	Grandpa's Boogie (Jones)	Ki 812		Ki 554; St 3008

Cincinnati, 4 Nov. 1949
Grandpa Jones, vocal and banjo; Cowboy Copas, vocal and guitar; prob. Red Herron, fiddle; Hank Garland, el. guitar; Wayne Raney, harmonica; Jerry Byrd, steel guitar

| 2954 | Mule Train (Lango–Heath–Lickman) | Ki 835 | | Ki 809 |
| 2995 | The Feudin' Boogie (Bernard–Schroder) | Ki 835 | | Ki 844, 967; PP 301; NA 2097 |

Cincinnati, 10 April 1950
Grandpa Jones, vocal and banjo; Ramona Jones, fiddle and vocal; Billy Grammer, lead el. guitar; Jackie Phelps, rhythm guitar and bluegrass banjo; Ernest Ferguson, mandolin; others unknown

3012	Uncle Eph's Got the Coon (Jones)	Ki 867		Ki 554, 813, 1006, 1042; Na 2097; St 3008
3013	Dark as a Dungeon (Jones)	Ki 896		Ki 823
3014	Come and Dine (Widemeyer–Bolton)	Ki 896		Ki 822
3015	Stay in the Wagonyard (Jones)	Ki 912		Ki 625; Na 2069
3016	Grandpa's Getting Married Again (King–Douglas–Arend)	Ki 890		Ki 625
3017	Melinda (Joe Maphis)	Ki 912		Ki 625, 1042

| 3018 | I Don't Know Gee From Haw (Pop Eckler) | Ki 890 | | *Ki 625; Na 2069* |
| 3019 | Five String Banjo Boogie (Jones) | Ki 867 | | *Ki 625* |

Cincinnati, 17 Dec. 1950
Grandpa Jones, banjo and vocals; Ramona Jones, vocal and bass; Billy Grammer, el. lead guitar; Tommy Jackson, fiddle; Jerry Bryd, steel guitar; possibly Jackie Phelps, guitar and banjo

3136	Chicken Don't Roost Too High (R. Jones–L. Jones)	Ki 976	Ki EP 407	*Ki 809; Na 2069; Ki 967*
3137	The Golden Rocket (H. Snow)	Ki 930		*Ki 809*
3138	What'll I Do with the Baby-O (R. Jones–L. Jones)	Ki 976		*Ki 625, 1042*
3139	Trouble, Trouble, Trouble (R. Jones–L. Jones)	Ki 934		*Ki 888*
3140	Send in Your Name and Address (Workman–Foots–Stotes)	Ki 934		*Ki 554*
3141	Jennie, Get Your Hoe Cakes Done (R. Jones–L. Jones)	Ki 930		*Ki 625, 845; PP 301; Na 2097*
3142	I'm Hog Wild Crazy Over You (Foots–Stotz)	Ki 948		*Ki 845*
3143	Nobody Loves Me Anymore (Wheeler)	Ki 948		

Cincinnati, 15 Aug. 1951
Grandpa Jones, banjo and vocals; Ramona Jones, vocals, bass, mandolin; members of Shorty Long band, unidentified; pro. Joe Wheeler, guitar

3224	You Done Me Mean and Hateful (Eloise Riggins)	Ki 1029		*Ki 621, 967*
3225	Fifteen Cents Is All I Got (Eloise Riggins)	Ki 1069	Ki EP 223	*Ki 726, 1042; PP 301; Na 2097; Ki 554; St 3008*
3226	Happy Little Home in Arkansas (Eloise Riggins)	Ki 992		*Ki 869, 947*
3227	The Rain Is Still Falling (Glover–Mann–Riggins)	Ki 992		*Ki 625*

Cincinnati, 28 Oct. 1951
Grandpa Jones, vocals; Red Turner, vocal and mandolin; Alton Delmore, vocal and guitar; Rabon Delmore, vocal and guitar (as: The Brown's Ferry Four)

| 3274 | The Judgement Day (A. Delmore) | Unissued | | |
| 3275 | There's a Page in the Bible (A. Delmore) | Ki 1059 | | *Ki 590, 943; PMR 220, PMR 251* |

3276	We Should Walk Together (A. Delmore)	Ki 1059	Ki 590; PMR 250
3277	I Am a Weary Pilgrim (A. Delmore)	Ki 1032	Ki 943; PMR 220
3278	Heaven Eternal for Me (Jones)	Ki 1032	Ki 922, 943; PMR 220, PMR 22; St 3017
3279	I'm Travelling Home (A. Delmore)	Unissued	

Cincinnati, 29 Oct. 1951
Grandpa Jones, vocal and banjo; Ramona Jones, vocal and bass; Louis Innis, guitar and harmony vocal; Jerry Byrd, steel guitar and harmony vocal; Jackie Phelps, guitar; Tommy Jackson, fiddle

3280	Time, Time, Time, Time (Eloise Riggins)	Ki 1061	Ki 809, 907, 1042
3281	Fix Me a Pallet (Jolly Joe Parish)	Ki 1069	Ki 625
3282	Down in Dixie (Where They Say 'You All') (Jones–Coley–Wilson)	Ki 1061	Ki 625
3283	That Memphis Train (Delmore–Jones)	Ki 1029	Ki 697; Na 2097; PP 301; Ki 869

RCA VICTOR RECORDINGS

Nashville, 10 Jan. 1952, Brown Radio Production, 1:30–5:30 P.M.
Grandpa Jones, banjo and leader; Eddie Hill, guitar; Chet Atkins, el. guitar; Ernie Newton, bass; Tommy Jackson, fiddle; Ramona Jones, vocal and mandolin

E2-VB-5030-1, 1A	Stop That Ticklin' Me (Mapis)	Vi 20(47)-4660	
E2-VB-5031-1, 1A	Mountain Laurel (Childton Price)	Vi 20(47)-4505	
E2-VB-5032-1, 1A	Retreat (Cries My Heart) (Boyer–Fransworth–Furtado)	Vi 20(47)-4505	RCA SPD-3
E2-VB-5033-1, 1A	T.V. Blues (Ruby Wheeler)	Vi 20(47)-4660	

Nashville, 20 May 1952, Brown Radio Production, 9:30 A.M.–12:30 P.M.
Grandpa Jones, leader, banjo, vocal; Chet Atkins, guitar; Henry "Homer" Haynes, guitar; Kenneth "Jethro" Burns, mandolin; Tommy Jackson, fiddle; Ernie Newton, bass

E2-VB-6286-1,	I'm No Communist (Scotty Wieman)	Vi 20(47)-	

	1A			4771	
E2-VB-	Sass-A-Frass (Swafford–Villines)	Vi	Cam
6287-1,			20(47)-	ADL2-
1A			4956	0701e
E2-VB-	The Closer to the Bone (The Sweeter is the	Vi	RD 678ES19
6288-1,	Meat) (Louis M. Jones)	20(47)-
1A			4956
E2-VB-	Pickin' on Me (Cy Cohen)	Vi	RCA SPD-3
6289-1,			20(47)-
1A			4771

Nashville, 16 Oct. 1952, Brown Radio Production, 9 A.M.–12 noon
Grandpa Jones, leader, vocal, banjo; Henry Haynes, guitar; Chet Atkins, guitar; Kenneth Burns, mandolin; Tommy Jackson, fiddle; Jerry Byrd, steel guitar; Charlie Green: bass

E2-VB-	Bread and Gravy (Latham, Raff, Jaffe)	Vi	
7635-1,		20(47)-
1A		5234
E2-VB-	Dear Old Sunny South by the Sea	Vi
7636-1,	(Rodgers–Cozzens)	20(47)-
1A		5113
E2-VB-	Pap's Corn Likker Still (Jones)	Vi	Cam
7637-1,		20(47)-	ADL2-
1A		5234	0701e
E2-VB-	Old Rattler's Son (Jones)	Vi	Cam
7638-1,		20(47)-	ADL2-
1A		5113	0701e;
			RCA
			SPD-3

Nashville, 16 May 1953, Thomas Studio, 1 P.M.–4 P.M.
Grandpa Jones, banjo, vocal; Chet Atkins, guitar; Eddie Hill, guitar; Jerry Byrd, steel guitar; Thomas Jackson, fiddle; Ramona Jones, bass

E3-VB-	You Aint' Seen Nothing Yet (Grandpa	Vi	Cam
0635-1,	Jones)	20(47)-	ADL2-
1A		5357	0701e
E3-VB-	You're Never Too Old for Love (Cy	Vi
0636-1,	Cohen)	20(47)-
1A		5357

Nashville, 9 Sept. 1953, Thomas Studio
Grandpa Jones, vocal, banjo, guitar; Louis Innis, guitar; Tommy Jackson, fiddle; Jerry Byrd, steel guitar; Chet Atkins, el. guitar

E3-VB-	My Heart Is Like a Train (Lee–Welch)	Vi	Cam
19590-		20(47)-	ADL2-
1, 1A		5475	0701e

E3-VB-1960-1, 1A	Some More Mountain Dew (M. Wiseman–S. Wiseman	Vi 20(47)-5685	Cam ADL2-0701e
E3-VB-1961-1, 1A	That New Vitamine (S. Wiseman)	Vi 20(47)-5475	
E3-VB-1962-1, 1A*	Old Rattler	Vi 20(47)-5648	Cam CAL/CAS-689e; RCA 3192, 6015; Cam ADL2-0701e; RCA EPB-3192

*On 5/25/54, sound effects added to above and result given new mx. E4-VB-3454; this version appears on CAL/CAS-689, LPM-3192.

Nashville, 30 November 1953, Thomas Production, 2:00 P.M.–5:00 P.M.
Grandpa Jones, banjo, vocal; Tommy Jackson, fiddle; Ramona Jones, bass; Chet Atkins, guitar; Louis Innis, guitar; Claude J. Phelps, steel guitar

E3-VB-2664-1	You-All Come (Arlie Duff)	Vi 20(47)-5576	Cam ADL2-0701e
E3-VB-2665	The Trader (Nick Nicholas)	Vi 20(47)-5576	
E3-VB-2666	In the Future (Bryant–Barclay)	Vi 20(47)-6179	

Nashville, 18 Feb. 1954, Thomas Studios
Grandpa Jones, banjo, vocal; Ramona Jones, bass; Chet Atkins, guitar; Velma Smith, guitar; Hall Smith, fiddle; Odell McLeod, harmonica

E4-VB-3628-1	Standing in the Depot (Louis M. Jones)	Vi 20(47)-5789	Cam ADL2-0701
E4-VB-3629-1	Old Blue	Vi 20(47)-5685	RCA CPL20466
E4-VB-3630-1	High Silk Hat	Vi 20(47)-5789	

Nashville, 19 May 1954, Thomas Studio, 10:00 A.M.–1:00 P.M.
Ruby Wells and Grandpa Jones, vocals; Johnny Wright, guitar; Louis Innis, guitar; Grady Martin, guitar; Harold Jackson, steel guitar; Ernest Newton, bass; Murray Harmon, drums; Benny Martin, fiddle

E4-VB- 4195-1	Lookin' Back to See (Jim Ed Brown–Maxine Brown)	Vi 20(47)- 5770	

NOTE: Other sides from this session do not include GJ.

Nashville, 23 Sept. 1954, Thomas Studio, 9:30 A.M.–12:30 P.M.
Grandpa Jones, leader, banjo, vocal; Ramona Jones, bass, vocal;* Chet Atkins, el. and rhythm guitar; Billie W. Grammer, el. guitar; Claude J. Phelps, rhythm guitar and fiddle

E4-VB- 5514	Old Dan Tucker (PD)	Vi 20(47)- 6006	
E4-VB- 5515	Some Little Bug is Gonig to Find You (PD)	Vi 20(47)- 5939	
E4-VB- 5516	Keep on the Sunny Side of Life* (Ada Blankhorn–J. Howard Entwistle)	Vi 20(47)- 5939	
E4-VB- 5517	Gooseberry Pie (PD)	Vi 20(47)- 6006	

Nashville, 23 Sept. 1954, Thomas Studios
Grandpa Jones, banjo, vocal; Minnie Pearl, vocal; Chet Atkins, el guitar; Jerry Byrd, steel guitar; John Gordy, piano; Ernie Newton, bass; Ray Edenton, rhythm guitar; Farris Coursey, drums (as Grandpa Jones and Minnie Pearl)

E4-VB- 5518	Gotta Marry off Our Daughter (Connie Taylor)	Vi 20(47)- 5891	
E4-VB- 5519	Papa Loves Mambo (Al Hoffman–Dick Manning–Bix Reichner)	Vi 20(47)- 5891	*Cam* *ADL2-* *0701e*

Nashville, 2 March 1955, RCA Victor Studios
Grandpa Jones, banjo, vocal; Minnie Pearl, vocal; Eddie Hill, rhythm guitar; Jerry Byrd, steel guitar; Chet Atkins, el. guitar; Floyd Chance, bass; Murray Harmon, drums (as Grandpa Jones and Minnie Pearls)

F2-WB- 0268	Kissin' Games (Minnie Pearl–Grandpa Jones)	Vi 20(47)- 6474	*Cam* *ADL2-* *0701e*
F2-WB- 0869	Matrimony Ridge (E.C. Mac McCarthy)	Vi 20(47)- 6088	

F2-WB- 0270	Spring Fever (Grandpa Jones–Minnie Pearl)	Vi 20(47)- 6088	

Nashville, 28 April 1955, RCA Victor Studios
Grandpa Jones, banjo, vocal; Jackie Phelps, steel guitar; Bob Moore, bass; Eddie Hill, rhythm
guitar; Tommy Vaden, violin

F2-WB- 2244	The Champion (Irving Rousch)	Vi 20(47)- 6263	
F2-WB- 2245	Herd O' Turtles (Grandpa Jones)	Vi 20(47)- 6179	
F2-WB- 2246	I'm Gettin' Gray Hair (Virgil Whitehurst)	Vi 20(47)- 6474	
F2-WB- 2247	What She Has Got (Cy Coben)	Vi 20(47)- 6263	

M I S C E L L A N E O U S

"GRANDPA JONES" label. Nashville ca. March 1956
Grandpa Jones, vocal and banjo; Ramona Jones, bass and vocal; others unknown

NR 5570-1	The Kicking Mule (PD), Grandpa Jones Banjo Course	GJ 1001	
NR 5570-1	Pretty Little Pink (PD), Grandpa Jones Banjo Course	GJ 1001	
NR 5570-2	Cindy (PD), Grandpa Jones Banjo Course	GJ 1001	
NR 5570-2	Rose Don-O-Lee (PD), Grandpa Jones Banjo Course	GJ 1001	ACE-001

> NOTE: The above was a custom-made EP record designed to accompany a mail-order banjo instruction course.

KING label. Cincinnati, 14 March 1956
Grandpa Jones, vocal, guitar and banjo; Jackie Phelps, guitar; others unknown

4043	Rock Island Line (Lonnie Donegan)	Ki 918	Ki 809, 869
4044	Hello Blues (L.M. Jones)	Ki 918	Ki 625
4045	Fast Moving Night Train (Rudy Toombs)	Ki 5321	Ki 869; Na 2069
4046	A Night Out (Innis–Jones)	Ki 5335	Ki 726

RCA VICTOR label. Nashville, 9 Sept. 1956
Grandpa Jones, vocal, banjo, guitar; Johnny Wright, vocal and guitar; Jack Anglin, vocal and
guitar; others unknown

G2WB-	When My Blue Moon Turns to Gold Again	Vi	

5358	(Walker–Sullivan)		*EPA-4053, LPM-1587, VPM-6022*

Nashville, 12 Sept. 1956
Grandpa Jones, banjo; Johnny Wright and Jack Anglin, vocal and guitars; others unknown

G2WB-5439	The Banana Boat Song	Vi 20(47)-6777	*Vi VPM 6022, SPD 26*

DECCA RECORDINGS

Nashville, 28 Nov. 1956
Grandpa Jones, vocal, guitar, and banjo; Ramona Jones, vocal, bass, fiddle; others unknown

101210	Rattler's Pup (L. M. Jones)	Dec 30523	*Dec 4364; MCA/C 20060; Voc 73900*
101211	Eight More Miles to Louisville (Jones)	Dec 30264	*Dec 4364; MCA/C 20060; Voc 73900; Dec (7)4671*
101212	Mountain Dew (Lunsford–Wiseman)	Dec 30523	*Dec 4364; MCA/C 20060; Voc 73900*
101213	Dark as a Dungeon (Travis)	Dec 30264	*Dec 4364; MCA/C 20060, Voc 73900*

Nashville, 14 April 1958
Grandpa Jones, vocal, guitar, and banjo; Ramona Jones, vocal, bass, fiddle; others unknown

104829	Don't Look Back (?)	Dec 30655		
104830	Daylight Saving Time (L. M. Jones)	Dec 30655	*Dec EP 2648*	*Dec 4364*
104831	When the Jones Get Together (Jones)		*Dec EP 2648*	*Dec 4364*

Nashville, 18 Dec. 1958
Grandpa Jones, vocal, guitar, and banjo; Ramona Jones, vocal, bass, fiddle; others unknown

106276	The Huntin's Over for Tonight (Jones)		Dec EP 2648	Dec 4364; MCA/C 20060; Voc 73900
106277	Falling Leaves		Unissued	
106278	Come Pickin' Time (Cash)	Dec 30823		Dec 4364; MCA/C 20060; Voc 73900
106279	The All-American Boy (Parsons–Lunsford)	Dec 30823	Dec EP 2468	Dec 4364; MCA/C 20060; Voc 73900

Nashville, 14 April 1959

107136	It Takes a Lot of Living (?)	Decca 30904	
107137	Don't Bring Your Banjo Home (Jones–Cash)	Decca 30904	Dec 4364; MCA/C 20060; Voc 73900
107138	Old Towzer (B. Chaplin–L. Jones)		Dec 4364; MCA/C 20060; Voc 73900
107139	Waiting for a Train (Rodgers)		Dec 4364; MCA/C 20060; Voc 73900

MISCELLANEOUS

RCA VICTOR label. Nashville, 19 May 1959
Grandpa Jones, banjo; Johnny Wright, vocal and guitar; Jack Anglin, vocal and guitar; others unknown (as Johnny and Jack with Grandpa Jones)

K2WB-0532	Sailor Man	RCA 47-7545

MONUMENT RECORDS

Nashville, 29 Sept. 1960, RCA Victor Studios, 7 P.M.–10:30 P.M.
Grandpa Jones, leader, vocal, banjo; Bob Moore, bass; Merle Travis, guitar; Jack Phelps, el. guitar; William Purcell, piano; Harold Bradley, guitar; Murrey Harmon, drums; Homer Randolph, saxophone

| MO 587 | The Thing | Mon 422 |
| MO 588 | Ladies Man | Mon 422 |

Nashville, 21 Feb. 1961, Bradley Recording Studio, 11:30 P.M.–3:00 A.M.
Gandpa Jones, leader, vocal, banjo; Floyd Cramer, piano; Ray Edenton, lead guitar; Murrey Harmon, bass; Jerry Byrd, steel guitar; Hank Garland, lead guitar; Harold Bradley, rhythm guitar

MO 612	I Don't Love Nobody	Mon 430
MO 613	The Hip Cat's Wedding (Boudleaux Bryant)	Mon 430
MO 646	These Hills (Jones)	Mon 440
MO 647	Billy Yank and Johnny Reb (Driftwood)	Mon 440

Nashville, 23 Aug. 1961, Bradley Recording Studio, 10 A.M.–1 P.M.
Grandpa Jones, leader, vocal, banjo; Murrey Harman, bass; Hargus Robbins, piano; Jerry Byrd, steel guitar; Merle Travis, lead guitar; Harold Bradley, rhythm guitar; Ray Edenton, guitar

MO 729	Make the Rafters Ring (Paul Clayton)	Mon 4006
MO 730	Raining Here This Morning (Jones)	Mon 4006
MO 731	My Darling's Not My Darling Anymore (Jones)	Mon 4006
MO 732	Groundhog (Arr: Jones)	Mon 4006

NOTE: Selections in this session and the next may not exactly match up to mx.

Nashville, 23 Aug. 1961, Bradley Recording Studio, 2:30 P.M.–5:30 P.M.
Grandpa Jones, leader, vocal, banjo; Floyd Cramer, piano; Jerry Byrd, steel guitar; Ray Edenton, guitar; Merle Travis, lead guitar; Murrey Harman, drums; Harold Bradley, guitar

MO 733	All Night Long	Mon 4006
MO 734	Going Across the Sea	Mon 4006
MO 735	I Guess You Don't Remember Now (Jones)	Mon 4006
MO 736	Might Long Way to Travel (Jones)	Mon 4006

Nashville, 24 Aug. 1961, Bradley Recording Studio, 10:00 A.M.–1:00 P.M.
Grandpa Jones, leader, vocal, banjo; Harold Bradley, Murrey Harmon, drums; Floyd Cramer, piano; Jerry Byrd, steel guitar; Ray Edenton, guitar; Merle Travis, lead guitar; Ramona Jones, vocal and mandolin

MO 725	Count Your Blessings (Jones)	Mon 4006
MO 726	Banjo Sam (Jones)	Mon 4006
MO 727	I've Just Been Gone Too Long (Jones)	Mon 4006
MO 728	East Bound Freight Train (Jones)	Mon 4006

Nashville, 14 Sept. 1962, RCA Victor Studios, 7–10 P.M.
Grandpa Jones, leader, vocal, banjo; Jerry Byrd, steel guitar; James Isbell, bass; Norris Wilson, paino; Ray Edenton, lead el. guitar; Helen Carter, guitar; Maybelle Carter, autoharp

| Mx. | T for Texas | Mon 801 | Mon |

unknown			MLP-8001, MSP 001 *
Mx. unknown	Waiting for a Train		Mon MLP-8001
Mx. unknown	You and My Old Guitar		Mon MLP-8001
Mx. unknown	Tritzen Yodel	Mon 801	Mon MLP-8001, MSP 001 *

* MSP-001 is a special 7-inch LP album.

Nashville, 6 Dec. 1962, RCA Victor Studios, 7–10 P.M.
Grandpa Jones, leader, vocal, banjo; Jim Isbell, bass; Norris Wilson, piano; Ray Edenton, lead el. guitar; Jerry Byrd, steel guitar; Maybelle Carter, autoharp

A12W-138	My Caroline Sunshine Girl	Mon 811	Mon MLP-8001, MSP 001 *
A12W-139	Dear Old Sunny South		Mon MLP-8001
A12W-140	My Little Lady	Mon 820	Mon MLP-8001, MSP 001 *
A12W-141	Brakeman's Blues		Mon MLP-8001
A12W-142	Lullaby Yodel		Mon MLP-8001, MSP-001 *

Nashville, 17 Dec. 1962, RCA Victor Studios, 7–10 P.M.
Grandpa Jones, leader, vocal, banjo; Jim Isbell, bass; Ray Edenton, guitar; Jerry Bryd, el. guitar; Norris Wilson, piano; Joe Tanner, guitar

A12W-146	Peach Picking Time in Georgia		Mon MLP-8001
A12W-147	Hobo Bill		Mon MLP-8001
A12W-148	Away Out on the Mountain (Harrell)	Mon 820	Mon MLP-8001, MSP-001 *

*MSP-001 is a special 7-inch LP album.

Nashville, Ca. April 1963
Grandpa Jones, vocal and banjo; others unknown

BAW-167	Night Train to Memphis (Rose)	Mon 811	Mon SLP 18083, Mon SLP 18131

Nashville, 12 Aug. 1963, RCA Victor Studios, 1–4 P.M.
Grandpa Jones, leader, vocal, banjo; Jim Isbell, bass; Ray Edenton, lead el. guitar; Harold R. Bradley, rhythm guitar; Jerry Byrd, steel guitar; Rita Faye Sinks, autoharp

B8W-339	Rosa Lee	Mon SLP-18021
B8W-340	Somewhere Somebody's Waiting for You	Mon SLP-18021
B8W-341	Willis Mayberry	Mon SLP-18021
B8W-342	Liza's Up the 'Simmon Tree	Mon SLP-18021

Nashville, 12 Aug. 1963, RCA Victor Studios, 5–8 P.M.
Grandpa Jones, leader, vocal, banjo; Jerry Byrd, el. guitar; Harold R. Bradley, guitar; Ray Edenton, guitar; Jim Isbell, bass; Rita Faye Sinks, autoharp; Ramona Jones, vocal and mandolin

B8W-343	Chicken Don't Roost Too High	Mon SLP-18021
B8W-344	Going from the Cotton Fields (Miller–Hall)	Mon SLP-18021
B8W-345	Tragic Romance	Mon SLP-18021
B8W-346	Methodist Pie	Mon SLP-18021

Nashville, 13 August 1963, RCA Victor Studios, 7–10 P.M.
Grandpa Jones, leader; Jim Isbell, bass; Jerry Byrd, el. gtr.; Ray Edenton, gtr.; Harold Bradley, gtr.; Rita Faye Sinks, autoharp

B8W-335	What Does the Deep Sea Say?	Mon SLP-18021
B8W-336	I'm Tying the Leaves so they Won't Fall Down	Mon SLP-18021
B8W-337	Oh Captain Captain	Mon SLP-18021
B8W-338	Devilish Mary	Mon SLP-18021, Mon SLP-18131

Nashville, 2 Nov. 1965, Fred Foster Sound Studios, 10–1 P.M.
Grandpa Jones, vocal, banjo, leader; Murrey Harman, Jr., drums; Jerry Byrd, steel or lead guitar; Ray Edenton, guitar; Floyd Cramer, piano; Merle Travis, guitar

D11W-675	Banjo Am the Instrument (Jones)	Mon SLP 18083, SLP 18131

D11W- 676	Springtime Comes But Once a Year		Mon SLP 18083
D11W- 677	Eight More Miles to Louisville (Jones)		Mon SLP 18083, SLP 18131
D9W-736	My Darling's Not My Darling Anymore		Mon 903

Nashville, 8 Dec. 1965, Fred Foster Sound Studios, 2–5 P.M., 6–9 P.M.
Grandpa Jones, banjo, lead vocal; Jerry Byrd, guitar; Merle Travis, guitar and vocal; Eugene
(Red) Rector, vocal and mandolin; Ramona Jones, vocal (tenor)

	(2–5 session)	
Mx. unknown	On the Jericho Road	Mon SLP 18041
Mx. unknown	I'll Meet You in the Morning	Mon SLP 18041
Mx. unknown	Gone Home	Mon SLP 18041
Mx. unknown	Keep on the Firing Line	Mon SLP 18041
Mx. unknown	Just Over in the Glory Land	Mon SLP 18041
Mx. unknown	Old Camp Meetin' Time	Mon SLP 18041
	(6–9 session)	
Mx. unknown	Empty Mansion	Mon SLP 18041
Mx. unknown	When I Get to the End of the Way	Mon SLP 18041
Mx. unknown	The Glory Land Way	Mon SLP 18041
Mx. unknown	Turn Your Radio On	Mon SLP 18041
Mx. unknown	No Tears in Heaven	Mon SLP 18041

Nashville, 12 March 1964, Fred Foster Sound Studios, 9:30 A.M.–12:30 P.M.
Grandpa Jones, leader, vocal banjo; Jerry Kennedy, steel guitar; Harold Bradley, bass guitar;
Ray Edenton, rhythm guitar; Jerry Byrd, steel or lead guitar; Jim Isbell, bass

C3W-479	Are You From Dixie?	Mon 903	Mon SLP 18083, SLP 18131
C3W-480	Root Hog Root (C. Walker)	Mon 844	
C3W-481	Falling Leaves	Mon 866	Mon SLP 18083
C3S-482	Here Comes the Champion	Mon 866	

Nashville, ca. 1966
Grandpa Jones, vocal, guitar, banjo; others unknown
| E8W-943 | The Little Old Lady (Jones) | Mon 973 |
| E8W-943 | Eight More Miles to Louisville (Jones) | Mon 973 |

Nashville, 27 Dec. 1966, Fred Foster Sound Studio, 10–1 P.M., and 2–5 P.M.
Grandpa Jones, vocal, banjo, guitar; Jerry Byrd, el. guitar; Harold Bradley, bass guitar; Leon Rhodes, el. guitar; Harold Rugg, bass; Doug Kirkham, bass; Merle Travis, el. guitar
Mx. unknown	Steady Drips of Water		*Mon SLP* 18083
Mx. unknown	Goin' Down the River		*Mon SLP* 18083
Mx. unknown	Heart Full of Love		*Mon SLP* 18083

Nashville, ca. 28 Dec. 1966, Fred Foster Sound Studio
Grandpa Jones, vocal, banjo, guitar; others probably same as 27 Dec.
E12W-1052	Moon of Arizona (Jones)	Mon 1000	
E12W-1053	These Hills		*Mon* KZ-32939
E12W-1054	Everything I Had Going for Me Is Gone (Cochran)	Mon 1000	
E12W-1055	Don't Look Back (Jones)	Mon 1043	*Mon SLP* 18083

Nashville, 28 Sept. 1967, Foster's Sound Studio, 10 A.M.–1:30 P.M.
Grandpa Jones, vocal, guitar, banjo; Larry Butler, piano; Buddy Harmon, drums; Ray Edenton, rhythm guitar; Fred Carter, Jr., guitar; Norbert Putnam, bass; Jerry Kennedy, steel guitar; Wayne Moss, guitar; Harold Bradley, bass guitar
F9W-2144	Trouble in Mind (Richard M. Jones)	Mon 1263	*Mon SLP* 18131
F9W-2145	That's What This Old World Needs (B. Turbet–D. Tapp)	Mon 1043	
F9W-2146	Bill's Gonna Soon Be Home (?)	Mon 1069	

Mt. Juliet, Tennessee, 26 Aug. 1968, Bradley's Barn, 2 P.M.–5:30 P.M.
Grandpa Jones, banjo, vocals, guitar; Wayne Moss, guitar; Ray Edenton, guitar; Billy Linneman, steel guitar; Jim Isbell, bass; Joe Edwards, guitar, fiddle
G9W-2409	Mountain Laurel (Chilton Price and Grandpa Jones)	Mon 1143
G9W-2410	Smoke, Smoke, Smoke #2 (Travis)	Mon 1108
G9W-2411	Leave That to the Lord (Jones)	Mon 1203

| G9W-2412 | Old Troup Dog (Ramona Jones) | Mon 1143 | Mon KZ-32939 |

Mt. Juliet, Tennessee, 30 Aug. 1968, Bradley's Barn, 10 A.M.–1 P.M.
Grandpa Jones, banjo, vocal, guitar; Buddy Harman, drums; Ray Edenton, guitar; Billy Linneman, bass; Joe Edwards, guitar, fiddle; Wayne Moss, guitar

G9W-2414	Sweet Lips (Battle of King's Mountain)		Mon KZ-32939
G9W-2415	I'm Just A-living Along	Mon 1108	
G9W-2416	Plans	Unissued	
G9W-2417	She's a Prisoner Behind Bars of Gold	Unissued	

Nashville, 29 July 1969, Monument Recording Studio, 10 A.M.–1 P.M.
Grandpa Jones, banjo, vocals, guitar; Harold Bradley, guitar, piano; Murrey M. Harman, drums; Hargus Robbins, piano; Ray Edenton, rhythm guitar; Joe Edwards, guitar or fiddle; Roy M. Huskey, bass

H7W-2859	King of the Cannon County Hills		Mon SLP-18131
H7W-2860	Mountain Dew		Mon SLP-18131
H7W-2861	Old Rattler		Mon SLP 18131
H7W-2862	Old Blue		Mon SLP 18131

Nashville, 5 Sept. 1969, Monument Recording Studio (overdub session)
Grandpa Jones, Bill Walker, Richard Morris, Diane Harriss, John Duke, Brenton Banks (contractor), Lillian Hunt, Doris Allen, Solie Fott, Martin Katahan, Sheldon Jurland, George Binkley, Carol Walker, Marvin Chantry, Gary Vanosdale, David Vanderkooi

H7W-2850	Christman Guest [Christmas Guest]	Mon 8556	Mon SLP 18125
H7W-2848	Kettles and Bells	Unissued	
H6W-2790	Sweet Little Jesus Boy	Unissued	

Nashville, 1 Oct. 1969, Monument Recording Studios, 10 A.M.–1 P.M.
Grandpa Jones, banjo, guitar, vocals; Ray Edenton, leader, rhythm guitar; Murrey Harman, Jr., drums; David Briggs, piano; Harold R. Bradley, guitar; Roy Huskey, Jr., bass

| H10W-2979 | Christmas Roses (Ramona Jones) | Mon GA 1939, 8556, 8677 | |

| H10W-2980 | Grasshopper McClain | Unissued |
| H10W-2981 | Old Bill | Unissued |

Cincinnati, Ohio, 30 Dec. 1969, 7–10 P.M. (recording of live performance)
Grandpa Jones, banjo and vocal; Ramona Jones, fiddle and vocals; Joseph Edwards, guitar;
Marshall Barnes, bass

H12W-3100	Fix Me a Pallet	*Mon SLP-18138; Har H-31396*
H12W-3101	Dooley	*Mon SLP-18138*
H12W-3102	The Air, the Sunshine, and the Rain	*Mon SLP-18138; Har H-31396*
H12W-3103	Castles in the Air	*Mon SLP-18138*
H12W-3104	Rattler's Pup	*Mon SLP-18138; Har H-31396*
H12W-3105	My Bonnie Lies over the Ocean	*Mon SLP-18138; Har H-31396*
H12W-3106	Rocky Top	*Mon SLP-18138; Har H-31396*
H12W-3107	I Don't Love Nobody	*Mon SLP-18138; Har H-31396*
H12W-3108	John Henry	*Mon SLP-18138; Har H-31396*
H12W-3109	The Last Old Shovel	*Mon SLP-18138; Har H-31396*

H12W- 3110	Southern Bound		Mon SLP-18138; Har H-31396
H12W- 3111	15¢ Is All I Got		Mon SLP-18138

Nashville, 22 July 1971, Monument Recording Studios, 6 P.M. –9 P.M.
Grandpa Jones, banjo, guitar, vocals; Joe Maphis, leader, guitar; Fred P. Carter, Jr., guitar; Roy M. Huskey, Jr., bass; James M. Vest, steel guitar; Kenneth Malone, guitar; Jerry D. Smith, piano; Dave C. Kirby, guitar; Roselee Maphis, vocals; Ramona Jones, fiddle, vocals, mandolin

J7W 3426	The Valley of the Never Do No Good	Mon 25-7-8528	
J7W 3427	Four Stone Walls		Mon KZ-32939
J7W 3428	A Dollar Short (Ray Jones)	Mon 25-7-8528	

Nashville, 8 Feb. 1972, Monument Recording Studios, 10 A.M.–1 P.M.
Grandpa Jones, vocal and banjo; James West, leader; Henry P. Strzelecki, bass; Jerry D. Smith, piano; Kenneth M. Malone, guitar; James Codand, guitar; Dave Kirby, guitar; George W. McCormick, guitar

K2W-3552	Coal Camp	Mon 25-7-8539	
K2W-3553	Here I Am Makin' Plans	Mon 25-7-8539	
K2W-3554	Green Hills of Home	Mon 45-1069	Mon KZ-32939

NOTE: Overdub session on these titles on 1 March 1972; added: Charles McCoy, harmonica.

Nashville, 10 May 1973, Monument Recording Studios, 10 A.M.–1 P.M.
Grandpa Jones, vocal, guitar, banjo; Murrey Harman, drums; Weldon Myrick, steel guitar; Billy Lineman, bass; Ray Edenton, rhythm guitar; George W. McCormick, guitar; Bill Carver, poss. guitar

M5W- 3840	Are You Sleepin' Daddy Darlin'		Mon KZ-32939
M5W- 3842	Nashville on My Mind (A. Hancock)	Mon 25-7-8599	Mon KZ-32939
M5W- 3842	The Mountain Man	Mon 25-7-8577	Mon KZ-32939

Nashville, 18 May 1973, Monument Recording Studios, 10 A.M.–1 P.M.
Grandpa Jones, vocal, guitar, banjo; Murrey Harman, drums; Weldon Myrick, steel guitar; Billy Linneman, bass; Ray Edenton, guitar; George W. McCormick, guitar; Bill Carver, poss.

guitar

M5W-3843	Deep Dark Corner of My Mind		*Mon* KZ-32939
M5W-3844	Baby-O		*Mon* KZ-32939
M5W-3845	My Old Lady	Unissued	
M5W-3846	Brown Girl and Fair Eleanor	MON 8599	*LC LBC-9; Mon* KZ-32939
M5W-3847	Four Winds A-blowin' (Jones)	MON 8577	*Mon* KZ-32939

WARNER BROTHERS RECORDS

Nashville, ca. 1974 or 1975
Grandpa Jones, banjo and vocal; others unknown

| Mx. unknown | Time | WBS 8016 |
| Mx. unknown | Freedom Lives in a Country Song | WBS 8016 |

SKYLITE RECORDINGS

Nashville, 1976, Nugget Studio
Grandpa Jones, banjo and vocal; Ramona Jones, vocal, fiddle, mandolin; Joe Zinkan, bass; George McCormick, guitar and vocals; Fred Carter, Jr., band leader; others unidentified Mx. unknown

Mx. unknown	Traveling Lite to Heaven (B. Miller)	*Sky C LP SC 7306*
Mx. unknown	I'll Meet You in the Morning (Brumley)	*Sky C LP SC7306*
Mx. unknown	Great Will Be the Coming of the Lord (Grandpa Jones)	*Sky C LP SC 7306*
Mx. unknown	Closer to God (J. Wheeler)	*Sky C LP SC7306*
Mx. unknown	Gone Home (B. Carlyle)	*Sky C LP SC7306*
Mx. unknown	It It's Good Enough for You, Lord (B. Miller)	*Sky C LP SC7306*
Mx. unknown	Precious Promises (B. Miller)	*Sky C LP SC7306*
Mx. unknown	Old Camp Meeting Day (E. Pace)	*Sky C LP SC7306*

Mx.	When I Get to the End of my Way (C.	*Sky C LP*
unknown	Tillman)	SC7306
Mx.	Come and Dine (Grandpa Jones)	*Sky C LP*
unknown		SC7306

CMH RECORDINGS

Charlotte, North Carolina, 1976, Arthur Smith Studios, Arthur Smith, Producer
Grandpa Jones, banjo, guitar, and vocals; Ramona Jones, fiddle and vocal;* Dayle Dykes, el.
lead guitar; Arthur Smith, fiddle and guitar; Tommy Faile, bass; Clay Smith, guitar; David
Brakefield, drums

Mx.	Sweet Dreams of Kentucky (Jones)	*CMH LP*
unknown		*9007*
Mx.	My Carolina Sunshine Girl (Rodgers)	*CMH LP*
unknown		*9007*
Mx.	Jesse James	*CMH LP*
unknown		*9007*
Mx.	It's Raining Here This Morning (Jones)	*CMH LP*
unknown		*9007*
Mx.	Eight More Miles to Louisville (Jones)	*CMH LP*
unknown		*9007*
Mx.	Tragic Romance (Jones)	*CMH LP*
unknown		*9007*
Mx.	Kentucky (C. Davis)*	*CMH LP*
unknown		*9007*
Mx.	Old Rattler (Jones)	*CMH LP*
unknown		*9007*
Mx.	Mountain Laurel*	*CMH LP*
unknown		*9007*
Mx.	I'm on My Way Back Home (J. Connor)	*CMH LP*
unknown		*9007*
Mx.	Sweeping Through the Gates*	*CMH LP*
unknown		*9007*
Mx.	There's a Hand That's A-waiting (Jones)*	*CMH LP*
unknown		*9007*
Mx.	Old Camp Meeting Time*	*CMH LP*
unknown		*9007*
Mx.	Closer to God Than Ever Before (J.	*CMH LP*
unknown	Wheeler)*	*9007*
Mx.	I'll Meet You in the Morning (Brumley)*	*CMH LP*
unknown		*9007*
Mx.	You'll Make Our Shack a Mansion (Jones)	*CMH LP*
unknown		*9007*

Mx. unknown	Dark as a Dungeon (Travis)*	CMH LP 9007
Mx. unknown	I'm on My Way Somewhere (Jones)	CMH LP 9007
Mx. unknown	Rosalee*	CMH LP 9007
Mx. unknown	Going Home (B. Carlisle)*	CMH LP 9007

Nashville, 1978, Hilltop Studios, Vic Willis and Grandpa Jones, Producers
Grandpa Jones, banjo, guitar, vocals; Ramona Jones, fiddle, mandolin, background vocals; Joe Maphis, lead guitar, fiddle, mandolin, tenor guitar, and background vocals; Doyle Dykes, el. and acoustic guitars, banjo, background vocals; Vic Willis, piano, mitre box, background vocals; Weldon Myrick, steel guitar; Billy Linneman, bass; George McCormick, rhythm guitar and background vocals

Mx. unknown	She Was Always Chewing Gum (M. Christian)	CMH LP 9010
Mx. unknown	When the Bees Are in the Hive (M. Christian)	CMH LP 9010
Mx. unknown	Young Charlotte (M. Christian)	CMH LP 9010
Mx. unknown	The All Go Hungry Hash House (M. Christian)	CMH LP 9010
Mx. unknown	The Code of the Mountains (K. Davis, H. Taylor, P. McAdory)	CMH LP 9010
Mx. unknown	I Don't Love Nobody (M. Christian)	CMH LP 9010
Mx. unknown	I Wonder Where My Darling Is Tonight (A. Delmore)	CMH LP 9010
Mx. unknown	Pap's Corn Liquor Still (L. M. Jones)	CMH LP 9010
Mx. unknown	Where the Silv'ry Colorado Wends Its Way (M. Christian)	CMH LP 9010
Mx. unknown	Alabam (L. Copas)	CMH LP 9010
Mx. unknown	Where the Mississippi Washes (M. Christian)	CMH LP 9010
Mx. unknown	Neighbors (C. Sandago, T. Simmons)	CMH LP 9010
Mx. unknown	Weary Lonesome Me. (M. Travis, T. Atchison)	CMH LP 9010
Mx. unknown	Driftwood on the River (J. Klenner, B. Miller)	CMH LP 9010
Mx. unknown	Dog and Gun (M. Christian)	CMH LP 9010

Mx.	Grandfather's Clock (M. Christian)	CMH LP
unknown		9010
Mx.	Cabin Just over the Hill (D. Hopkins)	CMH LP
unknown		9010
Mx.	I'm on My Way (L.M. Jones)	CMH LP
unknown		9010
Mx.	Open Up Them Pearly Gates for Me (C.	CMH LP
unknown	Robison)	9010
Mx.	When It's Time for the Whippoorwill to	CMH LP
unknown	Sing (A. Delmore)	9010
Mx.	Down the Old Plank Road (M. Christian)	CMH LP
unknown		9010
Mx.	I'm Getting Grey Hair (E. Rouse)	CMH LP
unknown		9010
Mx.	I Am a Pilgrim (M. Christian)	CMH LP
unknown		9010
Mx.	Thinking Tonight of My Blue Eyes (M.	CMH LP
unknown	Christian)	9010

Nashville, 12–14 Jan. 1979, Hilltop Studios, Grandpa Jones and Joe Maphis, Producers
Grandpa Jones banjo (−1), guitar, vocals (−2); Ramona Jones, fiddle (−3), mandolin (−4), guitar, vocals (−5); Marsha Jones, autoharp, vocals (−6); Eloise Jones Hawkins, vocals (−7); Mark Jones, banjo, 5-string dobro, guitar (−8); Alisa Jones, hammered dulcimer and vocals (−9); Joe Maphis, lead and rhythm guitar, fiddle, mandolin, vocals (−10); Rose Lee Maphis, vocals (−11); George McCormick, rhythm guitar, vocals (−12); Gene Wooten, dobro, guitar, banjo, 5-string dobro (−13); Billy Linneman, bass

Mx.	Old Mountain Dew (−1, −8)	CMH LP
unknown		9015
Mx.	Let Him Go, God Bless Him (−9, −13)	CMH LP
unknown		9015
Mx.	Autoharp Trilogy (−6, −10)	CMH LP
unknown		9015
Mx.	Cannonball Blues (−2, −10)	CMH LP
unknown		9015
Mx.	Red Haired Boy (−3, −8, −10, −13)	CMH LP
unknown		9015
Mx.	My Pretty Quadroon (−2, −3, −9)	CMH LP
unknown		9015
Mx.	I Gave My Love a Cherry (−2, −5, −12)	CMH LP
unknown		9015
Mx.	The Johnson Boys (−8, −10, −13)	CMH LP
unknown		9015
Mx.	Gold Watch and Chain (−9, −6, −2,	CMH LP
unknown	−5)	9015

Mx.	Pig in the Pen (−2, −5, −6, −7, −9,	*CMH LP*
unknown	−1, −3, −11)	*9015*
Mx.	Over the Waterfall (−3, −9)	*CMH LP*
unknown		*9015*
Mx.	There'll Come a Time (−2, −9, −4,	*CMH LP*
unknown	−10)	*9015*
Mx.	Muleskinner Blues (−2, −10)	*CMH LP*
unknown		*9015*
Mx.	The Flowers of Edinburgh (−9)	*CMH LP*
unknown		*9015*
Mx.	Nellie Bly (−2, −1, −8, −5, −12,	*CMH LP*
unknown	−10)	*9015*
Mx.	The Banks of the Ohio (−9, −2, −5,	*CMH LP*
unknown	−6)	*9015*
Mx.	10th of November (−8)	*CMH LP*
unknown		*9015*
Mx.	The Blind Girl (−2)	*CMH LP*
unknown		*9015*
Mx.	Billy Richardson's Last Ride (−2)	*CMH LP*
unknown		*9015*
Mx.	Autoharp Concerto (−6, −10)	*CMH LP*
unknown		*9015*
Mx.	Falling Leaves (−9, −2, −5, −12)	*CMH LP*
unknown		*9015*
Mx.	Ramona's Choice (−3, −8)	*CMH LP*
unknown		*9015*
Mx.	Clear the Kitchen (all)	*CMH LP*
unknown		*9015*
Mx.	Down Home Waltz (−9, −4, −10)	*CMH LP*
unknown		*9015*
Mx.	Who Will Sing for Me (−9, −2, −5)	*CMH LP*
unknown		*9015*

Albuquerque, New Mexico, ca. 1981, CMH Studio
Grandpa Jones, banjo, guitar, vocals; Ramona Jones, fiddle, mandolin, vocals; Marsha Jones, autoharp and vocals; Mark Jones, banjo and 5-string dobro; Alisa Jones, vocals, hammered dulcimer; Joe Maphis, guitar, fiddle, mandolin, or tenor banjo; Rose Lee Maphis, vocals (−1); Zen Crook, fiddle or piano (−2); Mike Auldridge, dobro (−3); Joe Carroll, rhythm guitar; Billy Linneman, bass; Paul Charon, drums; Merle Travis, guitar (−4)

Mx.	Come My Little Pink	CMH 9026
unknown		
Mx.	River (−3)	CMH 9026
unknown		

Mx. unknown	Bethesda (−3)	CMH 9026
Mx. unknown	Daylight Saving Time (−3, −2)	CMH 9026
Mx. unknown	Greensleeves	CMH 9026
Mx. unknown	Great Will Be the Coming of Our Lord (−4)	CMH 9026
Mx. unknown	Had a Big Time Today (−2, −3)	CMH 9026
Mx. unknown	Cluck Ol' Hen	CMH 9026
Mx. unknown	Charlene (−3)	CMH 9026
Mx. unknown	Come Thy Fount	CMH 9026
Mx. unknown	The Storms Are on the Ocean (−1, −3, −4)	CMH 9026
Mx. unknown	Don't Bite the Hand That's Feeding You (−1, −2, −3, −4)	CMH 9026
Mx. unknown	My Little Old Home Down in New Orleans (−3)	CMH 9026
Mx. unknown	Old Troupe Dog (−3)	CMH 9026
Mx. unknown	Darby's Ram	CMH 9026
Mx. unknown	Whiskey before Breakfast	CMH 9026
Mx. unknown	Ballad of Music Row (−2, −3)	CMH 9026
Mx. unknown	Pictures from Life's Other Side (−2, −3, −4)	CMH 9026
Mx. unknown	Sail Away Ladies (−3, −2)	CMH 9026
Mx. unknown	Just Plain Folks (−3)	CMH 9026
Mx. unknown	Kate's Tune (−3)	CMH 9026
Mx. unknown	Wish I'd Stayed in the Wagon Yard	CMH 9026
Mx. unknown	Red Bird	CMH 9026
Mx. unknown	Matthew 24	CMH 9026

HEE HAW LABEL

Nashville, ca. 1981
Grandpa Jones, vocal; Roy Clark, vocal and guitar; Buck Owens, vocal; Kenny Price, vocal;
Charlie McCoy (− 1), harmonica (as the Hee Haw Gospel Quartet)

Mx.	The Unclouded Day (PD)	HH-19801
unknown		
Mx.	The Old Country Church (J.W. Vaughan)	HH-19801
unknown		
Mx.	Where Could I Go But to the Lord (J.B.	HH-19801
unknown	Coates)	
Mx.	Only One Step More (John Lair)	HH-19801
unknown		
Mx.	The Glory Land Way (Bill Monroe)	HH-19801
unknown		
Mx.	Gone Home (Bill Carlisle)	HH-19801
unknown		
Mx.	We Are Going Down the Valley (Jesse	HH-19801
unknown	Brown–J.H. Fellmore)	
Mx.	O Come Angel Band (PD)	HH-19801
unknown		
Mx.	Sweet By and By (PD)	HH-19801
unknown		
Mx.	This World Is Not My Home (A.E.	HH-19801
unknown	Brumley)	
Mx.	Everybody Will Be Happy over There	HH-19801
unknown	(E.M. Bartlett)	
Mx.	Amazing Grace (PD) − 1	HH-19801
unknown		

Bibliography

Compiled by Charles K. Wolfe

HARMONIES OF THE HILL COUNTRY.

by Grandpa Jones. Music arranged by Loren Bledsoe. Charleston, W.V., 1938. 18 pp. Music and words.

On That Great Judgement Morning (w/m: Grandpa Jones)
Jennie Get Your Hoecake Done (w/m: Grandpa Jones)
Answer to the Maple on the Hill No. 2 (w/m: Grandpa Jones)
When Its Twilight in the Bluegrass Mountains (w/m: Grandpa Jones)
Our Heavenly Home (w/m: Grandpa Jones)
As the Years Go Rolling By (w/m: Grandpa Jones)
Memories of my Mother's Prayers (w/m: Grandpa Jones)
Take Me Back with You (w/m: Grandpa Jones)
Goodbye to Beautiful Brown Eyes (m: Grandpa Jones; w: Vion O'Niel)
Just for Tonight (w/m: Grandpa Jones)
Send Me Your Address from Heaven (w/m: Grandpa Jones)
There's a Place in the Circle Waiting (w/m: Grandpa Jones)
Go to Sleep (w/m: Grandpa Jones)
Prepare to Meet Your Savior (w/m: Grandpa Jones)
I Know My Lord Is Coming (w/m: Grandpa Jones)
Moving into Town (words only; no CC)

The Old Man in the Moon (words only; no CC)
Remembrances (words only; no CC)

* There were at least two editions of this book with no apparent changes in song texts: the earlier edition has a photo of Grandpa alone on the inside front cover; the later, a photo of "Grandpa and his Grandsons," Loren Bledsoe (Dale Parker) and Pete Rentcheler.

NOTE - Abbreviations key: w = words; m = music; CC = composer credits.

HARMONIES OF THE HILL COUNTRY, No. 2

by Grandpa Jones. Charleston, W.V., 1940. 24 pp.; Music, words, photos.

The Tragic Romance (w/m: Grandpa Jones)
I Love You Still (w/m: Grandpa Jones)
Don't Tear Down Our Log Cabin Home (w: Richard O. Liller; m: Grandpa Jones)
Upon the Blue Ridge Mountains (no CC)
Drifting Down the Moonlit Mississippi (w/m: Grandpa Jones)
Silent Church Bells (w: Richard O. Liller; no music)
If I Were Only You (words only; no CC)
You Done Me Mean and Dirty (w/m: Grandpa Jones)
Blue Eyes or Brown Eyes? (w: Richard O. Liller; no music given)
Beautiful, Beautiful Heaven (w: Richard O. Liller; m: Grandpa Jones)
Sweet Bird (words only; no CC)
Answer to Gypsy's Warning (no CC)
When You Reach the Golden Gate (no CC)
Answer to Maple on the Hill (words only; no CC)
Goin' Down the River (w/m: Sally Weaver)
The First Whippoorwill's Song (words only; no CC)
Somebody's Waiting for Me (words only; no CC)
Eternal Peace (words: Richard O. Liller; m: Grandpa Jones)
Jesus Has the Key to Set You Free (w: Richard O. Liller, m: Grandpa Jones)
Sweet Mem'ries of Mother and Home (w: Richard O. Liller, m: Grandpa Jones)
Build Me a Cabin, Old Timer (w: Richard O. Liller; no music given)
Happy Little Home in Arkansas (words only; no CC)

THE KENTUCK' YODELER

by Grandpa Jones. Chicago: M.M. Cole Publishing Co., ca. 1941. 64 pp. Words, music, biographical sketch.*

The Yellow Rose of Texas
We Sat Beneath the Maple on the Hill
I Believe It for My Mother Told Me So
Tell My Mother I'm in Heaven
Six Feet of Earth
The Little Rosewood Casket
Billy Boy
Bury Me Out on the Prairie
Cow-Boy Jack
Sweet Evalina
Hear Dem Bells
The Little Old Cabin in the Lane
Red River Valley
When It's Prayer Meetin' Time in the Hollow
Barbara Allen
I'll Take You Home Again Kathleen
Lorena
Be Kind to a Man When He's Down
Bury Me Beneath the Willow
The Cowboy's Dream
Put My Little Shoes Away
Froggie Went a'Courtin'
Sourwood Mountain

Carry Me Back to Old Virginny
Me and My Burro
Good-Bye, Maggie
Down in My Old Cabin Home
Careless Love
Nobody's Darling
Give My Love to Nell
Keep a Light in Your Window Tonight
Mother's Old Red Shawl
Golden Slippers
Are You Tired of Me Darling?
Oh Susanna
The Old Hickory Cane
She'll Be Comin' Round the Mountain
The Letter Edged in Black
Sweet By and By
Methodist Pie
Pretty Little Pink
The Lonesome Road
Down in the Valley
Trail to Mexico
Let the Lower Lights Be Burning
Barney McCoy
Silver Threads Among the Gold

* Grandpa has noted that this folio, and the following one, both published by M.M. Cole, were actually compiled by the publishers and do not necessarily constitute an accurate reflection of his performing repertoire at that time.

THE KENTUCK' YODELER Book No. 2

by Grandpa Jones. Chicago: M.M. Cole Publishing Co., ca. 1942. 66 pp.

Covered Wagons Rolling Along
I Only Want a Buddy—Not a Sweetheart
Over Yonder, Over There
Me and My Burro
Good-Bye, Maggie
The Yellow Rose of Texas

Charlie Brooks
Climbing up the Golden Stairs
Swing Low, Sweet Chariot
Wait for the Wagon
Silver Threads among the Gold
Sweet Kitty Wells
Oh Susannah

A Home on the Range

The Lone Rider

Those Desert Blues

Strummin' My Old Guitar

Manana Land

My Miss by the Swiss Chalet

There's a Coyote Howlin' to the Moon
    Tonight

Hittin' the Trail to Heaven

The Lonesome Road

Froggie Went a'Courtin'

Montana Nights

I Learned about Horses from Him

Since Pappy Lost His Corn Cob Pipe

Hello Central, Give Me Heaven

Whispering Hope

You've Been a Faithful Old Dog

When We Picnic 'Long the Mountain
    Trail

Little Dream Home on Dream Mountain

Hold Fast to the Right

The Boston Burglar

Let's Whoop 'Er Up Tonight

Pappy

My Little Prairie Queen

Camptown Races

Bouncing Baby

It Doesn't Seem Like Home Sweet
    Home

My Dream Girl

She's Just a Little Angel

I Want to Follow the Swallow Back
    Home to Colorado

Prairie Schooner Days

Sunshine Valley

The Snow Capped Mountains Seem So
    Near

The Good Old Farmer

Winding Road

Headin' Back to Old Wyoming

Sing Again That Sweet Refrain

You're a Flower Blooming in the
    Wildwood

The Rustler's Farewell

Hear Dem Bells

McDonald's Reel

Turkey in the Straw

Leather Breeches

Devil's Dream

Arkansas Traveler

Cackling Hen

Soldier's Joy

Pop Goes the Weasel

My Old Bronc Pete

Underneath the Prairie Skies

Back in Those Bicycle Days

HARMONIES OF THE HILL COUNTRY

by Grandpa Jones, Star of the Grand Ole Opry. Cincinnati: Lois Music
Publishing Company [1947]. 40 pp. Words, music, photos.

Are There Tears behind Your Smiles (w/m: Grandpa Jones)

Darling Won't You Love Me Now (no CC)

East Bound Freight Train (no CC)

Get Back on the Glory Road (w/m: Grandpa Jones)

Goin' Down to the Country (w/m: Grandpa Jones)
I'll Be Around If You Need Me (w/m: Grandpa Jones)
I'll Never Lose That Loneliness for You (w/m: Grandpa Jones)
It's Raining Here This Morning (w/m: Grandpa Jones)
I've Been All Around This World (w/m: Grandpa Jones)
My Darling's Not My Darling Anymore (w/m: Jones–White)
Ridin' on That Train (no CC)
She's Gone and Left Another Broken Heart (w/m: Grandpa Jones)
Tears That Make Believe (w/m: Grandpa Jones)
The Old Rail Fence (w/m: Grandpa Jones)
There's a Grave in the Waves of the Ocean (w/m: Grandpa Jones)
You Didn't Have to Leave Me (w/m: Grandpa Jones)
You'll Be Lonesome Too (w/m: Grandpa Jones)

HILL AND COUNTRY SONGS

by Grandpa Jones, Star of the Grand Ole Opry. New York: Tannen Music, Inc., 1954. 32 pp. Words, Music, Illustrations.

Mountain Dew (w/m: Bascomb Lunsford–Lulu Belle & Scotty)
Rotation Blues (w/m: Lt. Stewart Powell)
That New Vitamine (w/m: Scotty Wiseman)
Time, Time, Time, Time (w/m: Eloise Higgins)
Old Rattler (w/m: Louis M. Jones)
Pickin' on Me (w/m: Cy Coben)
You're Never Too Old for Love (w/m: Cy Coben)
In the Future (w/m: Boudleaux Bryant)
You Ain't Seen Nothin' Yet (w/m: Grandpa Jones)
Standing in the Depot (w/m: Louis M. Jones)
I'm No Communist (w/m: Scotty Wiseman)
Good Morning Judge (w/m: Louis Innis)
Jug Band Boogie (w/m: Louis Innis)
Some More Mountain Dew (words only; no CC)

METHOD OF OLD-TIME SOUTHERN STYLE 5-STRING BANJO

by Grandpa Jones. With Photographs, Songs, Etc. Nashville, Tenn., 1954. 31 pp. Words and chord symbols. *

Bile Dem Cabbage Down
Ring de Banjo
Golden Slippers
Oh! Susanna
Old Joe Clark

Pretty Little Pink
Darby's Ram
Camptown Races
Crawdad Song

*This was an instruction book developed as part of a mail-order package sold by Grandpa Jones.

GRANDPA'S FOLDER OF SONGS FOR THE BANJO

by Grandpa Jones. No date, no publisher listed, but apparently published in Nashville, ca. 1954. 4 pp. Words only.

Camptown Races
Nelly Bly
Free a Little Bird as I Can Be
Arkansas Traveller
Ring de Banjo
The Glendy Burk

I'll Be All Smiles Tonight
Red River Valley
Black Eyed Susan
Cripple Creek
Old Dan Tucker
Pretty Little Pink

GRANDPA'S SONG AND PICTURE ALBUM.

by Grandpa Jones. Publisher and place uncertain, ca. 1956. Words, illustrations.

Stop That Tickling Me (no CC)
Goin' Down in Town (no CC)
Rotation Blues (no CC)
Standing in the Depot (no CC)
11 More Months and 10 More Days (no CC)

11-Cent Cotton: 40-Cent Meat (no CC)
You Ain't Seen Nothing Yet (no CC)

Index

Everybody's Grandpa has been composed into type on the Linotron 202N digital phototypesetter in eleven point Goudy Old Style with two points of line spacing. Bookman Light with swash capitals has been selected for display. The book was designed by Jim Billingsley, composed by Williams of Chattanooga, printed offset by Thomson-Shore, Inc., and bound by John H. Dekker & Sons. The paper on which the book is printed carries acid-free characteristics with an expected shelf life of at least three hundred years.

THE UNIVERSITY OF TENNESSEE PRESS : KNOXVILLE